Praise for *Benefit Corporation Law and Governance*

"Important new ideas that can change the world are both misunderstood and fragile. Understanding makes them stronger but alone doesn't guarantee that they will make the difference they could and should. Benefit corporations are one of those new ideas and one sorely needed if the capital markets are going to contribute to, rather than detract from, sustainable development. Rick's book elegantly explains this idea to a wide range of audiences, thereby making it stronger. The work he and B Lab are doing makes it stronger still. Thanks to them, I am hopeful that the benefit corporation can be for the 21st century what the traditional corporation was for the 20th."

—**Robert Eccles, Founding Chairman, Sustainability Accounting Standards Board**

"This book is the most important book about corporate law in decades, if not ever."

—**John Montgomery, founder of Lex Ultima**

"The magnitude of the crises impacting our world, and particularly our country, is certainly not disputed—by liberals or conservatives, men or women, African Americans or White Anglo-Saxon Protestants, members of the 1 percent or the working poor. The nature of such crises is also not in doubt—the fact that the climate is changing and negatively impacting the environment, the fact that there is a wider gap between rich and poor in this country than at any time since 1929, the fact that there is a sweeping tide of gun violence, and the fact that the Black Lives Matter movement is needed to address continuing overt and covert discrimination. Rick Alexander clearly articulates the need for a new corporate form to effect the significant change that we so desperately need."

—**Suz Mac Cormac, Chair, Social Enterprise and Impact Investing Group, and Cochair, Energy and Clean Technology Groups, Morrison & Foerster**

"Alexander's new book covers both the theory and the practice of benefit corporation law in a practical guide that anyone interested in the subject should own."

—**Janine Guillot, Director of Capital Markets Policy and Outreach, Sustainability Accounting Standards Board**

"This book is an excellent study of the evolution of corporate governance and the emerging role of the corporation as a public benefit entity. I highly recommend it to those who want to understand the challenges of corporate governance as well as the opportunities for the corporation to have a meaningful social impact in the global economy."

—**Larry Sonsini, Chairman, Wilson Sonsini Goodrich & Rosati**

"As the CEO of a public benefit corporation, I really appreciate having a readily accessible, easily understood resource. This book explains both the 'how' and the 'why' of this new corporate form that will help us transform business and create long-term value for all our stakeholders. I am proud to endorse it."

—**Lorna Davis, CEO, DanoneWave, and Chief Manifesto Catalyst, Danone**

"Rick is a thoughtful and assiduous leader pushing the benefit corporation movement forward. With this book, he's written an indispensable guide for anyone seeking to learn more about the benefit corporation form. Any entrepreneur or executive setting his or her company down a path in pursuit of purpose would do well to pick it up."

—Michal Rosenn, General Counsel, Kickstarter

"An insightful, practical, enriching book for any attorney or executive looking for a guide on how best to navigate the world of benefit corporations."

—Margaret M. Foran, Chief Governance Officer, Senior Vice President, and Corporate Secretary, Prudential Inc.

"Rick Alexander's new book takes us through a review of the corporation and its role in society, pointing out some of the structural gaps implicated in the traditional form and making a case for the development of the benefit corporation. As one of the creators of this structure, Alexander is uniquely suited to write this book, and he does so effectively, concisely, and with intelligence."

—Hillary A. Sale, Sullivan & Cromwell Visiting Professor, Harvard Law School

"Rick Alexander has written a book that is of great importance to the field of responsible business and the benefit corporation movement. Not only does it succeed in explaining the basis and practical implementation of benefit corporations in lucid and engaging terms, but it also places them in the context of existing corporate law and theories of the firm. It does all this in a form that is both accessible to the general interested reader and relevant to the most knowledgeable legal expert. It is therefore a triumph of clear thinking and precise exposition from which we will all benefit immensely."

—Colin Mayer, Peter Moores Professor of Management Studies, Saïd Business School, University of Oxford

"AltSchool was created to advance innovation in education and to improve access to quality schooling. Becoming a certified B Corporation and a public benefit corporation helps codify and support our mission. In AltSchool's case, delivering a broad social impact goes hand-in-hand with creating a large and thriving business. This book should be a valuable resource for organizations interested in pursuing a more socially responsible way to do business now and in the future."

—Max Ventilla, founder and CEO, AltSchool

BENEFIT CORPORATION LAW AND GOVERNANCE

BENEFIT CORPORATION LAW AND GOVERNANCE

PURSUING PROFIT WITH PURPOSE

FREDERICK H. ALEXANDER

Berrett–Koehler Publishers, Inc.
a BK Business book

Berrett-Koehler Publishers, Inc.
1333 Broadway, Suite 1000
Oakland, CA 94612-1921
Tel: (510) 817-2277   Fax: (510) 817-2278   www.bkconnection.com

Ordering Information

Quantity sales. Special discounts are available on quantity purchases by corporations, associations, and others. For details, contact the "Special Sales Department" at the Berrett-Koehler address above.

Individual sales. Berrett-Koehler publications are available through most bookstores. They can also be ordered directly from Berrett-Koehler: Tel: (800) 929-2929; Fax: (802) 864-7626; www.bkconnection.com

Orders for college textbook/course adoption use. Please contact Berrett-Koehler: Tel: (800) 929-2929; Fax: (802) 864-7626.

Orders by U.S. trade bookstores and wholesalers. Please contact Ingram Publisher Services, Tel: (800) 509-4887; Fax: (800) 838-1149; E-mail: customer.service@ingrampublisherservices.com; or visit www.ingrampublisherservices.com/Ordering for details about electronic ordering.

Berrett-Koehler and the BK logo are registered trademarks of Berrett-Koehler Publishers, Inc.

Printed in the United States of America

Berrett-Koehler books are printed on long-lasting acid-free paper. When it is available, we choose paper that has been manufactured by environmentally responsible processes. These may include using trees grown in sustainable forests, incorporating recycled paper, minimizing chlorine in bleaching, or recycling the energy produced at the paper mill.

Library of Congress Cataloging-in-Publication Data
Names: Alexander, Frederick H., 1963– author.
Benefit corporation law and governance : pursuing profit with purpose / Frederick H. Alexander.
Oakland, California : Berrett-Koehler Publishers, [2017]
LCCN 2017032779 | ISBN 9781523083589 (hardcover)
LCSH: Business enterprises--Law and legislation--United States.
Stockholders--Legal status, laws, etc.--United States. | Corporation law--United States. | Corporate governance--Law and legislation--United States.
Classification: LCC KF1355 .A97 2017 | DDC 346.73/066--dc23
LC record available at https://lccn.loc.gov/2017032779

First Edition

24 23 22 21 20 19 18   10 9 8 7 6 5 4 3 2 1

Cover: Foltz Design
Design and production: Seventeenth Street Studios
Copyeditor: Todd Manza
Index: Richard Evans
Author Photo: Jordan Scheiner

This book is dedicated to the memory of 1,129 human beings who perished in the collapse of the Rana Plaza garment factory.

CONTENTS

Foreword

As someone who grew up under the heavy influence of George Orwell, I respect those who have the courage to look at the world the way it is and to get their hands dirty trying to make it a better one. For too long, an important perspective on the American corporate governance system has eschewed this clear-eyed approach. Rather than having the fortitude to fight to change the system we have, they bemoan the reality that corporate managers and directors who are accountable to only one corporate constituency—the stockholders who directly own their voting shares—seem to be focused on putting that constituency first. Rather than fighting to change the corporate law statutes that give stockholders the exclusive authority to elect directors, vote on transactions, and sue for breach of fiduciary duty, these good-hearted, but often faint-willed, commentators just urge the directors to "do the right thing."

In this debate has emerged a strain of realist courage in the form of the benefit corporation movement. Recognizing that it might be unrealistic in the current American political context to give other corporate constituencies the right to elect elements of the board, the benefit corporation movement has sought to move the legal power structure established by corporation statutes in another way to give corporations the ability to make legally enforceable commitments to social responsibility and fair worker treatment, and to put actual teeth behind those commitments.

Although the movement still depends critically on an evolution in not only the social responsibility but also the financial prudence of institutional investors who hold the capital of ordinary Americans if it is come to full flower, the benefit corporation movement represents a refreshing and substantial step forward for those who believe that corporations—and all business entities—not only can but should do well not only by their investors but also by their workers and the societies in which they operate. As Rick Alexander's comprehensive and learned overview explains, the benefit corporation model moves us in a positive direction through various means. But, most important of all, the model does so by changing the corporate power dynamic so that there is legal—and thus market—force behind the social responsibility commitments benefit corporations make.

Rather than just high-minded talk, the benefit corporation model represents a serious effort to match talk with important action. At a time when the irrationally tumultuous influences of volatile stock market forces are encouraging entrepreneurs to keep their companies private or to even go public without giving other stockholders a right to vote, benefit corporations also promise benefit to ordinary investors. End-user ordinary investors primarily save for two long-term objectives—paying for college for their kids and retirement for themselves. These long-term objectives depend on money made the old-fashioned way, in a steady, responsible manner that focuses on buying and holding the stock of a diverse array of companies that make and deliver real products that are of durable worth.

Through the more straightforward means of the benefit corporation model—as opposed to structures built on denying other investors real voting power—entrepreneurs and corporate managers who wish to do well by doing right have a credible means to establish a more rational accountability structure. Through this model, investors have a chance to invest in socially responsible corporations and to diminish the credibility of the argument that minimizing the voting power of institutional investors in public corporations is necessary if corporations are to be able to pursue long-term value in a socially responsible manner. No doubt that the biggest challenge remains making sure that the class of fiduciaries who directly hold most Americans' wealth—the money managers who control institutional investors like mutual and pension funds—act and vote in a manner consistent with those whose capital they hold. But the benefit corporation model will goad them in that direction and provide a foundation for further innovation.

For anyone who cares about our corporate governance system and whether it is delivering the results that America deserves, Rick Alexander's primer on the innovative benefit corporation model is well worth the effort. Dig in!

—Leo E. Strine, Jr., Chief Justice of the Delaware Supreme Court

Preface

This book provides business and law students, as well as practicing lawyers, with a guide for using and understanding a new legal tool: benefit corporation governance. It should also interest investment professionals, especially those who care about sustainability and responsible investing. I also hope this book will develop a broader audience among those interested in shaping public policy.

Although corporate governance may occupy a remote corner in our policy discussions, it has a profound effect on the economy. This book's theme is that in order to tackle issues like inequality and climate risk, we need to change the way we govern our corporations. One critical component of the message is that *shareholder primacy*—the dominant corporate doctrine that the primary purpose of corporations is to make profits for shareholders—threatens the long-term health of our society. Everyone, including shareholders, would be better served by a financial and legal system that respects the interests of all corporate stakeholders—including workers, the environment, and the community. Benefit corporation law is a tool for establishing such a system.

Such a varied audience will have differing knowledge of corporate law. Recognizing that, I have tried to include some basic law and theory, so that those who are less familiar can understand the differences between traditional corporate law and benefit corporation law. I have also included a general overview of the role played by corporations and investors in society, because those roles give critical context to the opportunity that the new benefit corporation statutes provide.

For practitioners, I hope the book can neutralize the fear factor in advising entrepreneurs, managers, and investors who want to use benefit corporation law, and also explain the imperative for using a different kind of corporate governance. Because traditional corporations have a long track record, there is a natural tendency to think that forming or investing in a benefit corporation will create unnecessary complexity and ambiguity. I hope that lawyers come away from this book seeing benefit corporation law as the best tool for integrating stakeholder values into a corporation's DNA, and feeling that they can comfortably guide a client forming a benefit corporation, by helping to draft a specific purpose, creating some operating guidelines, and helping it report periodically as required by the applicable statute. I hope that investment professionals come away believing that benefit corporations belong in their portfolios and that their stewardship obligations require them to understand that there is a responsible alternative to shareholder primacy. I hope that all readers come away convinced that corporate governance needs to be part of our public policy discussion, and that the investment professionals who represent our interests need to manage the systems they control for the benefit of all.

Because I know that readers will come to this book with different purposes and backgrounds, I want to provide a brief overview. The most important concept to keep in mind as you begin is this: the new benefit corporation statutes are intended to address shareholder primacy, the doctrine that the purpose of corporations is to make money for their shareholders, and that everything else they do must be in service of that goal. In order to understand benefit corporation law, you must understand how shareholder primacy permeates and undermines our financial and legal systems.

* * *

The introduction is a bit of personal history that explains how a corporate lawyer (me) came to understand the problem and to believe that benefit corporations offered the right solution.

Part 1 addresses shareholder primacy in law and finance. Chapter 1 presents a much-boiled-down description of the institutions of the corporation and the investing system, in order to give the reader some context. Chapter 2 digs more deeply into corporate law and spends time on the theory of who corporations are supposed to serve and on the history of that theory. Chapter 3 then examines how courts decide whether directors are meeting their duties to shareholders. It delves into the case law, and those who are mostly interested in the public policy aspects of benefit corporations may wish to simply review table 2, which summarizes the standards. Finally, chapter 4 discusses how this same idea—that corporations are managed only for the benefit of shareholders—is not sufficient to meet the needs of our modern investing channels.

Part 2 then describes the new benefit corporation statutes and how they address the problem of shareholder primacy. It includes chapters 5 and 6, each of which describes one of the two basic models of benefit corporation law that have been adopted in the United States and Italy and that are being considered in a number of other countries. Chapters 7 and 8 consider how the current standards governing traditional corporations may be adapted for benefit corporations and how corporate decision making will be affected.

Part 3 explores other options for eliminating shareholder primacy. Chapter 9 discusses the history and theory of constituency statutes, a precursor to benefit corporation legislation that was adopted in thirty-three states in the late twentieth century. It addresses how constituency statutes differ from benefit corporation legislation, and why they failed to address the problems created by shareholder primacy. Despite this failure, understanding the historical background of these statutes and how they fared in litigation is important to gaining a full picture of the legal response to shareholder primacy. Chapter 10 explains why conventional corporations cannot address shareholder primacy on their own through private ordering. The last chapter contains a brief discussion of how the benefit corporation concepts can be translated to alternative entities such as limited liability companies and limited partnerships. This chapter is likely to be of interest mostly to practicing lawyers.

* * *

Different sections of this book may have greater import to different readers. If you really just want to understand the policy issues, the introduction, part 1 and the epilogue will explain *why* we must change our system of corporate governance. If you are in private practice or an in-house lawyer, part 2 is intended to provide a deep understanding of the operation of benefit corporations and the differences between the competing versions. In addition, the appendixes are meant to be practice aids (although, for practical reasons, the appendixes only contain forms for Delaware corporations). Part 3 should be of interest to any reader who wants to understand the alternatives to benefit corporations.

At a number of points in the book, the discussion will highlight publicly traded corporations. Although the benefit corporation alternative is relevant to all businesses operating as corporations, it has particular resonance for publicly traded corporations because those are the entities where decision making is at its furthest remove from the shareholders, so that corporate governance law has the greatest importance. The public markets are also the place where shareholder primacy appears to have the strongest hold. Moreover, public companies represent an incredibly large slice of society's financial capital, so that the public policy issues addressed by benefit corporation law have the greatest salience at the level of the public markets. Nevertheless, the form can be used for companies backed by venture capital, private equity, angel investors, and other forms of outside equity.

I want to thank Donald Van Buren, Sean Herron, Coleen Hill, Elizabeth Muller, Daniel Menken, Emily Hagan, and Taylor Bartholomew, who did the research and drafting of an earlier version of this book, which focused solely on Delaware law. Several chapters in this book are based on that earlier work. I also want to thank Chief Justice Leo E. Strine Jr. of the Delaware Supreme Court, Lawrence Hamermesh, and Anne Tucker, who each read the draft of the first book and provided invaluable comments. The chief justice also graciously provided the foreword to this work. John Montgomery read the entire book and provided me with important ideas, some needed encouragement, and insightful comments. Jennifer Kassan generously reviewed the entire book as well, and challenged me with many questions that showed me some of my many blind spots. Elizabeth Babson also reviewed the manuscript and provided particular help on matters relating to the Model Benefit Corporation Legislation. Much that is good in this book is thanks to their contributions; the mistakes, needless to say, are mine. I also want to thank everyone at Berrett-Koehler Publishing (which is a benefit corporation), who first suggested the idea for this book, and who have provided much support and guidance along the way, and the terrific team at Seventeenth Street Studios. Thanks also to

Karen Jannie Landau, who input much of the text for that initial work. I also appreciate the support of my colleagues at B Lab, all of whom gave me the time to get this done, and especially Holly Ensign-Barstow, whose load got heavier as I devoted more time to this project. I also want to thank Debbie Fahey, who did most of the word processing with the same precision and grace that I have benefited from for over twenty-eight years. Finally, I must acknowledge that this book would never have come to be if my life partner, Elly Alexander, had not provided unwavering support and encouragement.

A Corporate
Lawyer's Journey

Many readers of this book will be familiar with traditional corporations and the law that governs them and may wonder why more than thirty jurisdictions in the United States, including Delaware, the center of U.S. corporate law for the past century, would introduce a new corporate governance model. They may be reading this book to discover the "why" of benefit corporation law as much as the "how." In light of that, I thought it might be helpful to tell a bit of my own history with the changes to the Delaware statute.

I have spent almost thirty years in private practice, advising clients on Delaware corporate law issues. As a partner in the transaction group of a leading Delaware law firm, I worked on preferred stock financings, initial public offerings, mergers, hostile takeovers, proxy contests, corporate governance, and fiduciary issues. My practice addressed anything in the life cycle of a corporation that involved the relationship between shareholders, directors, officers, and corporations. There was a great deal of complexity, but that complexity, for the most part, arose not from a profusion of laws and regulation but rather from the multiplicity of situations in which some fairly simple rules and principles were to be applied. In a nutshell, these principles are that (1) directors are elected by shareholders, and, once elected, have the full authority to manage the corporation; and (2) that authority is subject to the board's fiduciary duties of care and loyalty: the directors must prudently and unselfishly manage the corporation to create a financial return for shareholders.

Of course, there are a few other rules (how the director elections work, what charters and bylaws can include, and so on), but that basic structure—shareholder-elected directors manage the corporation but must do so carefully and loyally for the financial benefit of the shareholders—underlies nearly every question that comes up in corporate law disputes. This paradigm is often called the "shareholder primacy" model, and it drove much of the advice I gave.

Thus, in my practice it was critical to help directors understand the primacy of shareholder value, particularly when the company was being sold. While corporations could certainly be good employers and provide valuable resources to the community, that was not their raison d'être; corporate law was about creating value for the shareholders, who owned the corporation and who elected its managers to oversee their investment.

For corporate lawyers, these were simple, non-ideological facts. The corporate form was a brilliant legal technology that allowed entities to raise large sums of money from disaggregated investors, who could diversify their investments across many such entities, allowing many corporations to take risks and create value. The underlying ethos was that investors were willing to risk their capital with these complete strangers because they knew that there was a system in place to protect them: elected directors who were obligated to be loyal to shareholders.

A few years ago, when I was chairing the bar committee (the "council") that recommends changes to the Delaware General Corporation Law (DGCL), we were approached by B Lab, a nonprofit organization working to create a business infrastructure that encourages corporate conduct that benefits all members of society. B Lab certifies companies as being good corporate citizens (like a Fair Trade mark for companies). B Lab has requirements for certification: first, the company must meet a strict standard of social and environmental performance; second, the company must have a corporate governance model that mandates accountability for all stakeholder interests. For corporations, however, that second aspect violates the shareholder primacy model central to traditional corporate law, and B Lab was asking state legislatures to adopt a statute they had drafted called the Model Benefit Corporation Legislation (MBCL). The MBCL contains a number of provisions that require corporations to follow a broader fiduciary model. When a state adopts the MBCL or similar statutory provisions, corporations created under that state's general corporation law can opt into the new provisions and become "benefit corporations."

In Delaware, the council's immediate reaction to B Lab was far from positive. The corporate bar was very comfortable with the way that corporate law worked, and recognized the tremendous value the corporate form had produced over time. Even corporate lawyers who believed that corporate behavior with respect to social and environmental issues was a concern, and who believed that the profit motive could encourage behavior that damaged the public interest, did not think those issues should be addressed by changing corporate law. Instead, there was consensus that those issues could be better addressed with laws and regulations that protect society and the environment and with contractual provisions negotiated with creditors, customers, and other stakeholders. There was also concern that trying to add those concepts into a corporate governance model would enhance board discretion too broadly and provide management with a tool with which to impinge upon the rights of shareholders.

However, the council was encouraged by the governor and the secretary of state to undertake a review of the concept, particularly in light of Delaware's national leadership in corporate law, and the growing interest in the benefit corporation movement. With the assistance of B Lab, members of the council met with entrepreneurs and investors who championed the concept. As a result of this process, the council determined that an opt-in statute could offer the option of stakeholder-oriented governance for corporations, without impugning traditional shareholder rights. Members of the council found it particularly persuasive that there were business founders and investors who believed that benefit corporation law was a better fit for some businesses than conventional corporate law. In light of such demand, the council saw little reason to completely reject the benefit corporation model, as long as shareholders were adequately protected.

In 2013, Delaware adopted a statute that reflects that balance and that allows corporations to opt into a structure where the duties of directors extend beyond the consideration of shareholder interests to include the interests of all stakeholders. As I will discuss in chapter 6, however, Delaware's statute has some significant differences from the MBCL, and also uses slightly different terminology, so that a corporation using the Delaware version is called a public benefit corporation (PBC). I will try to use the term "PBC" when referring specifically to Delaware entities and "benefit corporations" when referring to the general concept. As of this writing, a total of thirty-five U.S. jurisdictions and Italy provide some form of benefit corporation legislation.

I wanted to write this book because I suspect that many corporate lawyers, investors, and policy makers are still where the council was when first approached by B Lab—suspicious that this is not a very good idea, and maybe thinking, *If it ain't broke. . . .* I want to share some of my thought process in moving from being first a strong skeptic, then one of the drafters of the PBC statute, and, finally, head of legal policy at B Lab.

First, I reexamined corporate theory as we studied B Lab's proposal. One idea that struck me came from Lynn Stout, a law professor at Cornell, who wrote an important book called *The Shareholder Value Myth*.[1] In that work, she notes that if a human being were to operate under the rule of always maximizing value for herself, no matter the cost to others, we would consider such a person a psychopath. As discussed in chapter 4, most corporations do not actually operate in a completely antisocial manner, but the question is whether the principle of profit value maximization makes any sense in a world where corporate activity dominates the economy. Do we really want directors to be guided by fiduciary duties that can justify child labor in their supply chain, or shifting costs to future generations, as long as they determine that such actions are legal and will increase shareholder value? One writer painted a particularly grim picture: "Somehow, at the beginning of the twenty-first century, the corporation had evolved to the point of being a sociopathic institution, at odds with the deep-rooted prosocial tendencies in human psychology and behavior."[2] Admittedly, the terms "psychopath" and "sociopathic" seem strong and certainly do not accurately describe the behavior of most corporations. The point, however, is that such behavior is the logical extension of mainstream corporate governance rules.

Another work I found significant was the book *Firm Commitment*, written by Colin Mayer, a finance professor at Oxford.[3] Mayer convincingly shows that the existence of the value maximization principle destroys trust, which paradoxically destroys value for the "value-maximizing" entity. He argues that third parties, including employees, customers, and communities, know that any commitment the corporation makes may be contingent on either legal compulsion (such as a contract right) or the commitment to continuing to create value for shareholders. Thus, rather than trusting the corporation as a partner, these third parties must always be on guard against the corporation's tendency to maximize shareholder value at their expense. This lack of trust creates antagonism and overly legalistic relationships that deter the creation of durable long-term value with trusted partners.

A third element that was important in my conversion was the position of the "universal owner." Large institutional owners, like pension funds and mutual funds, end up owning most of the market in order to be sufficiently diversified. Small asset owners, like an individual 401(k), would be wise to have the same diversification. The returns of such universal owners suffer from the commons-grazing effects of a corporate law regime that supports corporate managers who load negative externalities onto the system in order to "create value" for their individual shareholders. Hermes Investment Management, a well-known UK pension adviser, articulates this idea in its ownership principles: "Most investors are widely diversified; therefore it makes little sense for them to support activity by one company which is damaging to overall economic activity. . . . It makes little sense for pension funds to support commercial activity which creates an equal or greater cost to society by robbing Peter to pay Paul."

Yet traditional corporate law *requires* Paul Corp. to rob Peter Inc., even though they have the same shareholders. The fact is that institutional investors have emerged as an important force in corporate governance over the past two decades, and they are increasingly using their voice to act as stewards on behalf of their beneficiaries. This stewardship obligation will require institutions to manage not just companies but also the systems in which their portfolios are embedded, in order to prevent the Peter/Paul problem.

All of this led me to believe that there is good reason to provide an option where corporations can be managed for the good of all stakeholders rather than simply to provide a financial return to shareholders. Hopefully, by making room for such corporations, benefit corporation governance can create better opportunities for entrepreneurs and investors interested in corporations that operate in a responsible and sustainable manner, and place market pressure on other businesses to do the same.

I remain convinced that the for-profit corporation is the best vehicle for raising and allocating capital (other than for certain public goods that remain the responsibility of government and nongovernmental organizations). However, given the challenges that our planet and society face, I also believe we must find a way for that vehicle to recognize the interdependence of our complex globe, and the corresponding responsibility that corporations have. The benefit corporation provides a path.

Shareholder Primacy and Its Discontents

I suspect most Union Carbide shareholders would have been happy to accept a somewhat lower dividend if this allowed Union Carbide to adopt safety measures that would have prevented the deadly explosion in Bhopal, India, that killed 2,000 and severely injured thousands more.

Lynn Stout

We need to rethink exactly what we consider our wealth to be, what it is that we value, and whether it can or should be expressed only in terms of numbers and money.

Jane Gleeson-White

CHAPTER ONE

Corporations and Investors

SETTING THE STAGE

Chapter 1 provides context for the rest of the book. It includes a discussion of just what makes business entities like corporations so important to the global economy. It also explores the special privileges such entities enjoy, and the historical path that led to these privileges. Next is a brief exploration of the system through which savers channel their capital to the productive economy and of how that system interacts with corporations, which are often the final stop for capital flowing through the investment chain. Finally, the chapter raises the question whether the participants in the investment chain should have obligations to safeguard the vital systems they impact, in light of their powerful role in the economy. This question foreshadows the issue raised by benefit corporation law: Should the purpose of corporations encompass obligations to protect the systems that serve all of their stakeholders?

The Corporation

ROLE OF THE CORPORATION

This entire book is dedicated to the study of one form of corporation. The form is relatively new and still rare. As of the date of this publication, there are only five thousand benefit entities out of a total of 8 million business entities in the

United States.[1] Why then is the subject worthy of a book? More fundamentally, what is the significance of the distinction between benefit corporations and other entities?

Answering these questions requires an understanding of the importance of business corporations and the role they play in our economy.[2] In particular, it is important to understand the relationship between corporations and shareholders, who own the equity of such entities. These shareholders provide risk capital that drives the world economy. One source estimates that publicly traded equity has a value of $70 trillion, constituting 20 percent of the "value of everything."[3] By way of comparison, the same source estimates $100 trillion in fixed income securities and another $95 trillion in real estate value.

The ability of the corporation to organize capital and apply it to areas of need has long been recognized. A leading treatise from last century described the importance of the modern corporation to industrial society:

> Much of the industrial and commercial development of the nineteenth and twentieth centuries has been made possible by the corporate mechanism. By its use investors may combine their capital and participate in the profits of large- or small-scale business enterprises under a centralized management, with a risk limited to the capital contributed and without peril to their other resources and business. *The amount of capital needed for modern business could hardly have been assembled and combined in any other way* [emphasis added].[4]

The treatise goes on to say that the important elements of the corporate form are the right to hold property and otherwise deal with third parties as a separate person, limited liability for shareholders, continued existence when a shareholder dies or transfers shares, and centralized management and organization.

While this may all seem quite intuitive to a reader who has spent her entire existence in a society where transactions with artificial persons is routine, these corporate characteristics were quite disruptive. Without them, every enterprise that required the equity capital of more than one person would be subject to complex contracting issues, legal uncertainties, and financial risks that would make it extremely difficult to aggregate large amounts of financial capital. One leading English academic has noted the remarkable historical importance of the corporation:

That the corporation can explain the growth of nations around the world and the failure of others to progress is indicative of its macroeconomic significance. That the different nature of the corporation is associated with social benefits and ills and its changes over time with their emergence and eradication suggests that it is to the corporation that we should turn for the source of both our prosperity and our impoverishment.[5]

THE HISTORY OF THE CORPORATION

A very brief history of the corporation will help to explain why the development of the benefit corporation may be the leading edge of a critical turning point in economic history. Initially, when individuals wanted to engage in business enterprises, they could do so as individuals or, perhaps, as partners, but as such, they were subject to liability for everything that the enterprise did, and, whenever a partner left or a new partner was brought in, new contracts had to be established. This system did not work well for encouraging private enterprise that required large amounts of capital, but in the preindustrial age there was limited need for such capital formation.

Nevertheless, certain business enterprises did require significant financial capital. For example, trading companies required large amounts of risk capital to finance expensive operations abroad. Early English corporations were formed by royal act, creating charters for particular corporations to trade, such as the East India Company.[6] In Anglo-American history, these were followed by legislatively created charters that enabled corporations to collect sufficient capital to fuel the investments that brought about the industrial revolution.[7] Essentially, legislatures were choosing enterprises that they believed needed capital to deliver needed improvements—canals, bridges, railways, banks, and utilities. The enterprises were granted the advantages that came with incorporation. In exchange for these privileges, shareholders committed capital to enterprises that created social good.

Eventually, legislatures came to see the power of corporations to steer capital to productive use as an important public good, without regard to any particular industry. As a result, general incorporation laws were created, allowing any business to be structured as a corporation, without obtaining a charter from the legislature. This also had the salutary effect of depoliticizing incorporation, as access to the legislature was not a prerequisite to forming a corporation.

In 1811, New York became the first state in the United States to establish a general corporation law, but even that statute limited its use to corporations that manufactured textiles, glass, metals, or paint. Not until 1837 did a state adopt a general incorporation statute that could be used for any "lawful, specified purposes." Within these statutes, states initially imposed limits on corporate power, requiring strict statements of purpose, and limiting the right to own other corporations, but eventually these restrictions were lifted, due in part to competition among the states for charters.[8] As corporations grew in size and strength, they became the dominant players in the economy, and incorporation had fully shifted from a privilege to a right.[9] At the same time, the corporation shifted from being a public institution to a private one.[10] As a result, incorporation ceased to be viewed as a "concession" from the state.[11]

Corporations thus evolved as an institution created by government in order to benefit the societies they governed. They allowed investors to aggregate resources into an artificial person, without fear of personal liability. This, in turn, allowed for massive, efficient investment vehicles that create the goods and services that benefit society. As the economy became more complex, there were more instances in which these vehicles were advantageous. The end point of this evolution was general incorporation laws, which allowed any business to use the corporate form, without regard to social benefit.

The Investment Chain

THE STRUCTURE OF THE INVESTMENT CHAIN

The previous section discussed the history of the corporate form and touched on the rationale for granting it special rights. Corporate forms now dominate global business, with $70 trillion in equity capital invested in public companies, and more in private entities with corporate characteristics.[12] This section examines the context in which that equity is purchased and managed.

The history of the equity investor parallels the history of the corporation itself in many ways. As the economy grew beyond one based on land and agriculture, individuals who accumulated wealth needed ways to invest that wealth in new businesses beyond land ownership—first trade, then industry, and eventually all forms of business activity. Corporate shares provided a method to do this. Investors were able to save, but also to access their wealth by selling their shares. Moreover, they could invest in many different enterprises, without having to take on any of the burdens of managing the enterprises. Shares in corporations provided limited liability, liquidity, and diversification. Investors could fund an enterprise without concern that they could lose more than they invested. Shares of stock in business became a way to save, accumulate, and transfer wealth.

But although savings through stock ownership originated as direct ownership by individuals, the global capital system has become a vast and complex network. For example, in the United States, the value of publicly traded stocks in early 2017 was more than $25.6 trillion, much of which is held by "institutional owners."[13] These institutions include banks, mutual funds, pension funds, sovereign wealth funds, insurance companies, endowments, and foundations.[14] All of these institutions are holding that money on behalf of beneficiaries—insureds, pension beneficiaries, citizens, students, and others. Anne Tucker has pointed out that citizens' participation in the stock market through this system is not voluntary; in the United States, in particular, workers saving for retirement are forced to become "citizen shareholders."[15] Those institutions employ asset managers, who in turn employ consultants and additional managers.

In this system, the directors and officers of corporations are essentially the last line of fiduciaries in a long chain. For example, an individual may buy a mutual fund in a 401(k) plan.[16] That fund may employ asset managers, who in turn rely on outside consultants. Those consultants may recommend the purchase of shares in particular corporations, whose directors and officers finally deploy the assets that underlie the individual's retirement savings into the real economy. As table 1 (on page 14) shows, assets may go through every link in the chain, or skip one or more links, as when a human being invests directly in a public corporation, skipping the layers of asset owners and managers. In contrast, a human being's capital may flow through multiple links, encountering advisers at each level, and perhaps flowing through multiple layers of subadvisers.

TABLE 1: THE INVESTING CHAIN

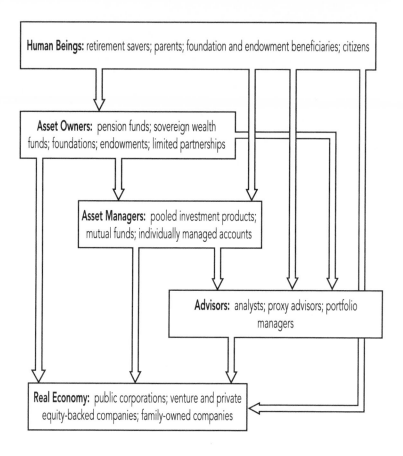

One author described this as a long chain of delegation in the investment management industry:

> At the top of the investment management industry are the individual investors, those who invest in pension funds and mutual funds or invest through bank savings accounts or insurance contracts. Individual investors are delegating most of their investment decisions to these asset owners. Asset owners then delegate asset management to in-house managers or external funds. These asset managers then delegate the decision on how to allocate capital

across productive projects to corporate executives. Corporate executives can thus be viewed as the bottom of the investment management industry.[17]

This chain of investment performs many important functions. It allows members of society to protect their savings throughout their own life cycle and to save for housing, for education, and for retirement. It allows society to channel savings into productive investments. Finally, and most importantly for the purposes of this book, this investment channel creates a mechanism whereby asset owners— or their representatives—can oversee and provide stewardship for those assets.[18]

THE ABSENCE OF SOCIETAL RESPONSIBILITIES IN THE INVESTMENT CHAIN

The allocation and use of these assets has tremendous effects on civic life and the environment—the corporate executives at the bottom of the investing chain must make decisions about treatment of workers, supply chains, and carbon emissions. In light of the tremendous amount of capital the financial industry oversees, one might believe that the asset managers along the chain would assume a certain level of societal responsibility. Yet, despite their critical role, these investment professionals often believe that their focus as investment fiduciaries must be on maximizing the return on the companies in the portfolios under their charge, and not on broader societal issues: "The majority of mainstream asset owners hold the view that it is not only appropriate, but required, to focus only on delivering financial returns to clients and beneficiaries."[19]

However, this limited view of investing can be self-defeating for beneficiaries, because the long-term financial cost of the externalities to diversified portfolios may outweigh any benefit gained at particular companies that create those external costs.[20] The chief justice of the Delaware Supreme Court has noted that the voice of the ultimate beneficiaries of institutional funds is not heard in this investing chain: "As a human investor, you turn your capital over every paycheck to funds available among fund families chosen by your employer. Those funds are effectively available to you only when you hit fifty-nine-and-a-half years old. Thus, for decades . . . you do not get to pick the shares of stock bought on your behalf or to express any view about how those shares are voted."[21]

The money managers and other intermediaries ignore the larger concerns that should be of most concern to those whom Chief Justice Strine calls "the human investor," and Professor Tucker the "citizen shareholder." Their focus on returns within the portfolios they manage means that they may ignore the effect that the components of those portfolios have on the system as a whole, including the markets themselves and the world in which the beneficiaries live. This leads to actions that can actually create systemic damage. Thamotheram and Ward compare the damage done by investment management that ignores systemic risk to doctor-induced illness:

> An iatrogenic illness is an illness caused by medication or a physician. By analogy iatrogenic risk is risk caused by the investment industry itself relating to the real world of the end-beneficiary, a world that investment intermediaries, especially the richest and most senior decision-makers, isolate themselves from. In a nutshell, the financial return from investment of, for example, a pension fund may fail to compensate for the costs imposed by environmental and social degradation owing to said investments.[22]

The evolution of this concern, and its interaction with the forces driving the adoption of benefit corporation legislation, are discussed in later chapters. However, this work is only focused on the changes that benefit corporation law effects with respect to the duties of directors. The foregoing discussion suggests that there should be a similar recalibration with respect to the fiduciary duties of asset managers and owners to the ultimate beneficiaries of the assets under management.[23] As with corporations themselves, investment fiduciaries may face problems of collective action and free riding when making decisions that have direct positive effects on investment returns and less direct, but negative, effects on the systems within which those investments operate.[24] Nevertheless, these investment fiduciaries ultimately control immense wealth that may be the only store of societal resources available to address our most pressing concerns: "Philanthropy is a powerful force for good. But the funds contributed by global philanthropy, even when combined with the development or aid budgets of many national governments (themselves facing budget constraints), add up to mere *billions*. The cost of solving problems such as water scarcity, climate change, and lack of access to health care, education, and affordable housing runs into the *trillions* of dollars."[25]

* * *

It is within this complex system of investment that corporations operate. The next chapter examines the ways that corporate law has traditionally protected the interests of shareholders within this system.

CHAPTER TWO

Fiduciary Duties for Conventional Corporations
ENFORCING SHAREHOLDER PRIMACY

Chapter 1 discussed the context in which the modern business corporation operates. This chapter focuses on one critical aspect of the modern conventional corporation: shareholder primacy. It begins with a discussion of some basic corporate law rules, establishing that corporations are a representative system, where shareholders elect directors who manage the corporation. It then discusses, in detail, the historical tug and pull between shareholder primacy and governance oriented toward the interests of all stakeholders. It then shows that, for now, shareholder primacy has emerged as the dominant model in the United States. The chapter then discusses how stakeholders fare in this model, including a specific discussion of how shareholder primacy impacts creditors and preferred shareholders. This latter discussion includes an illustration of the economic irrationality that shareholder primacy can create.

Basic Rules of Corporate Governance

As detailed in chapter 1, the corporation is the final link in the chain that takes financial capital from savers and channels it to productive uses in the economy. In this role, the corporation evolved to perform two essential functions in the modern economy. First, it allowed business to raise the large amounts of capital that are critical to building the large enterprises necessary to create an industrial society. Second, it provided a vehicle for individuals—and the institutions that represent their collective interests—to invest in multiple businesses in order to diversify their investments and maintain liquidity. This chapter discusses the relationship between these two functions. That is, how does corporate law ensure that businesses that possess the financial capital contributed by savers use that capital in a manner that furthers the interests of the business, but also protects the interests of the savers in accumulating and transferring wealth?

The answer lies in the legal concepts that have come to define the relationship between company, management, and shareholders. These include a variety of corporate governance rights that shareholders possess. Among these are the right to elect the directors who manage the business of a corporation, the right to remove directors under certain circumstances, and the right to approve changes to corporate constitutional documents, as well as mergers, assets sales, and dissolutions. Shareholders also have rights to inspect the corporate books.[1]

These governance rights are part of what is essentially a representative system, however. That is, while these mechanisms give shareholders the ultimate control over the corporation, they do not involve shareholders in the day-to-day, or even long-term, management of the corporate enterprise. That remains in the hands of the board of directors and the officers and employees of the corporation. This rule is established in Section 141 of the Delaware General Corporation Law, the statute that governs most publicly traded corporations in the United States: "The business and affairs of every corporation organized under this chapter shall be managed by or under the direction of a board of directors."[2]

Section 141 articulates a bedrock corporate law principle that directors manage the corporation.[3] This management function is regulated by duties that require directors to manage the corporation's assets carefully and loyally.[4] First, the duty of care requires the directors of a corporation to act deliberately, and on an informed basis.[5] Second, the duty of loyalty requires directors to focus on the best interests of the corporation and its shareholders, rather than on their own interests.[6] The duty of loyalty includes a requirement to act in good faith.[7]

A shareholder may challenge a director's loyalty by alleging that the director had a conflict of interest or was influenced by someone who did.[8] The principles underlying these duties are critical to understanding the problems created by conventional corporation law, and the solution that benefit corporation law offers. This chapter describes the relevant law for conventional corporations, including some areas of dispute that are particularly relevant when considering benefit corporations.

For Whom Is the Corporation Managed?

The preceding (very) simplified portrait of corporate governance represents a fairly basic construct: shareholders provide equity capital to corporations, and retain loose governance rights, but are handing over the management of the enterprise to others—directors and managers. These directors and managers are thus acting *on behalf* of the shareholders. In so doing, they are expected to hew to the conduct prescribed by the duties of care and loyalty—they must take adequate care, and must also not use the assets for their own selfish interests.

But once the assets are invested in a business enterprise, a host of other stakeholders quickly become relevant. In addition to its shareholders, a corporation has workers, customers, and neighbors. These are just some of the more obvious stakeholders. The operations of a corporation may create wealth and opportunity that benefits individuals around the globe, and future generations as well. By the same token, it may create risks to the global community by using a supply chain with human rights abuses, or create risks to future generations by wasting scarce resources or emitting environmentally harmful substances.

It thus seems that there are at least two ways to interpret what it means for a director to be both loyal and careful. First, they might view their fiduciary compact as extending solely to shareholders—that is, directors must carefully and loyally manage the corporation in order to provide the best possible return on capital for the shareholders. This manner of operation is known as "shareholder primacy." In contrast, a director might act carefully and loyally but aim to benefit a broader set of stakeholders, or even all of the corporation's stakeholders.[9] The rest of this chapter presents a detailed discussion of this distinction. The argument of the chapter is that traditional corporate law wavers between these two ideas, but has, in the past forty years, moved strongly toward share-holder primacy. Benefit corporation law, the subject of this book, is a tool to move in the other direction and require directors to consider the interests of all stakeholders.

This critical distinction between conventional contemporary corporate governance and benefit corporation governance can be articulated in terms of corporate purpose. Does the corporation exist solely for the benefit of shareholders, or for other stakeholders as well? This question has been the subject of debate for many years; the shareholder primacy and stakeholder models of the firm best encapsulate the competing visions of corporate purpose. Adolph A. Berle and Merrick Dodd were two famous scholars who argued in favor of one or the other model, with Berle arguing for shareholder primacy (sometimes called the "ownership" model of the firm) and Dodd arguing for consideration of other stakeholders (which is sometimes called the "enterprise" model).[10] Under the shareholder primacy model, the shareholders are considered the owners of the corporation and look to the directors to manage their assets solely for their benefit.[11] In contrast, the stakeholder model of the firm views the corporation as an institution whose purpose is to serve multiple constituencies.[12] As we discussed in chapter 1, the attributes granted to the corporation by the state—such as the ability to enter into contracts, to limit the liability of investors, and to have unlimited duration—are extremely advantageous to the corporation, which, the stakeholder theory posits, should correspondingly serve the interests of the state.[13]

THE SHAREHOLDER PRIMACY MODEL

The quintessential case cited in support of shareholder primacy is *Dodge v. Ford Motor Co.*, decided by the Michigan Supreme Court in 1919. In *Dodge*, the corporation stopped paying dividends to shareholders in order to produce less expensive products and to increase employee wages. In determining that the shareholders were entitled to the payment of dividends, the court articulated the basic tenets of shareholder primacy: "A business corporation is organized and carried on primarily for the profit of the stockholders. The powers of the directors are to be employed for that end. The discretion of directors is to be exercised in the choice of means to attain that end, and does not extend to a change in the end itself, to the reduction of profits, or to the nondistribution of profits among stockholders in order to devote them to other purposes."[14] Thus, the corporation has a single purpose: to maximize value for its shareholders (as "owners"), within the bounds of law.

In addition to ownership, the primacy model has been linked in academic literature to the "nexus of contracts" theory, which views the corporation as a legal fiction that facilitates complex transactions and views directors as agents for shareholders, who are most in need of protection in such a model.[15] Chancellor Allen explains that under this model of the corporation, stakeholders other than shareholders, such as employees or creditors, can enter into contracts with the corporation in return for things like salaries or agreed-upon interest payments.[16] These stakeholders, however, do not bear the same risk as the shareholder, who is not entitled to a fixed return like a salary or an interest payment but rather is only entitled to what, if anything, remains after all of the corporation's legal commitments are fulfilled.[17] Other stakeholders can also be protected by external laws that regulate the workplace, creditor rights, the environment, and many other areas in which corporate activity affects stakeholders.[18] Thus, the shareholders, as the residual risk bearers, can be understood as having "contracted for a promise to maximize long-run profits of the firm, which in turn maximizes the value of their stock."[19]

Under either the ownership or the contract theory, shareholders are like principals, relying on corporate directors and managers to act as agents on their behalf.[20] In the case of the modern corporation, this means that directors and management thus have control over large amounts of the capital that should be managed for the shareholders' benefit. This control creates a risk that managers will use corporate resources for their own purposes. This risk in turn creates two drains on the shareholders' capital: any resources actually appropriated by management, and the costs incurred to prevent such appropriation.[21] Shareholder primacy is sometimes justified as a solution to this "agency problem."

Worse still, this appropriation may come in the form of allocating the financial capital inefficiently, wasting scarce resources that could be used in a more productive fashion. For example, a CEO may expand a corporation by acquiring other companies, in a manner that decreases the shareholder return on equity, due to inefficiencies that come with combining incompatible businesses. The

CEO may be tempted to take these actions in order to increase her own salary, because compensation is correlated to business size.[22] Shareholder primacy is, in theory, a tool to combat this type of behavior, because it imposes a legal obligation on management to conduct the business in a way that benefits the shareholders, not the managers, which means applying the shareholders' capital to its most profitable use. Thus, it is argued, shareholder primacy is an efficient tool for allocating capital.

THE STAKEHOLDER MODEL

In contrast, the stakeholder model starts with the idea that the corporation is created by the government and therefore has a social function.[23] Thus, directors should consider not only shareholder returns but also all other constituencies that have a stake in the corporation, such as its employees, its debtholders, the environment, and the community.[24] Under this model, it is up to the board of directors to balance these competing interests. Lynn Stout is perhaps the most well-known and articulate contemporary proponent of this model within the legal academic community. In a piece coauthored with Margaret Blair, she described the board's obligation to the broad community: "Thus, the primary job of the board of directors of a public corporation is not to act as agents who ruthlessly pursue shareholders' interests at the expense of employees, creditors, or other team members. Rather, the directors are trustees for the corporation itself—mediating hierarchs whose job is to balance team members' competing interests in a fashion that keeps everyone happy enough that the productive coalition stays together."[25]

In the mid-twentieth century, the stakeholder model held sway, at least in popular culture, as this quote from a leading executive of the time demonstrates: "The job of management is to maintain an equitable and working balance among the claims of various directly affected interest groups . . . stockholders, employees, customers, and the public at large. Business managers are gaining professional status partly because they see in their work the basic responsibility [to the public]."[26]

Or, as *Time* magazine put it at the time, business leaders were willing to "judge their actions, not only from the standpoint of profit and loss on the balance sheet, but of profit and loss to the community."[27] This model challenges the basic tenet of shareholder primacy: that a corporation should be managed as if its primary purpose is to maximize profits. Instead, the postwar conception treated the corporation as an institution owned by all of the stakeholders: "In fact, in the first three decades following WW II . . . the large corporation was in effect "owned" by everyone with a stake in how it performed."[28]

Berle himself, often thought of as the quintessential champion of shareholder primacy, seemed to believe that although it was important for shareholders to retain the control of (and the corresponding benefit from) the corporation from managers, such an accomplishment was inevitably a step toward a broader conception of "ownership": "It is conceivable—indeed it seems almost essential if the corporate system is to survive—that the "control" of the great corporations should develop into a purely neutral technocracy, balancing a variety of claims by various groups in the community and assigning to each a portion of the income stream on the basis of public policy rather than private cupidity."[29]

However, the policy significance of the stakeholder model should not be lost in the semantic question of "ownership." The underlying assumption is that if society is to grant all the privileges of incorporation to business enterprises, then those enterprises, in return, should be managed to create a benefit for society. Accordingly, the rules for managing corporations should be structured to ensure that all of society benefits from those rules, not just shareholders.

One significant criticism of the stakeholder model is that it is simply unworkable. The concern is that there is no good way to balance the profusion of stakeholder interests, so that the model leaves directors with no clear mandate (and thus with ample room to abuse their authority, since there is no good way to measure their fidelity). Economist Michael Jensen describes this objection: "Any organization must have a single-valued objective as a precursor to purposeful or rational behavior. . . . It is logically impossible to maximize in more than one dimension at the same time. Thus, telling a manager to maximize current profits, market share, future growth profits, and anything else one pleases will leave that manager with no way to make a reasoned decision."[30]

Others refute this claim by reference to the multifaceted nature of general decision making.[31] This dispute—whether enterprises can ever efficiently serve all stakeholders and not just shareholders—illustrates that the proponents of shareholder primacy might accept the premise that corporate law should be fashioned to benefit society as a whole, yet still believe that the way to do that is, in fact, to maximize shareholder value. To a significant degree, that is the argument that has gained the upper hand, as discussed in the next section.

THE UNITED STATES GENERALLY FOLLOWS SHAREHOLDER PRIMACY

During the twentieth century, economies across the globe moved toward corporate capitalism, as large corporations with disparate shareholders began to control significant amounts of private capital. As we have seen, there has been a lingering question whether this capital is to be managed in the interests of all stakeholders or solely for the benefit of shareholders.

Although some academics would differ, shareholder primacy has essentially won out, particularly in the United States, the United Kingdom, and other jurisdictions that follow the Anglo-American legal tradition.[32] Economic theory, along with the liberalization of global capital markets, paved the way for this victory,[33] but it was a series of decisions by the Delaware courts that cemented the place of shareholder primacy.[34]

The most important of these was the *Revlon, Inc. v. MacAndrews & Forbes Holdings, Inc.* case decided by the Delaware Supreme Court in 1985.[35] As mentioned, Delaware is the preeminent corporate jurisdiction in the United States, and the decisions of its supreme court have resonance throughout the United States and beyond. In *Revlon*, the board of Revlon was faced with an acquisition proposal that appealed to the shareholders but that the board believed would result in a poor outcome for the corporate enterprise, including its bondholders. The board took measures to defeat the takeover bid and was sued for breaching its duty to shareholders. The board defended itself by arguing that the takeover would hurt bondholders.

However, the Delaware Supreme Court invalidated the defensive actions (which involved selling the company to a different bidder), rejecting the idea that the board had the duty, or even the option, to consider the interests of stakeholders other than shareholders in a sale process. The court found that, because the company was being sold, considerations of the interests of such stakeholders could in no way help the shareholders, because for them there was no "long run." Accordingly, the sole objective for directors had to be immediate wealth maximization for shareholders, even if the high bid might destroy large amounts of bondholder value (or, by extension, worker or community value).[36] Other Delaware authority has established that corporations exist primarily to generate shareholder value,[37] even though Delaware's corporate purpose statute broadly states that a corporation may undertake "any lawful business or purpose."[38]

eBay Domestic Holdings, Inc. v. Newmark is a more recent example of the Delaware focus on shareholder wealth maximization, even outside the sale context. In *eBay*, the directors of Craigslist employed defensive measures to prevent or, alternatively, slow eBay's ability to take control of Craigslist. In defending their actions, the Craigslist board argued that the defensive measures were put in place not for economic reasons but to protect the company's social values and community-centered culture. The court found that this motivation was inappropriate, and in doing so, clearly embraced shareholder primacy:

> The corporate form in which Craigslist operates . . . is not an appropriate vehicle for purely philanthropic ends, at least not when there are other stockholders interested in realizing a return on their investment. [Craigslist's directors] opted to form Craigslist, Inc. as a for-profit Delaware corporation and voluntarily accepted millions of dollars from eBay as part of a transaction whereby eBay became a stockholder. *Having chosen a for-profit corporate form, the Craigslist directors are bound by the fiduciary duties and standards that accompany that form. Those standards include acting to promote the value of the corporation for the benefit of its stockholders.* The "Inc." after the company name has to mean at least that. Thus, I cannot accept as valid for the purposes of implementing the Rights Plan a corporate policy that specifically, clearly, and admittedly seeks not to maximize the economic value of a for-profit Delaware corporation for the benefit of its stockholders—no matter whether those stockholders are individuals of modest means or a corporate titan of online commerce. . . . Directors of a for-profit Delaware corporation cannot deploy a rights plan to defend a business strategy that openly eschews stockholder wealth maximization—at least not consistently with the directors' fiduciary duty under Delaware law [emphasis added].[39]

The *eBay* case underlines the fact that the law requires that corporations operate for the benefit of their shareholders, and, for that reason, directors must perform their duties with the primary focus of increasing shareholder wealth.[40] Even in light of *eBay*, some commentators remain unpersuaded.[41] However, even proponents of the stakeholder theory will recognize the difficulty of ignoring the clear language of the case:

> The *eBay* case has the potential for a large impact similar to *Dodge v. Ford*, especially in the takeover defense arena, even if some academics feel that *eBay* was wrongly decided or should be limited to minority oppression fact patterns. . . . The *eBay* case will likely work itself into corporate lore and could push risk adverse social entrepreneurs, especially those using the Delaware for-profit form, in the direction of shareholder wealth maximization.[42]

In his academic writings, the chief justice of the Delaware Supreme Court has adopted a reading of the Delaware case law consistent with the shareholder primacy model and has summarized it with the following proposition: "The object of the corporation is to produce profits for the stockholders and . . . the social beliefs of the manager, no more than their own financial interests, cannot be their end in managing the corporation."[43]

As Delaware goes, so goes the nation; as a result of the *Revlon* decision, many felt that the law of the land was clearly shareholder primacy. In response, thirty-three states adopted specific provisions, called constituency statutes, that gave directors the ability (but generally not the obligation) to consider the interests of other stakeholders. (This will be discussed further in chapter 9.) Delaware, however, did not adopt such a provision.

With Delaware refusing to adopt a constituency statute, and those statutes continuing to permit (if not require) shareholder primacy, the United States remains dominated by shareholder primacy. Moreover, many jurisdictions around the world are heavily influenced by the doctrine, as shown by a series of papers recently drafted by experts in more than thirty countries in response to a 2015 questionnaire prepared by Professor Robert Eccles of the Harvard Business School. The questionnaire was answered for the United States by the American Bar Association's Task Force on Sustainable Development. That response concluded that: "The United States is a 'shareholder primacy' jurisdiction, meaning that the primary focus of corporations is to return profit to shareholders. If stakeholder needs are considered, they are a secondary concern."[44]

Whether the law in this area creates or reflects societal values is beyond the scope of this work. However, it is important to note the correlation between the two. As mentioned, the postwar attitude in the United States reflected a stakeholder bent: corporations were viewed as having broad purposes. More than a decade before *Revlon* was decided, however, that consensus had begun to recede. In 1970, Milton Friedman penned an article in the *New York Times Magazine* with the title "The Social Responsibility of Business Is to Increase Its Profits."[45] A deep analysis of the multiple strands of finance, political, and business trends leading to this shift is set out in Pavlos E. Masouros's *Corporate Law and Economic Stagnation*.[46] Contemporary business culture in the early twenty-first century largely accepts this role. In a *New York Times* article exploring whether ExxonMobil put the interests of shareholders before the global political interests of the United States, a company spokesperson was comfortable explaining, "Absent a law prohibiting something, we evaluate it on a business case basis."[47]

THE STATUS OF STAKEHOLDERS IN THE CONVENTIONAL CORPORATION

Each of the *Ford*, *Revlon*, and *eBay* cases was unusual, in that there was testimony from management stating that corporate action was taken for the primary benefit of stakeholders. In contrast, directors can usually tie action that benefits stakeholders to a corresponding shareholder value motive. For example, directors may assert that a charitable giving program, while benefiting the recipients of the charities, is ultimately aimed at enhancing the corporation's reputation in order to improve product sales and employee recruitment and retention. Accordingly, directors retain substantial discretion to consider all stakeholders in determining how to best achieve long-term shareholder wealth maximization under the "business judgment rule," which we will discuss in detail in chapter 3.[48] However, the Delaware courts have made it clear that directors may consider other constituencies only if such considerations coincide with the maximization of long-term shareholder value.[49]

Some argue that Delaware case law—specifically, the supreme court's decision in *Unocal v. Mesa Petroleum Co.*[50]—has explicitly recognized the legitimacy of directors considering non-shareholder interests as a primary concern when making business decisions. *Unocal* involved a hostile takeover, that is, a situation where an acquirer was attempting to gain control of the corporation even though the board of directors opposed the transaction. This type of situation often tests the question of what stakeholders a board may consider, because changes in control can result in large premiums being paid to shareholders but, at the same time, may result in corporate restructurings that damage other stakeholders, such as workers and communities.[51] Where the board resists a hostile takeover, it is not uncommon for shareholders to claim that the board is resisting the takeover in order to benefit a constituency other than shareholders. In *Unocal*, the court recognized this concern but found that a board *could* consider other stakeholders, *as long as that consideration was in service of shareholder value in the long run*.

In *Unocal*, the court acknowledged the "basic principle that corporate directors have a fiduciary duty to act in the best interests of the corporation's stockholders," but the court also legitimized the consideration of other concerns when facing a hostile takeover, including "the impact on 'constituencies' other than shareholders (i.e., creditors, customers, employees, and perhaps even the community generally)."[52] Some have claimed that *Unocal* demonstrates that the board may consider "the corporation," separate and apart from shareholders, implying that all stakeholders have equal dignity: "The court opined that the corporate board had a 'fundamental duty and obligation to protect the corporate enterprise, which includes stockholders,' a formulation that clearly implies the two are not identical."[53] However, others persuasively argue that the decisions in *Revlon* and *eBay* explicitly reject any such interpretation.[54] The chief justice of the Delaware Supreme Court lends credence to the latter interpretation through an anecdote from the *Revlon* oral arguments: "The Revlon directors argued that it was proper for them to consider the interests of [other constituencies] under the Supreme Court's recent ruling in *Unocal*. . . . The lawyer who argued for the directors, A. Gilchrist Sparks III, indicated that this argument was quickly dispensed with by the Justices at oral argument, when Justice Moore said in words or substance that *Unocal* did not mean that."[55] Instead, the Delaware Supreme Court has held that the rights of other constituencies such as creditors, employees, and the community, are limited to the protections offered by statutory, contractual, and common law rights.[56]

This view, that stakeholder interests are a valid board consideration when related to shareholder value, is consistent with the court's interpretation of the express statutory power that corporations have to make corporate donations for "charitable, scientific, or educational purposes."[57] The courts have limited this power with the principle that such gifts must benefit the shareholders in the long run. According to *Theodora Holding Corp. v. Henderson:*

> It is accordingly obvious, in my opinion, that the relatively small loss of immediate income otherwise payable to plaintiff and the corporate defendant's other stockholders, had it not been for the gift in question, is far outweighed by the overall benefits flowing from the placing of such gift in channels where it serves to benefit those in need of philanthropic or educational support, thus providing justification for large private holdings, thereby benefiting [stockholders] in the long run.[58]

Thus, the Delaware courts have made it clear that other constituencies may be considered, but only when their interests align with the long-term wealth maximization of the corporation's shareholders. As *Theodora* makes clear, however, the tie to shareholder value may be quite tenuous.

MULTIPLE INVESTOR CONSTITUENCIES

In addition to common shareholders, preferred shareholders and creditors may have direct investments in a corporation. These constituencies often have interests that conflict with those of the common shareholders, because they may receive different rewards from the corporation's success and may suffer different levels of loss in the case of poor performance. For groups other than common shareholders, the protections offered by Delaware law are limited when a corporation remains solvent. In some respects, the limited obligations of directors toward the holders of preferred stock and debt are analogous to the limited director obligations to stakeholders under traditional corporate law. This analogy may serve to highlight the weakness of a governance model that insists on favoring one constituency over all others.

As the *Revlon* case established, directors do not generally have fiduciary duties to consider the interests of creditors. Traditionally, creditors are "afforded protection through contractual agreements, fraud and fraudulent conveyance law, implied covenants of good faith and fair dealing, bankruptcy law, general commercial law and other sources of creditor rights,"[59] and the general rule is that directors do not owe creditors duties beyond the relevant contractual terms and commercial law, such as fraudulent transfer statutes.[60] However, creditors have tried to claim that, as a corporation approaches insolvency, the creditors should take the place of shareholders in the fiduciary scheme, because at that point it is creditors who bear the "residual risk," as described in the contract theory, discussed earlier.

Creditors have tried to use this argument to create fiduciary duties to creditors when a corporation is in the "zone of insolvency," but the Delaware courts have rejected such arguments.[61] When a corporation is actually insolvent, however, courts have held that its creditors do take the place of the shareholders as the residual beneficiaries of any increase (or decrease) in value of the corporation. Accordingly, the corporation's insolvency "makes the creditors the principal constituency injured by any fiduciary breaches that diminish the firm's value."[62] Due to this shift, the Delaware Supreme Court has recognized a creditor's ability to bring a derivative claim against a corporation for a breach of fiduciary duty when the corporation is insolvent, but has nevertheless expressly rejected any direct claims against a corporation by individual creditors for breach of fiduciary duty.[63]

The position of preferred shareholders with respect to director fiduciary duties is less clear. Their rights are generally contractual in nature.[64] However, the corporation may owe fiduciary duties to preferred shareholders when the right claimed is shared equally with the common shareholders.[65] (This might involve a claim for breach of the duty of care, for example.) When the interests of the common and preferred shareholders diverge, however, "the directors generally must 'prefer the interests of common stock—as the good faith judgment of the board sees them to be—to the interests created by the special rights, preferences, etc., of preferred stock.'"[66] The Delaware courts have also suggested that preferred shareholders may be owed certain fiduciary duties when the preferred shareholders have no contractual protection.[67]

The implication of this requirement of "common shareholder primacy" can be quite stark, and perhaps counterintuitive, because the fact that creditors and preferred shareholders are paid off before common shareholders creates strange incentives if a corporation's value barely covers the priority due to the preferred shareholders. Indeed, cases such as *Trados* and *LC Masterfund* suggest that directors are required to take actions (such as engaging in high-risk trans- actions) that benefit common shareholders over creditors or shareholders with preferences, *even where the actions do not create the most value for the enterprise as a whole.* In such situations, if the corporation's assets would only be enough to pay off the creditors and the preferred stock, the common shares will gain most of the upside if a risky decision creates value, while the downside of such a decision is mostly suffered by those with preferred returns, including credi- tors and preferred shareholders. This asymmetric risk allocation means a board charged with maximizing common share value may make a bet with a negative risk adjusted return, because the downside risk is borne by security holders to whom no duty is owed, while the security holders to whom a duty is owed receive any upside.

Interestingly, earlier case law suggested that directors should ignore the risk profiles of particular investors when the company was near insolvency, and should take actions that create the most value for the enterprise as a whole, in order to avoid inefficient decisions.[68] The evolution of the cases toward a single constituency (the common shareholder, as residual risk-bearer) with a single goal (high share value) follows the post-*Revlon* shift to promote shareholder interests over those of all other stakeholders. From a holistic perspective, each of these narrow focal points can lead to similarly inefficient outcomes.

DIRECTORS CANNOT PROTECT IDIOSYNCRATIC COMMON SHAREHOLDER GOALS

Even common shareholders may have goals other than maximizing share value. For example, a controlling shareholder may have a preference for a transaction that promises liquidity, which could create a conflicting interest.[69] Nevertheless, courts have noted that a controlling shareholder's desire for liquidity rarely creates a "disabling conflict of interest" when all shareholders receive the same pro rata consideration in a transaction. In addition to liquidity concerns, a controlling shareholder could favor a transaction for tax or other idiosyncratic reasons.[70] For example, a director might want to promote the interests of another stakeholder in the corporation, regardless of any connection to shareholder value, or have an interest in preserving the environment or the local community. Supporting such an interest to the detriment of shareholders could be "conscious disregard" for the interests of shareholders and thus constitute "bad faith."[71] Accordingly, even nonfinancial interests of the common shareholders themselves must be subordinated by directors bound by the shareholder primacy model.

* * *

In this chapter, we have seen how shareholder primacy has come to dominate corporate law. Chapter 3 will explain how courts enforce this rule.

CHAPTER THREE

Standards of Review

HOW JUDGES DECIDE WHETHER DIRECTORS ARE PUTTING SHAREHOLDERS FIRST

I n chapter 2, we showed that in the United States, and particularly in Delaware, courts have settled on the rule of shareholder primacy. In this chapter we will discuss the details of how courts enforce that rule. In corporate law, the critical question in enforcing fiduciary duties is the "standard of review," which is the formula that a court will use when a shareholder brings a lawsuit claiming that directors have violated their obligations. Understanding the enforcement mechanism is critical to understanding how both shareholder primacy and benefit corporation law operate. This chapter discusses how the standard of review operates under conventional corporate law. Later in the book, after discussing the new benefit corporation statutes, we will return to this subject and address how those standards are likely to operate for benefit corporations. In addition, chapter 9 includes a discussion of how those standards have been interpreted in states that have adopted "constituency statutes," which reject shareholder primacy but do not include the purpose, accountability, and transparency requirements imposed by benefit corporation statutes.

Function of Standards of Review

Standards of review establish the role of a court in determining whether a challenged board decision was made consistently with fiduciary obligations.[1] Delaware courts generally use one of three standards when reviewing most actions taken by the board of directors. These three standards are the business judgment rule, the entire fairness standard, and the "intermediate" or "enhanced" scrutiny standard. Determining which standard of review to apply is a fact-specific inquiry. Although these three standards are used in most cases, the courts on occasion use other standards for judging actions that interfere with the free exercise of voting rights by shareholders.

In deciding which standard to apply, a court must first determine whether the directors were disinterested and independent. If so, the business judgment rule will apply, giving great deference to board decisions. In the absence of such independence—where the board has conflicts of interest—a very strict standard of review will apply: entire fairness. In intermediate situations, where structural conflicts are inherent—such as company sales and hostile takeovers—an intermediate standard of review—enhanced business judgment—will apply.[2]

Table 2 (on page 37) summarizes the different standards that courts will apply, depending on the situation. These standards will be applied to benefit corporations as well, and it is important to understand the underpinnings of the standards, as their application to benefit corporations may require certain modifications, and these changes will affect the viability of the benefit corporation form.

The Business Judgment Rule

Under the business judgment rule, disinterested directors are given very broad discretion to make decisions. While the business judgment rule functions as a litigation standard, it also implements an important substantive law concept: in order to effectively fulfill their management role, directors should be able to make rational judgments and take calculated risks without fear of judicial second-guessing. David Yosifon explains the substantive policy rationale for this procedural rule:

> Several justifications are given for the business judgment rule. Most simply it is seen as giving force to the statutory injunction that "the business and affairs of every corporation . . . shall be managed by or under the direction of a board of directors." Del. Gen. Corp. L.

§ 141(a). Since somebody has to have the last word on what corporate decisions are legitimate, the business judgment rule sees to it that, per the statute, it is the directors who decide, not complaining shareholders, not other stakeholders, and not indifferent courts. Directors are likely to know more about the particulars of problems their firms face than are relatively ignorant shareholders, stakeholders, and judges.[3]

In order to support director authority, the business judgment rule provides that initially only the directors' decision-making *process* can be reviewed—not the substance of the decision itself. Accordingly, the first question in a proceeding challenging a business decision made by directors is whether they were independent, careful, and acting in good faith.[4] If so, then under the business judgment rule, the analysis is ended—the court does not examine the substance of the decision.[5] The business judgment rule provides that a decision will not

TABLE 2: STANDARDS OF REVIEW		
Situation	**Standard of Review**	**Effect**
Normal business decision	Business judgment rule	Very limited, if any, review of substance; court only reviews board process.
Selling the company	*Revlon* enhanced business judgment rule	Court reviews substance to determine if board took reasonable steps to maximize share value; stakeholders not considered.
Actions to defend against changes in control	*Unocal* enhanced business judgment rule	Defensive actions must not be preclusive or coercive and must be reasonable in relation to threat to shareholder interests. Stakeholder interests may be taken into account to extent they relate to shareholder value.
Conflict transactions	Entire fairness standard	Strict substantive review by courts to ensure directors and controlling shareholder do not receive benefit to detriment of shareholders.
Shareholder voting issues	*Blasius* test	Court will review to ensure board is not taking action in order to thwart shareholder votes or preserve its own control.

be interfered with by the courts, even if it appears to have been unwise or to have caused loss to the corporation or its shareholders, so long as the board is independent and informed and acts in good faith.[6] However, when applying this rule, courts do not permit decisions that are "irrational" to stand.[7]

Although this ability to review decisions for "rationality" might appear to be a review of substance, courts have explained that this minimal standard of substantive review is a means by which to detect bad faith.[8] It will be important to bear this minimal substantive test in mind when applying the business judgment rule to decisions made by directors of benefit corporations, where this substantive test may be the only litigation tool available to challenge any "trade-off" decisions made among stakeholders.[9]

Thus, although directors are required to pursue value maximization for the corporation's shareholders, the business judgment rule affords directors wide leeway in deciding how to accomplish this goal. With the substantial deference afforded to their business decisions, directors are able to sacrifice short-term corporate profits and provide benefits to other stakeholders so long as these actions serve a shareholder value maximization strategy, even if that strategy is long term, and does not immediately maximize share value.[10] For example, a board may decide to increase employee salaries based on a judgment that such an action will promote the long-term productivity of the company, despite the fact that the action will temporarily decrease the corporation's short-term profits, and (perhaps) consequently lower the company's stock price.[11]

Some commentators have suggested that the business judgment rule is so broad that it essentially eviscerates the shareholder primacy view of governance inherent in the ownership model.[12] It is very likely the case that directors do, in some instances, consider the interests of stakeholders without directly tying that consideration to shareholder value.[13] Moreover, it is also true that, if challenged in litigation, such decisions may be fairly easy to defend as related to long-term shareholder value, regardless of the actual motive of the directors. This circumstance does not, however, suggest that no change in the law is needed to permit directors to serve all stakeholders. First, there may be stakeholder benefits that cannot be linked to shareholder value, no matter how long term. Nor should directors be forced to lie, whether in their deliberations or in legal proceedings, even if they can "get away with it." Finally, such arguments conflate the standard of conduct with the standard of review and are not applicable in enhanced scrutiny or entire fairness cases, where most litigation occurs.

The Entire Fairness Standard

Whereas the deferential business judgment rule applies when there is no conflict of interest, there is no such deference where the directors (or controlling shareholders) have an economic interest that materially conflicts with the interests of the shareholders; in such cases, courts do review the substance of board decisions under the strict entire fairness standard.[14] Under the entire fairness test, the directors must demonstrate that the transaction is entirely fair—as to both price and process[15]—to the corporation and its shareholders.[16] In establishing that a transaction was entirely fair, a board must show more than an honest belief that the transaction was fair; instead, "the transaction itself must be objectively fair, independent of the board's beliefs."[17] Thus, unlike transactions governed by the business judgment rule, conflict transactions receive very substantial judicial scrutiny if challenged. In chapter 8, we will address how a court might apply such scrutiny to a conflict transaction involving a benefit corporation.

Intermediate Standards of Review: Enhanced Business Judgment Rule

Courts apply an intermediate standard of review when a board takes actions to defend against unwanted acquisitions of the corporation or when the corporation undergoes a change in control. In such situations, even if there is no traditional financial conflict, there may be subtle pressures that undermine the integrity of the board's process, so courts have found that some extra judicial scrutiny of such situations is appropriate, even though the strict entire fairness test is not applied.[18] Generally, when enhanced scrutiny applies, the defendants "bear the burden of persuasion to show that their motivations were proper and not selfish" and that "their actions were reasonable in relation to their legitimate objective."[19] When considering how this standard will be applied to a benefit corporation, it is again important to focus on the substantive element of the test: decisions that might favor one stakeholder over another may be subject to this reasonableness standard in defensive and change-in-control situations.

REVLON STANDARD: CHANGES IN CONTROL

Following the *Revlon* decision, which established that directors must maximize shareholder value in a sale of the company, the courts have imposed a heightened standard on directors who approve any transaction involving a change in control of the corporation.[20] This heightened standard does not apply once a transaction has been approved by a fully informed vote of a majority of disinterested shareholders.[21] The question whether a change in control has occurred focuses on the loss of the value of control. Thus, if a corporation is sold for cash, the sale is said to represent the only chance for shareholders to recognize the full value of the company, including any control premium. Similarly, if a corporation without a controlling shareholder merges with another company and its shareholders receive stock in a combined company that is controlled by a particular group or individual, the *Revlon* standard applies to board action.[22]

When there is a change in control, directors must show that they acted reasonably to obtain the best value reasonably available for shareholders.[23] This measured scrutiny of director decisions is grounded in the fact that, in a change-in-control situation, a corporation's shareholders have no long-term future, and, therefore, only short-term wealth maximization of the shareholders may be considered.[24] Because stakeholder interests *do* survive such a transaction, courts will have to reconsider the application of the *Revlon* test to a change in control of a benefit corporation. This question is addressed in chapter 8.

THE *UNOCAL* STANDARD: DEFENSIVE ACTIONS

The intermediate standard of judicial review, including the substantive test of reasonableness, also applies when a board adopts measures to defend against an unwanted acquisition of control. Board action in such circumstances is subject to the enhanced scrutiny standard established in two cases decided by the Delaware Supreme Court.[25] A threatened acquisition of control may include a hostile takeover, a proxy contest, or other situation in which the directors take action that might appear to interfere with the ability of shareholders to freely sell their shares or exercise their voting power.[26] *Unocal* scrutiny also may apply if a board adopts defensive measures to ensure the success of a merger.[27] The *Unocal* standard requires the board to demonstrate that it had reasonable grounds for believing that the takeover attempt posed a danger to corporate policy and effectiveness and that the defensive action taken was reasonable in relation to that threat.[28] A defensive measure will be found disproportionate if it is either coercive or preclusive, or if it falls outside a range of reasonable responses.[29] A response is "coercive" if it is aimed at forcing upon shareholders a management-sponsored alternative to a hostile offer. A response is "preclusive" if it deprives shareholders of the right to receive all tender offers or precludes a bidder from seeking control by fundamentally restricting proxy contests or otherwise.[30]

As we discussed in chapter 2, directors of conventional corporations may consider the interests of other stakeholders when responding to a threat. However, consideration of other stakeholders is permitted only if it relates to shareholder interest: "While concern for various corporate constituencies is proper when addressing a takeover threat, that principle is limited by the requirement that there be some rationally related benefit accruing to the stockholders."[31] Accordingly, when determining whether to take defensive measures against a hostile takeover attempt, directors may consider the interests of other constituencies, but only as they are "rationally related" to value for shareholders, and only where *Revlon* duties are not also applicable. Benefit corporation law should cut this tie: directors of benefit corporations should be permitted to consider the interests of all stakeholders, for their own sake, in taking defensive action. This change will be discussed in chapter 8.

Standards of Review for Shareholder Voting

The Delaware courts have applied strict standards to situations where the shareholder voting rights are threatened by board action. Thus, when the primary purpose of board action is to prevent the effectiveness of a vote, the board must show a "compelling justification" for taking such action in order to defend the action.[32] This is known as the *Blasius* standard, and it expands on the Delaware Supreme Court's prior holding in *Schnell v. Chris Craft Industries, Inc.* In *Schnell*, the court held that even though advancing the company's meeting date was in compliance with the relevant statute and the company's bylaws, the court would not uphold the action because it had been taken for the purpose of obstructing shareholder voting rights. The courts thus place special emphasis on protecting voting rights.[33]

What the cases mean, essentially, is that there is no "balancing." Even if the directors have good faith and reasonable business reasons for obstructing a shareholder vote, they cannot do so, because the very legitimacy of their power comes from the election process and the shareholders' franchise rights: "It is clear that [the vote] is critical to the theory that legitimates the exercise of power by some (directors and officers) over the vast aggregations of property that they do not own. Thus, when viewed from a broad, institutional perspective, it can be seen that matters involving the integrity of the shareholder voting process involve consideration not present in any other context in which directors exercise delegated power."[34]

The *Blasius* standard, however, is applied sparingly. Instead, the more flexible *Unocal* standard is applied when a board takes defensive action that interferes with, but does not thwart, the shareholders' franchise rights. In *Yucaipa Am. All. Fund II, L.P. v. Riggio*, then–Vice Chancellor Strine reviewed the adoption of a shareholder rights plan (often called a "poison pill") under the *Unocal* standard of review.[35] This action made it harder for a shareholder to succeed in a proxy contest by simply buying more shares in the market. However, such action did not directly interfere with the ability of each shareholder to effectively exercise voting rights. Accordingly, the court applied *Unocal* (and not the strict *Blasius* standard) to the adoption of the rights plan:

> If a board can meet its burden under *Unocal* to show that a rights plan is not unreasonable in the sense that its trigger is at such a reasonable threshold that the owner of a bloc up to the trigger level can effectively run a proxy contest, the pill would not work the type of disenfranchisement that both invokes *Blasius* review and almost invariably signals a ruling for the plaintiff.[36]

These standards may be particularly significant for shareholders of benefit corporations: such shareholders may look to franchise rights as more significant than in traditional corporations, given that the directors' fiduciary obligations to shareholders may in some sense be diluted by the broad stakeholder mandate in the benefit corporation statute. The question how this strict standard protecting voting rights might be altered (or preserved) under a benefit corporation governance model is discussed in chapter 8.

* * *

In the next chapter, we will leave the legal system and consider shareholder primacy from the investor perspective.

CHAPTER FOUR

The Responsible Investing Movement

Chapter 1 set the stage by discussing the role of corporations and the investment chain in the global economy. Chapters 2 and 3 took a closer look at how conventional corporations are operated on the basis of shareholder primacy. This chapter will examine the effect of that operation on the investment channel. From a public policy perspective, this may be the most important part of the book, as it is intended to explain why shareholder primacy fails investors, even though it originated as a doctrine meant to protect their interests.

We will first examine the contemporary movement among investors to think more holistically and "responsibly" and will examine what the motives behind that movement might be. We then turn to the ways that investors can use benefit corporation governance as a tool to act responsibly and manage the systems upon which their portfolios depend.

Responsible Investors

As we will discuss in chapters 5 and 6, one simple idea undergirds benefit corporation governance: corporations should be managed for the benefit of all stakeholders affected by their operation, and not just for shareholders. But because shareholders get to decide where their capital is invested, one threshold question must be whether shareholders will ever choose to invest in benefit corporations.

Shareholders might believe that they will always be better off investing in conventional corporations that follow shareholder primacy. If so, it may be unrealistic to suppose that a significant amount of capital will ever be invested in corporations that adopt a stakeholder model.

In fact, however, there is a current movement among many investors to seek investments that have more positive impact on all stakeholders. There are a host of phrases used to describe this phenomenon: socially responsible investing (SRI); environmental, social, and governance investing; responsible investing; impact investing; and others. This investing movement is closely tied to a call for expanded corporate disclosure that recognizes the importance of stakeholder impact and corporate sustainability. This is sometimes called integrated reporting or sustainability reporting. For ease of reference, I will use the term "responsible investing" as a term that encompasses all of these related ideas, using more specific terms only as necessary.

The responsible investing movement helps to put the benefit corporation concept into context. Many investors have come to believe that a greater focus on other stakeholders is important. These responsible investors may believe that such a focus is a better way to create shareholder value, or, in contrast, they may simply believe that other values should share priority with shareholder value. Teasing out some of the different threads motivating responsible investors may help to predict how benefit corporations are likely to fare.

Significant amounts of capital are invested in responsible investing of some form.[1] For example, some investors refuse to invest in companies that engage in certain industries, such as alcohol, tobacco, weapons, or fossil fuels. Others look for investments that will create specific positive effects, such as providing goods, services, or employment to underserved populations or creating technologies that address climate change or resource scarcity concerns.

Others seek to invest responsibly not just by choosing the right companies but also by providing stewardship to the companies they own. This latter type of responsible investing might mean voting for shareholder resolutions that encourage companies to measure their environmental footprint or voting to increase the diversity of a corporation's board of directors. Globally, institutions are signing on to the Principles for Responsible Investment, a U.N.-sponsored project that has signed up asset owners and managers with \$62 trillion in assets under management, under which signatories pledge to incorporate environmental, social, and governance principles into their investing.[2]

Concessionary Versus Non-Concessionary Responsible Investors

These trends all raise the same issue: Why would shareholders, who presumably seek to maximize their returns, focus on social or environmental issues, either from a substantive perspective or from a reporting perspective? There is no single answer to this question, as each investor has its own perspective. It is useful, however, to initially focus on one significant distinction: concessionary versus non-concessionary investors. The former are the easiest to explain: they are willing to accept a lower financial return that leads to positive impacts on other stakeholders. There are at least two motivations for accepting such a trade-off.

The first, which is purely self-interested, involves a recognition that some investments that promise a favorable return nevertheless involve companies that are conceding some return. For example, an investor might buy stock in a company that has a unique technology, even though the founder and controlling shareholder has made it clear that shareholder value will not be maximized if such maximization imposes certain environmental or societal costs. Even with such a built-in "cost" to shareholder value, the investment may present a favorable risk/reward balance. In contrast, some concessionary investments might reflect a willingness to accept below-market returns in order to create positive social and environmental impacts. This second form of concessionary investment is closer to what might be viewed as "altruistic."

In contrast, non-concessionary investors may believe that, over the long term, they will enjoy better returns as shareholders by investing in companies that are socially and environmentally conscious and that treat the community and their employees as well as shareholders. The motivations for non-concessionary investors to engage in responsible investing can be broken down into three categories, and, of course, these categories reflect the arguments that entrepreneurs and managers can make in favor of running their businesses with stakeholder values. The motivations, together with the motivations for concessionary investors, exist along a spectrum and tend to overlap, rather than existing discretely. Table 3 illustrates the spectrum of motivations.

TABLE 3: INVESTOR STYLES AND CORPORATE GOVERNANCE

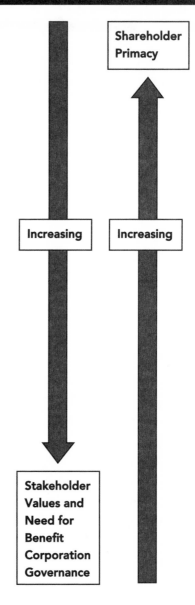

Modern Portfolio Theory: Focus on financial bottom line only. May include investments that concede some return in order to achieve positive social impact if the return is still competitive.

Enlightened Self-Interest: Do well by doing good; benefit stakeholders in order to increase long term financial performance of company

Purposeful Companies: Make authentic commitment to stakeholders in order to receive authentic commitments back and create shared value

Universal Ownership: Consider multiple bottom lines and the effect of corporate actions on multiple capitals in order to manage and protect social and environmental systems

Altruistic Concessionary Investing: Accept lower financial returns in order to achieve higher positive impact on other stakeholders.

Shareholder Primacy

Increasing   Increasing

Stakeholder Values and Need for Benefit Corporation Governance

Doing Well by Doing Good: No Concession

The first argument of non-concessionary responsible companies and investors is simply that a business can "do well by doing good." For example, a company might use a more expensive but well-audited supply chain and argue that consumers are willing to pay a premium to buy goods that are ethically sourced. The prospectus of Laureate Education, a benefit corporation incorporated in Delaware, includes a good example of this argument as it applies to becoming a benefit corporation. In that document (discussed in more detail later), Laureate explains how its status as a corporation that has obligations to students and communities will cause it to be viewed more positively by regulators than would an entity driven by shareholder primacy.

There are several strains to this idea. The first is that stakeholders, including customers, workers, and communities, will want to have a relationship with a company that is responsible to society and the environment—millions of consumers express this sentiment both in surveys and through practice, as evidenced by the rise of certifications such as "fair trade," and "organic."[3] In addition, there is an important element of risk mitigation involved. On this front, the BP oil spill in the Gulf of Mexico and the Bhopal tragedy and its monetary and reputational cost to Union Carbide are often cited as examples. The argument is straightforward: had these companies invested in safe practices that protected workers, adjacent communities, and other stakeholders, their shareholders would have been financially better off in the long run.[4] There is also evidence that companies with social and environmental practices are likely to be better managed, so that such practices may be an indicator of good management that will create long-term value.[5]

This view emphasizes the creation of value over the long term. Thus, cost cutting on safety or environmental matters may boost the financial bottom line immediately, which may in turn boost share price in the short term (because companies are often valued on the basis of a multiple of profits or cash flow). But investing in sustainability measures, while reducing short-term profits, can pay off later, years into the future. It is worth noting that this argument suggests that markets are mispricing stocks, since owning a share entitles a shareholder to all future cash flows, not just short-term flows. In other words, this argument suggests that the markets are not "efficient."[6]

In other words, considering the interests of all stakeholders is just good business. Numerous studies purport to support this claim. One important non-profit group, the Sustainability Accounting Standards Board, has developed an entire set of reporting metrics, on an industry-by-industry basis, that requires disclosure on environmental and social issues that are material to financial performance in each industry.[7] This reporting system is designed to provide environmental and social information to non-concessionary responsible investors. (In contrast, the International Integrated Reporting Council establishes standards that encourage companies to report on how their operations affect not only financial capital but also social, human, natural, and other capitals, without regard to their effect on financial return.)[8]

In this view, the value to shareholders of lowering their priority may simply be a paradoxical artifact of the real world in operation:

> Although traditional corporations provide broad leeway to pursue nonshareholder interests as a competitive advantage *when profit is explicitly sought after*, traditional corporations preclude directors from "doing good for good's sake"—which may in fact, somewhat paradoxically, prove to create an economic, profit-maximizing competitive advantage. One of the most interesting aspects of the economic implications of the statute is whether doing good *without regard to shareholder interests* will actually result in long-run profitability and more sustainable shareholder gains.[9]

The Paradox of the Value of Commitment: The Concession that Isn't

There is a second, related argument that a requirement to act in the interests of stakeholders will benefit shareholders as well. This idea focuses specifically on the value to a corporation that is derived from the commitment made to those other stakeholders. This value means that companies that commit to making concessions need not be concessionary investments. If corporations make strong commitments to important constituencies, including workers and communities, and those commitments induce firm-specific commitments in return, the company may create value that would not be obtainable if the company were committed only to shareholders. In short, commitment to stakeholders can create value for shareholders.[10] This idea is supported by social science research demonstrating that people tend to act generously when others are perceived to do so, but may retaliate if others act unfairly, even if such retaliation compromises their own interests.[11]

One UK fund manager has published a paper suggesting that the trust created by a company both certifying its social and environmental impacts and embedding purpose into its organizational documents builds resilience and value:

> One significant factor here is the degree of trust these businesses can build with their stakeholders—a trust that should, if anything, be bolstered by their willingness to have their societal mission validated by a third party and embedded in their governance articles. Certifying in this way makes it very clear to potential customers (and employees) that the company's commitment to social and environmental goals is a fundamental part of its strategy—not just a specious marketing exercise.[12]

Indeed, the chairman of Laureate Education, the first company to go public as a benefit corporation, made the point in its initial public offering prospectus that being a benefit corporation was a way for it to explain its commitments:

> I believe that balancing the needs of our constituents has been instrumental to our success and longevity, allowing us to grow even in challenging economic times. For a long time, we didn't have an easy way to explain the idea of a for-profit company with such a deep commitment to benefitting society. So we took notice when in 2010 the first state in the U.S. passed legislation creating the concept of a Public Benefit Corporation, a new type of for-profit corporation with an expressed commitment to creating a material positive impact on society. We watched this concept carefully as it swept the nation, with 31 states and the District of Columbia now having passed legislation to allow for this new class of corporation, which commits itself to high standards of corporate purpose, accountability and transparency.[13]

The advantage of being able to build such reciprocal relationships has been described by Lynn Stout in her book *The Shareholder Value Myth*, and by Colin Mayer, a leading finance professor at Oxford's Said Business School, in his book

Firm Commitment. This theory is particularly important with respect to the consideration of benefit corporation governance, because without a shift from shareholder primacy, all stakeholder commitments are legally contingent on a continuing positive relationship to shareholder value, and this weakens the strength of the commitments.

This legally imposed contingency creates antagonism that prevents corporations from creating value through mutual commitment. Mayer uses the following example to illustrate this conundrum:

> If there is an active labour market and it is easy for them to obtain alternative employment at any time, then it is the firm not the employees which is exposed. The employees have made no commitment, whereas it may be costly for the firm to train new workers every time that an existing one resigns. Now it is the potential employees who would like to be able to demonstrate commitment to gain employment but are incapable of doing so on their own. The firm offers a means of achieving this. It can do it financially by delaying payment of their wages, thereby making it costly for them to depart prematurely before the firm has recovered its investments in training them. Alternatively, it can encourage commitment by making employment in the firm a valued attribute in its own regard, reflecting strong employee affinity with the goals and values of the organization. Critical to both forms of control of firms over their employees is their corresponding trust in the firm—trust that the firm will not expropriate their deferred payments by, for example, engaging in reckless investments and trust that it really will uphold the values to which it aspires. That is why the balancing of commitment and control in the firm is so vital to it successful operation.[14]

Stout describes the problem as a conflict between current (*ex ante*) shareholders and their future (ex post) selves. The ex ante shareholders want the up-front value of committing, while the ex post shareholders want to get even more value by defecting:

> There is an inevitable conflict between shareholders' ex ante interest in "tying their own hands" to encourage their own and other stakeholders' firm-specific contributions, and their ex post interest

in opportunistically trying to unbind themselves to unlock capital and exploit others' specific contributions. This conflict—a conflict between shareholders' ex ante selves and their ex post selves, if you will—puts public corporations governed by the rules of stockholder primacy at a disadvantage when it comes to projects that require firm-specific investments. Rejecting shareholder value thinking, and instead inviting boards to consider the needs of employees, customers, and communities, allows boards to usefully mediate not only between the interests of shareholders and stakeholders, but between the interests of ex ante and ex post shareholders as well.[15]

As we noted in the discussion of the business judgment rule in chapter 3, some commentators believe that current law already allows directors to make such commitments, because the business judgment rule is so broad that it actually does allow director decisions that favor stakeholders over shareholders. Indeed, Professor Stout, in her discussion of the interests of ex ante and ex post shareholders, makes that very claim. As discussed in chapter 3, the claim that the business judgment rule allows such decisions is dubious, especially when a company is sold, and what good is a commitment to employees that evaporates upon the sale of the company? More importantly, however, even if directors could take the interests of stakeholders into account at the ex ante moment, there is certainly no argument that current law would compel them to do so. As discussed in detail in the chapters discussing the new benefit corporation statutes, such consideration is *compulsory* for benefit corporations. This compulsory nature of the statutes is the element that makes the commitments authentic and separates benefit corporation law from traditional corporate law in terms of potential to create value through mutual commitments, even if traditional law were interpreted to *permit* the consideration of stakeholder interests.

Universal Owners: Making Concessions to Preserve the Commons

Each of the two foregoing arguments might be characterized as corporate "enlightened self-interest." That is, by treating stakeholders well, and by committing to treat them well, corporations, if they are patient, can reward their shareholders with more value over the long term. Thus, under the prior two theories, there is no overall "concession" involved in treating stakeholders well. However, these ideas go only so far; despite the presence of opportunities to create value with stakeholders, there will continue to be opportunities for individual corporations to create even more value for shareholders with less cooperative strategies, which often create "negative externalities," or costs borne by stakeholders other than shareholders.[16] In other words, there will always be opportunities to "do well by doing bad."

Is there a non-concessionary argument that would lead investors to want the corporations that they own to forgo such strategies, or to pursue strategies that create positive externalities, even if they do not maximize the financial return provided by the company's directly to its shareholders? There is, in fact, such an argument, and it is the third reason that investors should favor benefit corporation governance.[17]

This strategy is concessionary, *but only on the level of individual corporations.* It is a strategy that springs from the perspective of the investor that is diversified, with broad shareholdings across the entire market, and that has a long time horizon. Such investors are often called "universal owners"; pension funds, with broadly diversified portfolios and very long-term obligations, are classic examples of this type of investor.[18] Indeed, this is the perspective of most beneficiaries of the institutional asset owners that dominate the market.[19] These investors earn most of their return not by successfully picking stocks that "beat the market" but rather by being invested in a healthy market; generally, at least 80 percent of an investor's return comes from the behavior of the market, often called "beta" in this context.[20] In fact, the significance of beta is not restricted to portfolios; most of the return at the individual company level is based on market performance.[21] Accordingly, investors are actually hurt when a company in which they are invested tries to improve the return to its shareholders by externalizing costs in a manner that hurts the market. One writer captured this idea as follows:

> Because the world's asset owners have a stake in the prosperity of the economy as a whole, there is a strong argument that part of the role of an asset owner should be to push for policies and frameworks that reduce negative externalities. In practical terms, this would point to asset owners having a rationale to push investee companies

to set minimum standards and certifications and to support sensible public policy (pollution control, emissions trading schemes, etc.) that would result in the most efficient allocation of environmental and social resources.[22]

David Wood summed up the idea of universal ownership, crediting its creator and elaborators:

> Among the more prominent theories used in support of responsi-
> ble investment is that of Universal Ownership, proposed by Robert
> Monks and elaborated by James Hawley and Andrew Williams. . . .
> The theory suggests that investors at scale (and the investment
> market in the aggregate) are so large that they are invested not just
> in a set of companies, but also in the interrelated network of social
> systems that make up society. Their portfolio performance depends
> on the economic growth and social value that their investments, and
> therefore society, create in aggregate. Costs externalized by one set
> of investments onto society are likely to weigh down performance
> in other parts of the portfolio. By extension, "universal owners" will
> only benefit when investments have positive social value.[23]

For example, universal owners were hurt by the "value-maximizing" activities of those financial companies that created the market crash in 2008. Moreover, these investors have nonfinancial interests as well: they would prefer to live in a world that is peaceful, prosperous, and stable, and such a world is much more likely to exist if corporations are not externalizing costs and risks in order to increase the financial return of a single company.[24] This latter concept of investors' multiple interests recognizes that what we often label "capitalism" is actually "monocapitalism," focused solely on financial capital. Universal ownership makes room for "multicapitalism," so that success is measured not only against financial capital but also against human, natural, and other capitals as well.[25]

Continued healthy markets will depend on responsible investors recognizing their own universal ownership and working to improve the beta of their portfolios (not to mention the health of their society and planet), rather than only viewing responsible investment as a means by which to increase individual company performance: "In our view, while alpha can sometimes be found in ESG [environmental, social, and governance] arenas, and this may serve a legitimation function that ESG/RI [responsible investment] factors matter and are material, it also has the potential to undermine what is critical: the change of the whole market (beta) to minimize and mitigate negative externalities. Such externalities, if left alone, undermine the ability to create sustainable long-term development."[26]

Steve Lydenberg further suggests that modern portfolio theory, the framework for professional investors that emerged in the 1970s, operates on the assumption that systemic risk is exogenous to portfolio management, so that investors focus (and reward portfolio managers) only on their performance as measured *against* the market, and that investors and managers ignore their effect *on* the market. This may lead investors to focus on maximizing the value of individual companies or portfolios as compared to the market, while ignoring, and perhaps even damaging, the systems within which those companies and portfolios are embedded: "But while the assumption that portfolio decision-making could be treated as independent and disconnected from the markets that these decisions take place within—and, by implication, from the world at large—may have been appropriate during early stages of MPT [modern portfolio theory], it now appears increasingly reasonable to raise questions about the system-wide impacts of these decisions."[27]

One clear implication of the idea that investors need to monitor systems is that government is failing to do so with law and regulation. There are many reasons this may be the case, including the use by corporations of strategies to limit the effect of laws and regulations, such as bare compliance, regulatory arbitrage, and lobbying efforts to limit the effect of such efforts.[28] For example, the pharmaceutical industry uses the capital of its shareholders to employ lobbyists in order to maintain high profits, which may well do long-term damage to our social system by contributing to inequality, as well as imposing short-term suffering on those in need of medicine.[29] Indeed, one commentator has noted that the ability of corporations to lobby the government undermines the claim that the presence of government controls can justify shareholder primacy: "The claim that shareholders should be prioritized because the availability of external laws mitigates non-shareholder conflicts with shareholders only makes sense if the firm itself cannot eliminate or modify those laws."[30]

In addition to corporate strategies to avoid regulation, there is the simple problem that law and regulation often come too late to address the external costs of corporate behavior. For example, innovation in the financial industry can create systemic risks that are unregulated due to their novelty. If corporations had a duty to consider externalities when innovating, this regulatory lag would be addressed.[31] Table 4 contrasts the corporate governance implications of universal ownership principles with the implications under Modern Portfolio Theory.

Shareholder Primacy and Responsible Investing

Many in the responsible investing movement, as well as many entrepreneurs, are concerned that shareholder primacy is an obstacle to the goal of responsible corporate conduct.[32] Of course, shareholder primacy runs directly counter to pure concessionary responsible investing, where investors are simply willing to take a decreased financial return in exchange for owning shares in a corporation that provides a greater social return. But even for investors who believe that the corporations that they invest in can act responsibly toward all stakeholders without conceding financial return (for one or more of the three reasons outlined above), shareholder primacy may create an obstacle. This concern becomes more acute as the motive for responsible conduct moves from the idea of doing well by doing good to making firm commitments to stakeholders and, finally, to principles of universal ownership. Table 3 (on page 46) illustrates this relationship.

TABLE 4: SHAREHOLDER PRIMACY V. STAKEHOLDER GOVERNANCE		
	Shareholder Primacy	**Stakeholder Governance**
Form	Conventional corporation	Benefit corporation
Purpose	Provide return on investment for shareholders	Create value for all Stakeholders
Investing theory	Modern Portfolio Theory	Universal ownership
Stakeholder interests	Considered to extent they relate to shareholder value; "enlightened self-interest"	Primary concern, along with shareholders
Capitals approach	Monocapitalistic: only financial capital is accounted for	Multicapital: Financial, human, natural and social capitals are accounted for

Clearly, shareholder primacy at the level of a single corporation is incompatible with principles of universal ownership, which requires individual companies to avoid taking profitable actions that impose costs on other companies and on the system generally. Similarly, it is difficult for a corporation to take advantage of the value of making authentic commitments to stakeholders if the law (i.e., shareholder primacy) appears to require reneging on those commitments if opportune. Even with respect to responsible strategies that are simply good long-term investments for shareholders, the reputational stigma of shareholder primacy may interfere with the complete integration of such strategies.

Shareholder primacy is a particularly difficult obstacle to overcome for publicly held entities, which are subject to significant pressure to deliver increased share value over the short term.[33] These organizations control roughly $70 trillion of equity capital, so that to the extent concepts of shareholder primacy dominate public markets, addressing this obstacle is of critical importance.[34] Operating as a universal owner requires investors to insist that companies in their portfolios forgo shareholder value maximization if such maximization creates significant negative externalities. However, without a governance model that mandates stakeholder governance in place of shareholder primacy, universal ownership principles will run counter to the rules governing the individual companies that make up an owner's portfolio. For example, a short-term, concentrated investor can claim that it is a breach of fiduciary duty for a conventional corporation to reduce carbon output if the indirect costs to the company of the emissions do not outweigh the direct benefits of maintaining cost savings by continuing to emit carbon at a globally unsustainable rate. Accordingly, introducing benefit corporations into the public markets could have a tremendous impact by allowing long-term, diversified owners to ensure that the systems in which they invest are robust and stable.

A number of commentators disagree with this conclusion. Their arguments take a number of forms, and it is worth addressing each of them here, because it is easier to understand the structure of benefit corporation legislation discussed in subsequent chapters if the contours of the arguments around its necessity are well understood.

Argument 1: There is no such thing as shareholder primacy in the law.[35] This argument is surprisingly resilient in light of the fact that the Delaware Supreme

Court has declared that shareholder primacy is the law, that the chief justice of that court has adopted this view in his academic writings, and that thirty-three states felt it necessary to adopt constituency statutes that reject primacy, whereas Delaware and other important jurisdictions have not.[36] Perhaps the best form of this argument is that the law is unclear, even in jurisdictions like Delaware that are purportedly primacy jurisdictions. But directors are not generally interested in taking legal chances.[37] A longtime corporate law practitioner makes this clear in a commentary:

> Directors who reject this notion [shareholder primacy], who take actions that are for the primary benefit of so-called "stakeholders" in the corporation—be they employees, customers, the communities served by the corporation or others—have their ideas rejected in the boardroom, may be the subject of scorn and derision in the business press and with their peers, can be voted out of their positions by shareholders and even found to have breached their fiduciary duty to the company and its shareholders.[38]

Argument 2: There are many nonprimacy jurisdictions. There are many jurisdictions where primacy is clearly not the law, including the thirty-three states that have adopted constituency statutes, and the many non-U.S. jurisdictions where consideration of non-shareholder interests, as a primary concern, is permitted (as we will discuss further in chapter 9). Couldn't companies just move to jurisdictions where the law clearly permitted consideration of stakeholder interests?

This argument cannot carry the day, however; reincorporating in another jurisdiction involves many risks and costs. For example, other available jurisdictions may be viewed by investors as less favorable.[39] In addition, there may be questions as to whether contracts would transfer to the new entity.[40] Even if these obstacles could be overcome, the transfer to a constituency jurisdiction will not mandate consideration of non-shareholder interests because in all U.S. jurisdictions without shareholder primacy, stakeholder consideration is *permissive* rather than *mandatory*, and there are no remedies or accountability measures protecting stakeholder interests.

This is not to say that constituency statutes do not make it easier for corporations to behave more responsibly with respect to stakeholders in jurisdictions where constituency statutes have replaced shareholder primacy. However, without an actual obligation to stakeholders, it will be much more difficult for companies to resist the types of rent-seeking behavior that shareholder primacy thinking at the investor level engenders; because current financial markets favor a primacy mentality, directors and other managers are very likely to continue to strongly favor shareholder interests, as will the many intermediaries in the investing chain, despite the applicability of constituency statutes.[41]

Argument 3: The business judgment rule permits directors to favor stakeholders over shareholders. The business judgment rule provides that courts do not generally interfere with business decisions; as a result, directors have extremely broad discretion in managing a corporation. So it is true that corporations can act responsibly and claim that such actions will benefit the shareholders in the long run.[42] But taking comfort in the business judgment rule and making this claim does not address the core concern: the ability to take an action to protect stakeholders, even if that action reduces the company's financial return to shareholders. It should not need to be said that we must not manage our capital markets on the basis of dissembling, nor could directors really be comfortable making decisions on the basis of an agreed-upon fiction.[43] Moreover, the business judgment rule does not apply in change in control transactions, which involve some of the most critical decisions in the lifetime of a corporation.[44] But more critically, as noted in response to argument 2, while the aggressive use of the business judgment rule might allow corporations to act responsibly in many situations, it would not require it. Without the accountability created by such a requirement, shareholder primacy thinking is likely to dominate the boardroom, particularly at public companies, in light of the short-term, share price focus of the current markets. For all these reasons, the business judgment rule simply does not provide the benefits of stakeholder governance.

Argument 4: Stakeholder governance cannot work, because there are too many interests for corporations to reconcile; this will allow managers to simply act in their own interest, because there will be no clear standards.[45] The fact is that managers must constantly think about all of their stakeholders in order to efficiently manage a business; benefit corporation governance merely allows them to give those interests a priority not available in shareholder primacy settings. Moreover, directors of benefit corporations are not able to ignore shareholder interests because shareholders retain all their corporate governance rights—including the right to elect the board that controls the management of the corporation.[46]

The concept of too many interests to balance ignores the fact that, for the most part, that is how life works: we must always balance a number of competing interests.[47] This is true for all businesses, not just those that are governed by stakeholder values. Eric Beinhocker explains that to be successful, a business must attract capital, manage employees, create relationships that are profitable for suppliers, provide goods and services that satisfy customers, meet legal obligations, pay taxes, and generally ensure that society continues its license to operate.[48] In other words, all businesses must manage many interests; under shareholder primacy, the only difference between shareholder interests and other stakeholder interests is that the former is an objective whereas the latter are constraints. In a benefit corporation, that objective is transformed into the additional constraint of providing shareholders with a competitive return; despite this change, however, there are not any "new" interests to manage in a benefit corporation.

Finally, it also is worth noting that, even for corporations operating under shareholder primacy, there is no one-size-fits-all answer as to what maximization is; indeed, given the very different perspectives of equity holders, that is far from the case.[49]

Argument 5: Creating corporations that are specifically designated as stakeholder friendly will give greater license to conventional corporations to act irresponsibly and create negative impacts on society and the environment. Traditional corporations already have such license, and many take advantage of it, underpaying workers, polluting the environment, and ignoring the negative effects of their operations.[50] As long as such activities are not illegal, the only path to improving corporate behavior is market pressure. The creation of benefit corporations lies on a critical path to increase that pressure by highlighting the legal distinction between companies that are legally required to protect their stakeholders and those for whom decent treatment of such stakeholders is always contingent on legal compulsion or shareholder value.[51] Denying corporations the opportunity to legally prioritize societal interests will only serve to slow any such market pressure.

But it is not just directors and investors who can drive this change. Once the flag is planted, other markets can serve to drive capital to corporations that are governed for the benefit of all stakeholders:

> When the dinosaurs of old-world financial primacy find that they can no longer attract the talent they require, they may discover their epoch is over. The market will indeed carry out capital allocation, but it will not be the financial market. It will be the talent market. Talented individuals will seek out organizations whose own values are transparent and who favor balance and sustainability over "profit-maximization at all costs."[53]

* * *

Part 1 has described shareholder primacy and the reasons why corporations and investors might want to shift to more stakeholder-oriented governance. Part 2 examines how benefit corporation laws provide a tool for doing so.

PART II

Governing for Stakeholders

You cannot abandon the emphasis on "the view that the business corporation exists for the sole purpose of making profits for stockholders" until such time as you are prepared to offer a clear and reasonably enforceable scheme of responsibilities to someone else.

Adolf Berle

Change comes from owning a problem that is systemic and fixing it with intentionality.

Cary Krosinsky

CHAPTER FIVE

The Model Benefit Corporation Legislation

Part 1 of this book has argued that conventional corporate law makes it difficult for corporations and investors to implement strategies that rely on commitments to stakeholders and that seek to manage critical social, environmental, and economic systems. In chapter 5, we begin to explore how the adoption of benefit corporation statutes addresses this concern. In particular, chapter 5 describes the operation of the Model Benefit Corporation Legislation, which was drafted and promoted by B Lab, a nonprofit organization that works to establish paths for business to operate as a force for good. Chapter 6 describes a second model, adopted in Delaware and several other states.

The Model Benefit Corporation Legislation eliminates shareholder primacy by requiring directors to consider a broad group of stakeholders when making decisions and by imposing a corporate purpose of creating a "general public benefit," which must be measured against a third-party standard that addresses the interests of all relevant stakeholders. The statute makes benefit corporations accountable by (1) requiring them to report annually against that third-party standard and (2) allowing shareholders to bring lawsuits challenging whether that purpose is being met.

Prelude: The Benefit Corporation Movement

A NEED IS RECOGNIZED

A growing number of investors and entrepreneurs have become uncomfortable with the shareholder primacy model.[1] One response could be to follow the "constituency statute" model, which allows, but does not require, directors to consider the interests of stakeholders. These provisions are discussed in detail in chapter 9. However, constituency statutes do not fully address the concerns created by shareholder primacy because they only *permit*, but do not require, corporations to alter shareholder primacy behavior. By contrast, benefit corporation legislation requires a change in corporate purpose and creates accountability and transparency with respect to stakeholder concerns.

Beginning in 2010, U.S. jurisdictions began to adopt legislation authorizing benefit corporations. A majority of the legislation adopted has generally followed the Model Benefit Corporation Legislation. Since 2013, several states have adopted an alternative model originating in Delaware, which is the subject of chapter 6. Like constituency statutes, benefit corporation laws allow directors to consider the interests of all stakeholders, but unlike constituency statutes, they mandate such consideration, and provide mechanisms to create accountability for these interests.

The benefit corporation movement focuses on broad corporate purposes and on expanding the obligations of corporate managers to include the interests of all stakeholders. However, benefit corporation governance can also be conceptualized as a way to recognize that shareholders have interests beyond financial return.[2] Clearly, the models of benefit corporation statutes adopted to date encompass this concept to some degree, because while expanding purpose and obligation, they do not empower any constituency beyond the shareholders to enforce those expansions, either through litigation or through corporate governance rights. Alternatively, the benefit corporation legislation may be viewed through the lens of concession theory, in which the state's interest in the public good must be satisfied by corporations in exchange for the privileges of limited liability, free transferability, and perpetual existence.[3]

Throughout this chapter and the rest of part 2, it is important to remember that all benefit corporation law is *optional*. None of the statutes discussed impose stakeholder governance. Instead, they provide an option, so that entrepreneurs and investors who believe that shareholder primacy is harmful, either to their business or to their portfolio, can choose another option. Thus, benefit corporation legislation does not impose stakeholder values on the corporate or investor community. Instead, by providing a viable option to shareholder primacy, the legislation allows entrepreneurs, investors, workers, suppliers, customers, and others to express a preference for accountable stakeholder governance, an option that was not available in the United States prior to 2010.

THE BIRTH OF THE BENEFIT CORPORATION AND THE DRAFTING OF THE MBCL

The MBCL was originally drafted on behalf of B Lab, a nonprofit corporation that promotes business as a force for creating positive social value.[4] B Lab provides tools that assist businesses seeking to have positive impacts on all of their stakeholders. Among other programs, B Lab awards the trademarked designation Certified B Corp to companies that achieve high scores on its proprietary impact assessment tool. However, B Lab believes that even businesses with positive social and environmental performance should adopt a corporate governance structure that will ensure that impact performance is maintained, even through changes in management or ownership, control changes, or significant events such as initial public offerings. This belief arose from the understanding that shareholder primacy plays a dominant role in the current legal systems and capital markets, so that good impact performance is always at risk, especially in changed circumstances.[5] In order to earn B Lab's certification, businesses must make a legally binding commitment to pursue positive social and environmental impact, as long as it is legal to do so.

However, after consultation with a number of corporate lawyers, B Lab concluded that it was difficult for corporations to make legally binding commitments to stakeholders, particularly in states that had not adopted constituency statutes. In states with constituency statutes, they believed that it might be acceptable for corporations to add a provision to their articles of incorporation that turned the permissive consideration of stakeholder interests into a mandate to do so and to pursue a material positive impact on society and the environment.[6] For limited liability companies (LLCs), a more flexible form of business entity, B Lab determined that binding commitments to stakeholders *could* be made in the operating agreement, the primary constitutional document of an LLC.

Although many businesses start as LLCs, a business often must migrate to the corporate form as it scales and seeks outside capital—many investors insist on the corporate form as a more reliable protector of investor rights. From B Lab's perspective, then, there was a need to change the law so that corporations could make authentic, enforceable commitments to all stakeholders. This was especially true in states that did not have constituency statutes, but even where there was a constituency statute, the fix of changing "may" to "must" was imperfect. One concern is that the mandate does not have a statutory imprimatur, and, without a precedent interpreting a private ordering provision, the enforceability of the mandate is uncertain. In addition, without the specific director protections that are included in the benefit corporation statutes (as discussed in this chapter and in chapter 6), there could be an increased risk of liability for directors. Finally, there is the concern that if corporations must individually opt in to mandatory stakeholder obligations, there will be a lack of uniformity and it will be difficult for stakeholders to ascertain the strength of the corporate commitment.

In order to address this gap, B Lab asked William Clark, a corporate law partner at Drinker Biddle & Reath LLP (B Lab's pro bono legal counsel) with significant experience in drafting entity law statutes, to create the MBCL.[7] Once the statute was drafted, B Lab and Clark worked together to persuade legislatures around the country to adopt the provisions, and met with fairly rapid success. In 2010, Maryland became the first state to adopt a version of the statute, which was signed into law on April 13, 2010.[8] B Lab's white paper on the subject includes the following summary of its pitch to legislatures:

> The sustainable business movement, impact investing and social enterprise sectors are developing rapidly but are constrained by an outdated legal framework that is not equipped to accommodate for-profit entities whose social benefit purpose is central to their existence. The benefit corporation is the most comprehensive yet flexible legal entity devised to address the needs of entrepreneurs and investors and, ultimately, the general public. Benefit corporations offer clear market differentiation, broad legal protection to directors and officers, expanded shareholder rights, and greater access to capital than current alternative approaches. As a result, the benefit corporation is also attracting broad support from entrepreneurs, investors, legal experts, citizens, and policy makers interested in new corporate form legislation.[9]

Largely through the efforts of Clark and B Lab, benefit corporation legislation has now been adopted in thirty-three jurisdictions within the United States.[10] Five of those states (Colorado, Delaware, Kansas, Kentucky, and Tennessee)[11] have adopted a model with substantial differences from the MBCL (including use of the slightly different term "public benefit corporation"), and a similar model has also been recommended by the American Bar Association's Corporate Laws Committee.[12] The Delaware model will be discussed in chapter 6.

Entrepreneurs are clearly excited by the opportunity to use this form. According to B Lab's internal database, states report the formation of more than five thousand benefit entities, although states are likely overreporting the number in some cases.[13] In Delaware, where very accurate numbers are reported, 927 benefit corporations have been formed as of May 2017.[14] Although many of these are small companies, without outside investment, a number of these entities are large enterprises or have raised outside capital. Companies with well-known brands, including Plum Organics (infant food), Patagonia (outdoor wear), and Eileen Fisher (women's fashion) are benefit corporations. Alliant International University is a large, for-profit education benefit corporation funded by Bertelsmann, a German media corporation. Haskell Murray reports on seven benefit corporations that have raised between $4.5 and $100 million from venture capitalists and corporations.[15] In 2016, Laureate Education, a benefit corporation, raised almost $400 million in a private fund-raising round, including investment from Apollo Global Management, a leading private equity firm. Then, in early 2017, Laureate raised $490 million in the first initial public offering of a benefit corporation.[16] In all, benefit corporations have raised more than $1 billion from venture and private equity funds, corporations, and the public markets.

It has been suggested that fiduciaries subject to strict rules, including institutional investors covered by the Employee Retirement Income Security Act, cannot invest in benefit corporations because such fiduciaries are required to seek the highest return possible for their beneficiaries.[17] The concern is that the rules prohibit trustees from pursuing an investment for any reason other than maximizing returns; that is, such trustees should never be concessionary investors, as described in chapter 4. This concern is misguided. As we have seen, there are numerous non-concessionary reasons for using the benefit corporation form. Most importantly, even if a corporation is making a concession with respect to shareholder return by balancing stakeholder interests, *it is a category error to attribute that concessionary view to investors.* From the investor perspective, any internal corporate concession is simply an expense to be factored in, just like the expense of taxes in a high-tax jurisdiction or a charitable giving program engaged in by a conventional corporation. Indeed, a similar issue arose in the 1980s and 1990s, when a number of states adopted "constituency statutes" that permitted, but did not require, directors to consider the interests of all stakeholders (which we will discuss further in chapter 9). Researchers have found that the Employee Retirement Income Security Act and similarly situated fiduciaries did not alter their behavior with respect to investments in entities subject to these changed laws in any statistically significant way.[18] This research strongly suggests that the fiduciary obligations of institutional investors do not require that they invest only in entities governed by shareholder primacy.

Provisions of the MBCL

A current version of the MBCL is maintained on B Lab's website and is included here as appendix A. This draft has evolved since 2010, when the first statute was adopted, so some of this discussion may reflect the language that was in place when a majority of the statutes were adopted but that no longer appears in the MBCL. More importantly, each state has made changes from the MBCL in their statutes, so it is important to review the specific text of the relevant statute when advising a benefit corporation. The discussion here does not move sequentially through the statute but rather begins with the critical distinction that makes a benefit corporation different—the requirement that directors consider all stakeholders—and then discusses how that requirement is enforced and reported.

SECTION 301(A): THE HEART OF THE MBCL
EXPANDS THE DUTIES OF DIRECTORS

Section 301(a) establishes a standard of conduct for directors that places all stakeholders at the center of governance. Most importantly, it mandates that directors consider the interests of a specific list of stakeholders as well as the ability of the corporation to accomplish its general benefit purpose (and its specific benefit purpose, if there is one). The definition of general benefit purpose is set out in Section 102 and is defined as "a material positive impact on society and the environment, taken as a whole, assessed against a third-party standard, from the business and operations of a benefit corporation."[19] Here is the text of Section 301(a):

(a) Consideration of interests.—In discharging the duties of their respective positions and in considering the best interests of the benefit corporation, the board of directors, committees of the board, and individual directors of a benefit corporation:

    (1) shall consider the effects of any action or inaction upon:

        (i) the shareholders of the benefit corporation;

        (ii) the employees and work force of the benefit corporation, its subsidiaries, and its suppliers;

        (iii) the interests of customers as beneficiaries of the general public benefit or a specific public benefit purpose of the benefit corporation;

        (iv) community and societal factors, including those of each community in which offices or facilities of the benefit corporation, its subsidiaries, or its suppliers are located;

        (v) the local and global environment;

        (vi) the short-term and long-term interests of the benefit corporation, including benefits that may accrue to the benefit corporation from its long-term plans and the possibility that these interests may be best served by the continued independence of the benefit corporation; and

        (vii) the ability of the benefit corporation to accomplish its general public benefit purpose and any specific public benefit purpose.

Under Section 301(a), directors of a benefit corporation *must* consider the effect the corporation has on shareholders, employees, customers, the community where the corporation operates, the local and global environment, and its ability to create a material positive impact on society and the environment.[20] To the extent that officers of a benefit corporation have discretion, they are charged with taking the same interests into consideration.

Paragraph 2 of Section 301 goes on to provide that the board *may* consider other interests set out in the constituency provisions of the corporate statute (in states that have such a provision), or any other "factors or interests" the board deems "appropriate." Finally, paragraph 3 establishes that the board is not required to prioritize among these interests, unless the corporation's articles of incorporation provide for such prioritization: "[Directors] need not give priority to a particular interest or factor referred to in paragraph (1) or (2) over any other interest or factor unless the benefit corporation has stated in its articles of incorporation its intention to give priority to certain interests or factors related to the accomplishment of its general public benefit purpose or of a specific public benefit purpose identified in its articles."

This language accomplishes two critical goals. First, it eliminates any argument that a benefit corporation is subject to shareholder primacy. Nevertheless, the white paper makes it very clear that the structure created is not intended to subvert the interests of shareholders but rather to place all interests, including those of shareholders, on equal footing:

> It is important to note that shareholders are among the stakeholders whose interests the directors of a benefit corporation are required to consider; in fact they are listed first, and remain the only stakeholder entitled to bring a legal action against the corporation or its directors. Therefore, directors of benefit corporations may not simply disregard financial stakeholders in pursuing their stated purpose; rather they must balance the interests of shareholders as financial stakeholders with the enumerated other interests.[21]

Second, the language establishes that no particular stakeholder interest has primacy. This reinforces the general nature of a corporation's public benefit purpose. In addition to eliminating shareholder primacy, it was important to the drafters that no other constituency be able to achieve primacy. For example, a governance model that subverted environmental interests to worker interests could create the same systemic risks as a regime that subverted environmental interests to shareholder interests. The white paper provides additional examples:

> The entrepreneurs, investors, consumers and policy makers interested in new corporate form legislation are not interested in, for example, reducing waste while increasing carbon emissions, or

reducing both while remaining indifferent to the creation of economic opportunity for low-income individuals or underserved communities. They are interested in creating a new corporate form that gives entrepreneurs and investors the flexibility and protection to pursue all of these public benefit purposes. The best way to give them what they need is to create a corporate form with a general public benefit purpose.[22]

Despite the mandatory nature of the provision, it is important to emphasize that the mandate in Section 301 is *procedural* in nature. The director provision only mandates that the board consider a wide range of constituencies; it does not mandate any particular outcome.[23] In this respect, the MBCL follows the contours of conventional corporate law: courts protect shareholders not by second-guessing the substance of decisions but rather by ensuring that directors are acting consistently with their fiduciary obligations.[24] This is a critical point, and we will return to it in our discussion of other provisions of the MBCL that take a different approach, as well as the Delaware model.

SECTION 201: CORPORATE PURPOSE BEYOND VALUE MAXIMIZATION

Expanding corporate purpose to include achieving public benefits

Under conventional corporate law, corporations have power to take actions to the extent provided by statute. By the twentieth century, most corporations were incorporated with the power to engage in any lawful activity.[25] This avoided cumbersome "ultra vires" litigation, in which corporations, shareholders, or third parties might dispute whether certain activities were legally permissible for a certain corporation.[26] It is important to note that purpose clauses, including the modern broad purpose clause—define only the *type* of activities that corporations can undertake, not what their *goal* might be in undertaking those activities. This means that shareholders cannot bring lawsuits to enforce shareholder primacy as a matter of corporate purpose, because primacy is a matter of *why* a corporation undertakes activity, not *what* activity it undertakes. Instead, shareholder primacy is enforced through application of the fiduciary duty concepts, and not as a matter of corporate power (discussed in chapter 3).

Section 301 thus parallels conventional corporate law by focusing on fiduciary duties and board procedures to enforce the stakeholder mandate. There is, however, a deviation from this correspondence in Section 201 of the MBCL, which specifies that "a benefit corporation shall have a purpose of creating general public benefit."[27] In addition, a benefit corporation may, in its articles, add a specific benefit purpose. *Section 201 suggests that there is possibly a goal-oriented element to corporate purpose under the MBCL, which is quite different from conventional corporate law.*

This suggestion is confirmed by the remedy provisions of the MBCL, which do call for substantive court review of the question whether a benefit corporation is satisfying its benefit purpose—even if the directors have satisfied their fiduciary duties. In this respect, the MBCL uses the concept of "purpose" very differently from conventional corporate law. This difference allows corporate action to be challenged as not adequately addressing stakeholder interests, even if the directors have satisfied their obligations with respect to all stakeholders. This aspect of the legislation is discussed further in the section on remedies.

General public benefit: Environmental and social concerns

Every corporation created under the MBCL has the purpose of creating "general public benefit," defined as "a material positive impact on society and the environment, taken as a whole, assessed against a third-party standard, from the business and operations of a benefit."[28]

The critical starting point for understanding the general benefit is the definition of "third-party standard."[29] Although the board of a benefit corporation is entitled to select the standard, the statutory definition is rigorous. The most important aspect of the third-party standard requirement for this purpose is its comprehensiveness: the standard must address all of the interests that directors must consider under Section 301. The additional requirements of independence, credibility, and transparency (all of which are subject to judicial review) are intended to ensure that public benefit status will not be abused. Returning to the definition of general public benefit, the board (or court) is to look for a positive impact "on society and the environment, taken as a whole" assessed against that standard. The "as a whole" language, paired with the use of an assessment that includes the aspects that a board must consider under Section 301, conveys that *all* interests with which directors must concern themselves are to be considered in the creation of positive impact.[30]

The term "as a whole" might be read to suggest netting all the positive and negative effects enumerated in the chosen third-party standard (which, by definition, would incorporate the stakeholder considerations required by Section 301). The white paper, however, initially indicates that it is only the positive effects that are to be included in the calculation:

> Some observers have expressed concern that "material positive impact" takes no account of potential "negative impacts" of the business or operations of a benefit corporation. This is true and intentional. A "net positive impact" would imply that one could add and subtract impacts from diverse activities (e.g., add 2 units for reducing energy usage per unit of production, subtract 1 unit for a discrimination lawsuit, etc.) based upon some common unit of measure. Such a unit of measure does not exist and is unlikely to exist at least for a considerable period of time.[31]

This is a fair point as to level of difficulty, but it is somewhat difficult to reconcile with the entire program of introducing broad stakeholder responsibility as a fundamental aspect of corporate governance. Considering only the positive effects could lead a company to champion a few good practices—for example, paying employees well, reducing solid waste, and making contributions to charity—while ignoring other concerns—such as human rights issues in its supply chain, large outputs of greenhouse gases, and discriminatory hiring practices—and yet still claim to produce a "material positive impact." The white paper suggests that use of third-party standards will ameliorate this concern and "moves the market closer to a desired net impact assessment."[32] Though the white paper is not explicit, this ameliorative effect presumably arises from the fact that negative impacts—such as those that arise from poor environmental or workplace practices—are likely to make it difficult to score well on a comprehensive third-party standard.

The best reading of the MBCL, the comments, and the white paper appears to be that the drafters did not contemplate any sort of rigorous mathematical netting process to arrive at a numerical benefit measurement but rather believed that the rigor of the definition of third-party standard, along with mandatory reporting, would force benefit corporations to do an analysis that did, in fact, account for negative effects on stakeholders, even if that accounting came in the form of failing to "score points" on an assessment of positive impacts.[33]

Specific public benefit: Tightening the focus

MBCL Section 201(b) also gives corporations the option to add a specific public benefit to the corporation's articles. "Specific public benefit" has a broad meaning, including a catchall: "conferring any other particular benefit on society or the environment."[34] Each of the items listed in the definition, as well as any matter encompassed within the catchall, clearly come within the definition of general public benefit, so the efficacy of adding a specific benefit is not immediately clear. The MBCL is very clear that this additional purpose should not dilute the corporation's general public benefit purpose.[35] However, this provision does allow a business to take on an obligation to achieve a particular goal that would not be mandated under the general public benefit obligation.

As with general public benefit, creation of the specific public benefit is deemed to be in the best interests of the corporation.[36] The term is then used throughout the statute, in parallel with general public benefit. Thus, the mandate under Section 301(a) that directors consider the ability of the corporation to accomplish its general benefit purpose is accompanied by an admonition to consider any specific benefit purpose in like manner. Similarly, Section 305(a) provides a substantive claim for failure of a benefit corporation to pursue or create its specific public benefit.

The option of choosing a specific public benefit might not be technically necessary, since anything that might be a specific public benefit would already seem to be included within the general definition that will be applicable to any benefit corporation that were to adopt a specific purpose. As we have seen, the white paper explains why it was important to mandate a general purpose, so that all stakeholders would be protected. It does not explain why, having determined that benefit corporations must pursue broad purposes, there was a need to also allow them to call out more specific purposes. The option of adopting specific purposes does provide an affirmative ability to supplement the broad aperture of general public benefit. If the creators of the corporation want to ensure that a particular interest—whether it is workers, stakeholders affected by climate change, or the local veterans population—are protected, there is no way to ensure that such a particular interest will play an important role in the general public benefit calculation. Thus, specifying a specific benefit is a way of making sure a fundamental interest does not get lost.[37]

There may be a second, somewhat subtler reason for including a specific purpose: to create stronger accountability where desired. Because the pursuit of "general public benefit" is so broad, there may be concern that corporations could take on the benefit label, measure against a standard, but still effectively obfuscate the benefit creation question by setting one stakeholder against another. Thus, a company might do just enough to scrape by in its pursuit of benefit, or at least to make a court hesitant to second-guess the board's conclusions. This is harder if the creators of the corporation include some specifics—such as greenhouse gas reduction or service to a particular underserved population. Interestingly, this is what appears to be behind the Delaware model's *requirement* that PBCs elect a specific purpose to go alongside their general stakeholder obligations (as we will discuss in chapter 6).

THE IMPORTANCE OF REMEDIES UNDER THE MBCL

Two types of claim

One of the most important innovations under the MBCL is the creation of the "benefit enforcement proceeding," a singular remedy for breaches of the stakeholder governance mandate. Section 102 defines such a proceeding as one to establish either that the benefit corporation failed in pursuing its benefit purpose or that the directors failed to adequately consider the interests of its stakeholders. Section 305 adds to this definition by limiting standing to bring such claims and by limiting corporate liability. Such a proceeding may allege:

(1) failure of a benefit corporation to pursue or create general public benefit or a specific public benefit purpose set forth in its articles; or

(2) violation of any obligation, duty, or standard of conduct under this [chapter].[38]

In keeping with the distinction between substantive and procedural remedies discussed above, clause 2 is focused on whether a standard of conduct was met, rather than on actual outcomes. Clause 1, however, is focused on substance:

Has the corporation itself failed to achieve (or to pursue) its benefit purposes? This is a critical departure from conventional corporate law—in some ways, as important as expanding the stakeholders who may be considered, because it changes the paradigm at the heart of corporate law.[39] Under that paradigm, a properly functioning board has the last word on business decisions. Allowing for substantive court review of independent board action represents a shift from the principles underlying the business judgment rule and gives courts a much stronger hand in corporate decision making. Despite the arguably radical conceptual change, the practical effect of clause 1 may be limited, due to its interaction with other provisions within the MBCL, as we shall discuss.

Exclusivity

The MBCL makes clear that the benefit enforcement proceeding is intended to be *exclusive*—it is the only remedy available with respect to general and specific public benefits, or with respect to the obligation to consider stakeholder interests (or certain other obligations we will discuss, such as reporting obligations).[40] Second, such a proceeding may be brought only directly by the benefit corporation itself, or derivatively by shareholders (or directors) of the corporation, or by an entity of which the benefit corporation is a subsidiary (unless the bylaws or articles of incorporation grant such a right to others). Corporate shareholders must own at least 2 percent of a class or series of stock in order to bring a claim; for parent shareholders, the ownership requirement increases to 5 percent of outstanding equity interests of the parent. Thus, other stakeholders cannot bring claims, and this limitation is consistent with the statement in Section 301 that directors do not have duties to beneficiaries of general or specific public benefits.[41]

The availability of the business judgment rule for fiduciary claims

The MBCL preserves the business judgment rule with respect to fiduciary claims:

> A director who makes a business judgment in good faith fulfills the duty
> under this section if the director:
>
> (1)   is not interested in the subject of the business judgment;

(2) is informed with respect to the subject of the business judgment to the extent the director reasonably believes to be appropriate under the circumstances; and

(3) rationally believes that the business judgment is in the best interests of the benefit corporation.[42]

This statutory imposition of the business judgment rule suggests that to the extent that stakeholder interests are to be protected by reference to fiduciary duties (i.e., claims brought under clause 2 of Section 305[a]), litigation under the MBCL will focus in the first instance on the procedure at the board level and not on the substance of the board's decision. As discussed in "The Business Judgment Rule" section of chapter 3, the business judgment rule strictly limits the ability of courts to second-guess business decisions made by disinterested directors. Unless a plaintiff can show that directors were conflicted, grossly negligent, or acting in bad faith, courts will not find a breach of duty, even if they disagree with the challenged decision and even if the results of the decision were disastrous.

Importantly, there is always room for some substantive showing under the business judgment rule, if the showing is made in order to demonstrate that the directors could not have met the procedural standard—that no rational, adequately informed person would have made the decision in question.[43] Moreover, if directors *do* have conflicts, a court may review the substance of a decision. Thus, a decision to support a charitable organization would likely be protected by the business judgment rule, but if it turned out that a controlling shareholder's spouse was the executive director of the charity and that a majority of the directors were not independent of the controlling shareholder, a court might apply the entire fairness test and review the substance of the decision.

In light of the limitations on standing, the imposition of the business judgment rule, and the exclusive nature of Section 303, it appears that the statute is intended to focus actions against unconflicted directors on challenges to board process, thus paralleling the rules in conventional corporation law. The difference, however, is that a benefit corporation board is required to consider many more interests than a traditional corporate board. These additional considerations were discussed above, and they include workers, customers, community, the environment, and the corporation's ability to accomplish its general benefit purpose.

Clause 1: The substantive claim—power to the courts?

Clause 1 of Section 305 provides that a claim may be brought for failure to pursue or create general public benefit. In such a proceeding, the business judgment rule will *not* apply, so that the court will *not* only be looking at whether the board was independent and followed all the right procedures. In such a substantive benefit proceeding, a court will instead determine whether the corporation is in fact pursuing or achieving a general public benefit, that is, a material positive impact on society and the environment as assessed against a third-party standard, as well as any specific public benefit set forth in its articles. This is potentially a radical change from conventional corporate law, giving courts greater reach into corporate decision making. Such a proceeding could examine several issues.

Did the corporation use a proper third-party standard? If shareholders bring a substantive benefit enforcement proceeding with respect to general public benefit under Section 305, the initial issue is likely to be whether the corporation is using a qualifying third-party standard. If the court were to find that the third-party standard chosen by the corporation did not satisfy the statutory standard, then it would appear that the shareholders would be entitled to relief. However, the only relief to which the shareholder would be entitled would be injunctive, as the statute exculpates benefit corporations from monetary liability in benefit enforcement proceedings.[44] Thus, a benefit corporation that was found not to have used a qualifying third-party standard to measure public benefit could be ordered to do so.

Must the corporation both pursue and create public benefit? What could be litigated if a court found that a corporation were using a qualifying third-party standard? The statutory test is creation of or pursuit of a general public benefit, as assessed against the standard (or a specific benefit listed in the articles). One initial inquiry is whether the test is disjunctive or conjunctive; in other words, what happens if a corporation pursues but does not create general public benefit? It seems unlikely that the drafters would have included the word "create" if there were not going to be an independent right to sue for failure to do so, even in the face of legitimate pursuit, since it seems extremely unlikely that there would be cases where a corporation achieved general public benefit without pursuing it.

In other words, if the statutory standard could always be satisfied by adequate pursuit, there would be no need to include the term "create." This is consistent with the white paper, which emphasizes that directors do not need to be concerned about monetary liability for failure to create general public benefit, because of the limitations on monetary liability (thus indicating that they did anticipate that shareholders could win some sort of relief where corporations failed to create public benefit).[45]

Who sets the standard? The next question, then, is how a court would determine whether there has been "material positive impact" assessed against the qualifying standard. In order to analyze this question, it is necessary to return to the third-party standard definition discussed earlier. In particular, it must be a "recognized standard for defining, reporting, and assessing corporate social and environmental performance." This language could be interpreted in three ways. First, it might be that the "assessment" aspect falls entirely on the corporation. That is, the standard need not include an assessment or a "score" but merely elicit enough information to allow the board (and, in a substantive proceeding, the court) to perform an assessment. Second, it might be that the standard should include a scoring mechanism but the board (or court) may determine whether any particular score signals achievement of general public benefit. Finally, the strictest interpretation would be one that contemplated that there must be a score and that the board (or court) must accept the standard setter's interpretation of whether the score represents a passing grade.

Two commentators suggested the latter, strict interpretation under a prior version of the MBCL. The initial version of the MBCL included the word "as" in the general public benefit definition, so that a corporation needed to have "a material positive impact on society and the environment, taken as a whole, as assessed against a third-party standard." The commentators' article, published in 2013, claimed that the word "as" created an ambiguity, suggesting that if a benefit corporation did not meet the requirements of its third-party standard, it would not have created general public benefit, as defined. In order to address this ambiguity and clarify that corporations and courts had greater flexibility, the authors proposed that the MBCL be changed to drop the word "as."[46]

The offending word has indeed been dropped from the MBCL. This still leaves the question whether there needs to be a *system of assessment* built into the standard, even if there is no concept of ranking or passing. Although the words of the MBCL might be read to suggest such a requirement, the better reading appears to be that no such system is required, and this is consistent with the white paper. The white paper names several standards that will meet the requirements of the MBCL, including the Global Reporting Initiative, Underwriters Laboratories ISO 26000, and B Lab's B Impact Assessment. Although the B Impact Assessment made available by B Lab does provide for scoring, the other two do not.[47]

Putting all of this together, it appears that a challenge under clause 1 of the benefit enforcement proceeding provision would examine the following issues:

1. Did the third-party standard meet the statutory definition?

2. Has the corporate process for satisfying its purpose of creating general public benefit taken into account all relevant factors from the standard?

3. Does the corporate goal for performance, if satisfied, create an actual positive impact, and has the company in fact pursued that goal?

4. Has the corporation met its goal, or otherwise created material positive impact?

Items 3 and 4 would both need to be satisfied if the "pursue or create" language were read to create a conjunctive test, while satisfying either would satisfy a disjunctive test. There are policy arguments that favor both interpretations. The strongest argument for a conjunctive test is that simply "trying" is not enough, and, moreover, is especially hard to measure. In order to prevent greenwashing, the argument runs, courts must be able to determine whether a company is in fact meeting its purpose. This argument draws some support from the fact that the only relief the statute contemplates is injunctive, so that the only result of a finding of liability for failure to create adequate benefit would be an order to do so, and, where the court found it appropriate, a mandatory injunction prescribing specific steps. For example, a particularly poor environmental performer might be enjoined to take specific actions with regard to reducing use of, reusing, and recycling nonrenewable resources.

On the other hand, it might be argued that the better policy would be to enforce the provision disjunctively. First, if a court were to find that a corporation had created adequate benefit for stakeholders, it would seem downright churlish to criticize them for not pursuing what they actually achieved. On the flip side, it would seem that if a corporation were in fact pursuing stakeholder benefits but was failing to achieve them, issuing an injunction would seem out of place. However, there may be less to this distinction than meets the eye. "Pursuing" without taking realistic steps to succeed should not be countenanced, but at the same time, failing to create benefit after putting in adequate effort is analogous to a well-functioning board taking calculated risks but failing to make a profit. Consider, for example, a company where a large element of benefit was a product that would allow customers to reduce energy use. If the product ultimately failed, would it make sense to find the company in breach of its benefit duties? This is likely to be an area where case-by-case development leads to the best law. The absence of risk of personal liability should ensure that directors are not discouraged from continuing to take entrepreneurial risks in creating general public benefit, even with this existing uncertainty.

A similar analysis should apply with respect to the "netting" question discussed earlier in relation to MBCL Section 201. Rather than viewing this as a simple binary issue, there is likely to develop a more nuanced case law that recognizes that significant failure to address one or more critical negative impacts arising from a corporation's conduct, when viewed through the lens of a comprehensive third-party standard, prevents it from claiming to have met the statutory standard.

TRANSPARENCY

The MBCL requires corporations to prepare and make available an annual benefit report.[48] This transparency requirement is a critical feature of the statute. Without some type of reporting, it would be very difficult for shareholders and other stakeholders to know whether a benefit corporation is in fact pursuing and creating public benefit.[49] There are three specific elements to the transparency requirement. First, the report must be sent to each shareholder. Second, the report must be posted on the website of the corporation or, if the corporation does not have a website, made available without charge to any person who requests it. Finally, the report must be filed with the corporate filing office. Although most states that have adopted the MBCL follow the first two requirements, more than half have not adopted the state filing requirement.[50] In addition, several states have added express penalties for failure to file the report.

There are really two critical elements to the transparency standard. The first, discussed earlier, is the third-party definition, which establishes the criteria for selecting a third-party standard against which to measure benefit performance. The second element is the annual benefit report itself.[51] The report has three critical pieces: a narrative, an assessment, and a compliance statement. In addition to these three elements, the annual report must include the name of the benefit officer and director, where applicable, and the compensation paid to directors.

In the narrative section, the report must detail the ways in which the corporation pursued and the extent to which it created general public benefit (as well as specific public benefits, if it has any). The narrative portion must also detail any circumstances that have hindered creation of benefit. The narrative must also explain the reasons for choosing the third-party standard used to assess performance. Next comes the heart of the report: the "assessment of the overall social and environmental performance of the benefit corporation against a third-party standard."[52] The compliance statement affirms that the corporation and the directors are properly pursuing benefit purposes.[53] For corporations that have a benefit director, the annual compliance statement is to be made by this director.

BENEFIT DIRECTORS AND OFFICERS

The MBCL permits the board of directors to include a benefit director, who must satisfy certain independence requirements.[54] Some states have adopted a requirement that there be a benefit director, or require such a director if the company is publicly traded. The only extra responsibility of a benefit director is the provision of an annual compliance statement, which must be included in the annual benefit report. The statement must indicate whether the corporation acted in accordance with its benefit purposes and whether the directors and officers acted in accordance with their obligations to consider the interests of stakeholders, and it must describe any failure to so comply. The MBCL also permits the designation of a benefit officer, who has the responsibility to prepare the annual benefit report and undertake any other duties related to public benefit that are delegated in the bylaws or by the board.

OPTING IN AND OUT

The MBCL requires a two-thirds vote of shareholders, by class, to authorize a transaction in which a corporation becomes a benefit corporation. The same vote is required for a transaction in which the benefit corporation ceases to be a benefit corporation or sells substantially all of its assets.[55] Unlike the Delaware benefit corporation statute, which will be discussed in chapter 6, the statute does expressly require a supermajority vote when a corporation is acquired in a merger and its shareholders receive stock in a benefit corporation. However, a supermajority role is required in a merger of a conventional corporation if the "surviving, [new, or resulting]" entity is to be a benefit corporation; this language could arguably apply to such a transaction. Some states have varied the vote requirement to bare majority, 75 percent, or 100 percent.[56]

* * *

In the next chapter, we will turn to the second important model of benefit corporation law, which was first adopted in Delaware in 2013.

CHAPTER SIX

The Delaware Public Benefit Corporation Statute

C hapter 5 described the Model Benefit Corporation Legislation, the first comprehensive attempt to address shareholder primacy in corporate law in the twenty-first century. (Constituency statutes, a less comprehensive solution adopted by many legislatures in the late twentieth century, are discussed in chapter 9.) This chapter will discuss a second model of benefit corporation, first adopted in Delaware in 2013 and now followed, to some degree, in five states. This version, known as the public benefit corporation, is important because Delaware is the jurisdiction most often chosen by companies that go public or raise significant equity from venture capital or private equity investors.

At the highest level, PBC law makes the same important changes to conventional law as the MBCL: it provides an option where directors must account for stakeholders just as they do for shareholders. There are, however, significant differences. First, PBC law mandates that, in addition to considering *all* stakeholders, a PBC must choose a specific public benefit to promote. Second, Delaware does not mandate the use of a third-party standard. Instead, the mechanisms to implement stakeholder values are left to the discretion of the board. Finally, the PBC statutes do not contemplate "benefit enforcement proceedings," and, as a result, any legal challenge as to whether a corporation is properly implementing stakeholder governance must consist of a fiduciary claim—unlike the MBCL, PBC law does not contemplate a separate substantive claim that a corporation has failed to pursue or create public benefit. Because of Delaware's role in U.S. corporate law, the question whether benefit corporation law will be adopted by large, widely held enterprises is likely to be a question of whether the PBC form is successful.

Delaware's Approach to Benefit Corporations

Delaware is the preferred choice for U.S. publicly traded companies, and it is also favored as a corporate home by many investors, so that many entities looking to raise outside capital incorporate there.[1] There is a rich literature discussing the reasons for this prominence, which posits items such as a flexible and well-maintained statute, access to an expert judiciary, and an attentive and modern secretary of state.[2] Whatever the reason, Delaware has special cause to maintain its prominence, given the importance of corporate business to its budget.[3]

Thus, when B Lab approached Delaware as it had other states in promoting the passage of benefit corporation legislation, the state, through the Corporate Law Section of the Delaware State Bar Association, took a different path than other states had. Rather than implementing the MBCL, Delaware took some of the key ideas from that model and incorporated them into an entirely different statute, which authorized what Delaware called a "public benefit corporation."

The Delaware model was driven by the need to craft provisions that could implement the stakeholder values inherent in benefit corporation governance in a manner that would appeal to public companies, private companies that raised significant outside capital, and investors. Brett McDonnell has described the delicate balance involved in crafting a stakeholder model for contemporary public markets:

> As one considers the leading unique benefits and costs of going public for benefit corporations, one sees that they must strike a difficult balance between maintaining the accountability of officers and directors (and thus avoiding self-dealing); reducing pressures to follow the dictates of profit-focused activist shareholders (and thus avoiding mission drift); while overall leaving managers the discretion to make difficult choices while still credibly committing to achieve both profits and social good.[4]

In contrast, the MBCL had been crafted with a view toward attracting entrepreneurs with a structure that allowed them to integrate responsible and sustainable practices into their businesses with great transparency to all stakeholders, and to ensure that the purposeful nature of the business would be preserved through time, even in the event of changes in management or control. The public benefit corporation statute (PBCS) seeks to accomplish similar goals, while taking into account the particular circumstances faced by institutional investors, by the directors and managers of public companies, as well as by venture- and private equity–backed companies that might anticipate going public. The states that have followed the PBC model have each made modifications to the Delaware version. The discussion in this chapter is specific to the Delaware version, so readers working with a PBC in a different jurisdiction should review the statute in question to understand any differences.

The PBC model gives such constituencies the choice to veer from the model of shareholder primacy, without giving up the key elements of conventional governance—including business judgment rule protection of transactions—and without imposing regulatory-like disclosure burdens on companies that may already be subject to a full regime of Securities and Exchange Commission (SEC) disclosure. In general, it is a less rigid model.[5] This chapter describes the PBCS (versions of which have been adopted in Colorado, Kansas, Kentucky, and Tennessee, as well).[6] The current version of the Delaware PBCS is included as appendix B. For practitioners, a Quick Guide to Becoming a Delaware PBC, and model provisions are included as appendixes C and D. Where relevant, contrasts will be drawn with the MBCL, in order to highlight the operation of the PBCS. Table 5 (on page 88) highlights a few important contrasts between the two models.

Responsible and Sustainable Management: The Balancing Obligation

The statute begins by establishing that the purpose of the law is to create responsible corporate governance: a PBC is "intended to produce a public benefit or benefits and to operate in a responsible and sustainable manner."[7] "Responsibility" can be understood as an acknowledgment that corporate operations affect many stakeholders, while the concept of "sustainability" recognizes that those operations have the potential to deplete (or expand) the resources those stakeholders

TABLE 5: DELAWARE PUBLIC BENEFIT CORPORATION STATUTE COMPARED TO MODEL BENEFIT CORPORATION LEGISLATION		
	Delaware	**Model Legislation**
CORPORATE PURPOSE	Corporation "intended to produce . . . public benefits and to operate in a responsible and sustainable manner. To that end, a public benefit corporation shall be managed in a manner that balances the stockholders' pecuniary interests, the best interests of those materially affected by the corporation's conduct, and the public benefit or benefits identified in its certificate of incorporation." Required to choose one or more specific public benefit purposes.	Businesses required to create general public benefit, defined as "a material positive impact on society and the environment, taken as a whole." Permitted to choose one or more specific benefit purposes.
DIRECTOR OBLIGATIONS	Required to balance the stockholders' pecuniary interests, the best interests of those materially affected by the corporation's conduct, and the public benefit or public benefits identified in its certificate of incorporation. Liability exculpation with respect to stakeholder balancing for all disinterested decisions —no "bad faith" exception for irrational choices.	Required to consider impact of decisions on all stakeholders. Liability exculpation for disinterested decisions with respect to stakeholder consideration if business judgment standard met, including rationality.
BENEFIT DIRECTOR	Not required.	Required for public company and, in some jurisdictions, a private company.
PUBLIC TRANSPARENCY	Required to report to stockholders once every two years, with an assessment of impact on the interests of those materially affected by the corporation's conduct and any named specific public benefit (no third party standard requirement). Permitted to report publicly more frequently using a third party standard and/or certification. No public disclosure requirement.	Required to report publicly and annually an assessment of overall impact on any named specific public benefit and all stakeholders as assessed against a third party standard.
THIRD PARTY STANDARD	Third party standard is permitted, but not required.	Benefit corporations must select and report against a third party standard that meets statutory standards for comprehensiveness, independence, credibility and transparency.
ENFORCEMENT	Board balancing decisions will not be disturbed by courts if board in independent, well-informed and acts in good faith.	Shareholders and directors may bring a lawsuit claiming the company is not pursuing or achieving its public benefit purposes.

need to thrive.[8] Though this provision is couched in precatory language, the statute goes on to prescribe *how* the company is to be managed in a manner that addresses the concerns of a broad range of stakeholders, and the precatory language gives content to the operative provisions. Specifically, a PBC must balance three considerations: the shareholders' pecuniary interests, the best interests of those materially affected by the corporation's conduct, and the specific public benefit or public benefits identified in its certificate of incorporation.[9]

This mandate expressly rejects the shareholder primacy model by elevating stakeholder interests to a level of importance equal to that of shareholders. The statute then specifically imposes on directors the obligation to conduct a balancing of all the relevant interests of both shareholders and other stakeholders.[10] While directors of a traditional Delaware corporation must act for the purpose of maximizing the economic wealth of shareholders and may consider socially beneficial actions only to further that end (as discussed in chapter 2), directors of a public benefit corporation must balance the interests of stakeholders other than shareholders as ends in themselves.[11]

BROAD PUBLIC BENEFIT: THE MATERIALITY TEST

The second part of the three-part balancing act invokes the "best interests of those materially affected by the corporation's conduct." This phrase does the same work as the phrase "general public benefit" in the MBCL. Although some have expressed concern that the PBC statute does not explicitly address the environment, this phrase clearly picks up any environmental issue that has an effect on people (since such people would be materially affected by degradation or improvement in their environment).

To understand the broad nature of this obligation, it is also important to consider the placement of the word "materially," which, together with "affected," identifies the stakeholders whom the board must consider. Thus, if a group of people is materially affected by the corporation's actions, the company must weigh their interests in the balance. There is no separate "materiality" test that applies each time a decision is made. This broad approach prevents a corporation from ignoring stakeholders who would be impacted by a series of actions even if each action in the series, standing alone, were immaterial; stakeholders cannot be "nickel-and-dimed."

It might also be suggested, however, that use of the term "material" could allow a corporation to be managed in a way that ignores broad societal and environmental concerns, because it might be argued one company's waste of scarce resources, or its small contribution to systemic instability, is not likely to matter very much—is not "material." In this narrow reading, the statute would only mandate responsible activity with respect to parochial interests, such as direct effects on the company workforce or perhaps on a community where the corporation deposits its waste, but not broad, global concerns, such as climate change or economic inequality at the macro scale.

This argument would undercut the purpose of the statute. The first sentence of Section 362 is explicit that PBCs are to be responsible and sustainable. The type of "free riding" that the "immateriality" argument presupposes is the very type of activity the statute was intended to address. The argument suggests that, where material harm is suffered or benefit received due to the aggregation of many individual actions by a group of actors, none of the actors is responsible in a "material" way. The far better understanding is that each actor, by continuing to participate, bears responsibility for the result.

Accordingly, the statute is likely to be interpreted so that citizens are viewed as stakeholders who are "materially affected" by a manufacturer's outputs, such as greenhouse gases, and that boards should accordingly include the effects of such output on the citizens in its decision-making balance. In this context, the statutory reference to "sustainable" operations can be understood as requiring a corporation to consider what constitutes its fair share of any common resource, whether environmental or social.[12] This conception is consistent with a 2015 United Nations Environmental Programme report, which declared that sustainability reports should be context-based and involve "fair share impacts."[13]

SPECIFIC PUBLIC BENEFIT

In addition to the broad mandate, each Delaware PBC must also choose one or more specific public benefits.[14] A public benefit is defined as "a positive effect (or reduction of negative effects) on one or more categories of persons, entities, communities, or interests," other than the pecuniary interests of the shareholders.[15] A PBC may choose to promote any public benefit as long as that benefit fits within the broad parameters of the statute, which are likely to be construed liberally if they are ever interpreted by a court.[16]

This mandatory specific benefit is another place where the Delaware model diverges from the MBCL, which permits, but does not require, a specific public benefit, as noted in the "Specific Public Benefit: Tightening the Focus" section of chapter 5. Given the broad nature of the consideration to be given to all stakeholders with a material interest, it is reasonable to question the need for selecting a specific public benefit, which is almost sure to fall within the broad general mandate. However, it appears that the requirement of specificity was an acknowledgment that creating accountability with respect to broad public benefit was a difficult proposition—that is, it might be very difficult to enforce board duties or transparency obligations with respect to every constituency that might be affected by a corporation's actions, because of the many different and competing interests involved.[17] For example, because the economic interests of one community might conflict with broader environmental interests, it may be particularly difficult to assess whether proper balancing has occurred. Though the specific benefit requirement does not relax the general requirement, it does potentially supply a more meaningful opportunity to hold a corporation accountable for a public benefit. We will return to this idea in the discussion of director duties.

The statute does not delineate a level of required specificity, but corporations should pick a specific benefit that is more restricted than a restatement of the general benefit that the statute requires. This specificity will ensure that the corporation has complied with Section 362, so that it will receive all the protections provided under the public benefit corporation provisions. It is also a best practice to provide a purpose that is broad enough to limit the need for future amendments to the specific goal. Thus, for example, if a company's specific public purpose involves ensuring that schoolchildren receive nutritious meals, it may be best to refer to that generic but specific purpose, rather than articulating the specific means by which the company currently achieves that purpose, since, as the company scales and evolves, its method for providing nutritious meals may also change.

Duties of Directors

INTEREST BALANCING

The board of directors is responsible for directing the business and affairs of a PBC.[18] However, unlike directors of conventional Delaware corporations, directors of PBCs are required to balance the pecuniary interests of shareholders with the best interests of stakeholders materially affected by the corporation and with the corporation's identified public benefit or benefits. Therefore, the directors of a PBC have a statutory duty to weigh concerns other than maximizing economic value for the shareholders of the corporation, and the directors must manage the corporation in a way that balances all of the relevant interests.[19] This obligation is analogous to Section 301 of the MBCL.

Although this provision adds obligations to the mandate of directors of Delaware corporations, its primary effect is to free them from the confines of shareholder primacy. Due to the strict language in the case law, and the absence of a constituency statute, directors of conventional Delaware corporations have a narrow range of purpose: as we saw in chapter 2, all of their decisions must consider shareholder value as the ultimate goal. Section 365 frees directors from that constraint. This is an enormous advantage for a Delaware corporation wishing to promote publicly beneficial objectives while remaining a for-profit entity. Although the directors of conventional corporations are provided some leeway as to social responsibility under the business judgment rule (discussed in chapter 3), they are required to view all decisions through the lens of value maximization for shareholders. In corporate sale situations, they are therefore required to act for the sole purpose of maximizing shareholder value in the short term (recall the *Revlon* standard with regard to changes in control, which we covered in chapter 3). Under the PBC model, directors not only may but *must* balance the interests of stakeholders other than shareholders in both sale and nonsale situations.[20] This obligation can be a powerful tool in winning the trust of stakeholders.

Though the statute mandates that this balancing occur, it does not mandate any particular outcome; compliance with the process outlined in the statute protects board decisions from substantive scrutiny.[21] This is critical to the efficient operation of the statute. As with constituency statutes, the board is permitted to make substantive decisions based on stakeholder interests. Moreover, unlike those statutes, the PBCS gives shareholders the ability to *require* that directors take such stakeholder concerns into account. However, as long as the directors act independently and in good faith, the courts are not authorized to judicially reject their balancing decisions. This could be an important distinction between the PBCS and the MBCL, because the latter specifically authorizes *substantive* challenges to decisions that affect stakeholders.[22]

One way to conceptualize the three-part balancing test is to think of it as imposing a mandate that directors balance the goals of (1) providing a competitive return to shareholders, (2) having a net positive impact on society and the environment, and (3) creating a net positive impact with respect to the benefits specified in the corporate charter. While balancing interests 1 and 2 might theoretically address policy concerns animating the adoption of the statute, it appears that the drafters may have believed that interest 2 was so broad as to limit accountability, which is why the third element was added: it will be more difficult for directors to avoid addressing specific benefits specified within the corporate charter.

STATUTORY BUSINESS JUDGMENT RULE

As we discussed in chapter 3, the business judgment rule is a doctrine developed by the courts, which prohibits interference with board decisions made by disinterested and fully informed directors acting in good faith. The PBCS states that this rule applies to all balancing decisions made by PBC directors.[23] Thus, if a shareholder initiates a derivative suit against the directors for failing to balance the three categories of interests recognized in the PBCS, the directors' action will be upheld by the court if the directors are informed and disinterested and if the balancing decision appears to be rational.[24]

The PBCS specifically provides, "With respect to a decision implicating the balance requirement . . . [a director] will be deemed to satisfy such director's fiduciary duties to stockholders and to the corporation if such director's decision is both informed and disinterested and not such that no person of ordinary, sound judgment would approve."[25] This language codifies the application of the business judgment rule to board balancing decisions (although in an admittedly awkward fashion, clearly drafted by a committee of lawyers).[26] The final phrase is meant to clarify that plainly irrational decisions will *not* be protected by the business judgment rule. "Rationality" is a concept that marks "the outer limit of the business judgment rule."[27] Irrationality, in turn, is defined as making a decision "that no person of ordinary, sound judgment" would undertake.[28]

Some practitioners have noted the distinction between the obligation to "balance" in the PBCS with the obligation to "consider" in the MBCL, and they question whether "balance" implies that at least some weight must be given to each factor. (Though it has alternatively been suggested that the term implies "equal" weight, this is far too formulaic a reading, as there is not a method by which to numerically compare the different interests involved in the process.) This requirement should only create incremental difference in light of Delaware's codification of the business judgment rule. This difference may also reflect the absence of a substantive remedy in the PBCS. Recall that, under the MBCL, the business judgment rule does not protect decisions in benefit enforcement proceedings brought directly against the corporation (discussed in chapter 5). Accordingly, the use of the light-touch term "consider" as the standard in the MBCL is counterbalanced by the fact that even if the consideration is cursory, the actual substance can be challenged. In contrast, the PBCS does not provide for a substantive review,[29] so that the slightly stronger formula for board action— an insistence that stakeholder interests are given some weight—helps to provide an increment of accountability through the potential for shareholder litigation.

ABSENCE OF SEPARATE BENEFICIARY OF PUBLIC BENEFIT CORPORATION DUTIES

The PBCS is carefully drafted to make it clear that the obligation of balancing does not create new holders of rights. Thus, the statute provides that the directors of a PBC do not owe a statutory duty to "any person" on account of that person's interest in a public benefit identified in the company's certificate of incorporation.[30] However, in order to maintain accountability for PBCs, shareholders are permitted to bring claims that directors failed to balance shareholder and public benefit interests correctly, as we will see in the next section.

This limitation on standing certainly makes the adoption of benefit corporation status more palatable to corporations; the chance of litigation from third parties would create a risk of fights among stakeholders that could make corporate operations difficult. But the standing bar is not simply a practical compromise; it reflects an idea that, while perhaps not explicit in either the PBCS or the MBCL, is a central theoretical underpinning of the benefit corporation:

shareholders have an interest in promoting the interests of all stakeholders and are adequate representatives for them. Under benefit corporation law, after all, shareholders retain the power to elect directors, to approve merger transactions, and to bring legal challenges. Stakeholders have no voice in any of these matters.

Why, then, is the benefit form considered to be an antidote to shareholder primacy? One answer lies in a concept discussed in chapter 4: the universal owner. By forming and investing in a benefit corporation, the shareholders and management have agreed to manage the corporation for the benefit of a broad group of stakeholders. Presumably, this means that the shareholders (or at least a supermajority of them) have determined that it is important to them that all stakeholders are accounted for in board decisions. And the simple fact is that shareholders (at least at the top of the investment chain outlined in chapter 1) are humans with broad interests—interests in a livable environment, interests in a stable society, and interests in a viable future for generations to come.

The goal of the benefit corporation is to bring all of these interests together at the shareholder level, because of shared interests:

> Because the world's asset owners have a stake in the prosperity of the economy as a whole, there is a strong argument that part of the role of an asset owner should be to push for policies and frameworks that reduce negative externalities. In practical terms, this would point to asset owners having a rationale to push investee companies to set minimum standards and certifications and to support sensible public policy (pollution control, emission trading schemes, etc.) that would result in the most efficient allocation of environmental and social resources.[31]

Of course, in the first instance, this balancing among stakeholders lies in the hands of directors: "Commitment by the board of directors to effectively mediated stakeholder primacy is likely to create the type of well-informed, longer-term horizon, collaborative behavior within the competitive firm that ultimately leads to durable corporate sustainability—a goal that rewards investors as well."[32]

In theory, then, the directors in the first instance, monitored by shareholders with the traditional tools of corporate governance—voting rights and lawsuits limited by business judgment principles—should be able to adequately represent the interests of all important stakeholders in the corporate enterprise. (None of this, of course, suggests that other stakeholders would not continue to have access to the political process as a way of addressing their legitimate interests.)

ACCOUNTABILITY THROUGH SHAREHOLDER DERIVATIVE SUITS

As noted earlier, the balancing requirement imposed by the PBCS does not create a duty to third parties. However, the statute does specifically allow a shareholder to bring a derivative action on behalf of the corporation itself for a failure to balance.[33] Such a lawsuit is the sole mechanism for enforcement of the balancing requirement.[34] There is, however, a minimum requirement for shareholders wishing to sue for violation of the directors' balancing duties.[35] In order to bring such a derivative suit, plaintiff shareholders must own, individually or collectively, at least 2 percent of the corporation's outstanding shares or, if the corporation's shares are publicly traded on a national securities exchange such as the New York Stock Exchange or NASDAQ, shares equaling at least two million dollars in market value.

As suggested previously, it would appear that a suit for failure to balance would need to allege that the directors simply failed to pursue one of the three interests (or perhaps engaged in a level of pursuit so weak as to constitute "conscious disregard" of that interest).[36] Thus, a plaintiff could allege that the directors were no longer pursuing shareholder return, were no longer trying to have a positive impact with respect to the corporation's specified purposes, or were no longer attempting to act in the best interests of the stakeholders affected by its conduct. Alternatively, a plaintiff might allege that, despite pursuit of all three goals, the board engaged in a trade-off that no rational person would engage in. As we will see in the next section, any such plaintiff would, absent a traditional conflict of interest, have to seek injunctive relief rather than monetary damages.

LIMITS ON DIRECTOR LIABILITY

The risk of personal liability for PBC directors in lawsuits challenging board balancing decisions is mitigated by Section 365(c), which allows PBCs to eliminate monetary liability for certain breaches of fiduciary duty.[37] Section 102(b)(7) permits traditional corporations to eliminate liability of directors for breaching their duty of care.[38] The PBCS extends the authority for exculpation to include disinterested directors making balancing decisions under Section 365(c). This extension can be accomplished through a charter provision that provides that the failure to make a proper balancing decision is neither a breach of loyalty nor considered "not in good faith." Just as almost every corporation formed in Delaware takes full advantage of the limitation on liability under Section 102(b)(7), all PBCs should take full advantage of Section 365(c) by including this liability limitation in its certificate of incorporation, unless a specific decision is made not to do so. (For an example of such an exculpation provision, see appendix D.)

Thus, unless they are receiving a personal benefit or are otherwise conflicted, directors protected by exculpation provisions can be liable for balancing decisions only if they are "interested." Under traditional Delaware law, a director is "interested" if "there are factors weighing upon the exercise of judgment with respect to that decision which conflict or are inconsistent with the concept of a single, uncompromised loyalty to the corporate interest." Self-dealing transactions, where the director has a personal financial stake in the outcome, fall within the ambit of interested transactions. A director is also interested if he or she receives a special material benefit from a transaction that is unavailable to other shareholders.[39]

Accordingly, while Section 365(b) provides that a director of a PBC satisfies his or her fiduciary duties if the director's judgment is, among other things, disinterested, Section 365(c)'s authorization of a protective provision in the corporation's certificate of incorporation provides further security to directors of public benefit corporations in making balancing decisions. Based on the scope of Delaware's protective provisions, self-dealing remains the likely focus of derivative challenges, and it is likely that the Court of Chancery will focus on whether directors' decisions were disinterested.[40] Although the scope of director obligations is expanded under Section 365 to include the effect of decisions on stakeholders, the statute remains shareholder-centric in many respects—no new beneficiaries are created, and only shareholders may bring lawsuits. Thus, the definition of "interested" should not change. In particular, the ownership of stock by a director should continue to be evidence of her alignment with the corporation, rather than creating a disabling interest.[41] This conclusion is reinforced by the requirement that plaintiffs own a material amount of stock before being permitted to challenge a balancing decision, because the requirement suggests that such ownership is *necessary* to balance competing, non-ownership

(stakeholder) interests in order to make a shareholder an adequately representative derivative plaintiff.

SUBSIDIARY PUBLIC BENEFIT CORPORATIONS
AND THE POTENTIAL FOR DOUBLE DERIVATIVE SUITS

While the PBCS provides for additional or different requirements for PBCs, it
also expressly states that PBCs are "subject in all respects to the [remaining]
provisions of [the Delaware General Corporation Law]."[42] This leaves open the
possibility that various traditional corporate law concepts will be applicable in
the PBC context, including the double derivative shareholder suit.

A standard derivative suit involves "a shareholder bring[ing] a lawsuit
asserting a claim belonging to a corporate entity in which the shareholder owns
shares."[43] A double derivative suit is brought by a shareholder of a parent corporation seeking enforcement of a claim belonging to a wholly owned or majority
controlled subsidiary corporation of that parent. Like a standard derivative suit,
the shareholders initiating a double derivative suit must either (1) first make a
demand on the parent corporation to take action to address or rectify the prob-
lematic conduct or circumstances, or (2) allege in the complaint for its double
derivative action that such a demand would be futile because the parent's board
could not properly exercise its independent and disinterested business judgment
in responding to a demand.[44] Corporate law geeks will recognize that the second
clause represents a tougher test than the test for a standard derivative suit: the
shareholder has to claim that a majority of the board has a conflict. They cannot
otherwise assert that the business judgment rule should not apply because of the
substance of the decision ("irrationality").

Under Delaware law, directors of a wholly owned conventional corporation
are obligated only to manage the affairs of the subsidiary in the best interests of
its sole shareholder. In contrast, directors of the wholly owned PBC would also
have a statutory obligation to balance the interests of all stakeholders as well as
the corporation's specific public benefit or public benefits.[45] Thus, it is possible that a shareholder of a traditional parent corporation could bring a double
derivative suit to hold subsidiary PBC directors accountable to their public
benefit purpose (provided, of course, that the shareholder satisfied the demand
requirements described above). Because the Delaware public benefit corporation statute only expressly allows for shareholders owning at least 2 percent of

the outstanding shares of the benefit corporation to bring a derivative action on behalf of the corporation, a double derivative suit that did not meet such requirement could be seen as a circumvention of this statutory protection. However, the statutory business judgment rule of the PBCS, combined with the strict test set forth by the Supreme Court in *Lambrecht v. O'Neal*, may make pursuit of such a claim largely impracticable, at least where a majority of the parent company directors are disinterested.[46]

Transparency

PUBLIC BENEFIT CORPORATION REPORTING REQUIREMENTS

PBCs must provide shareholders with a report assessing the corporation's promotion of its stated public benefit or benefits. The PBCS requires that the corporation provide such a report every other year.[47] The report must describe the board's goals and standards with respect to stakeholders; specifically, the report must include four elements:

1. the objectives the board has established to promote the best interests of stakeholders and the public benefit or benefits outlined in the certificate of incorporation;

2. the standards the board has adopted to measure the corporation's progress in promoting those interests and benefits;

3. objective factual information based on those standards; and

4. an assessment of the corporation's success in meeting its objectives.[48]

The PBCS is more flexible than the MBCL with respect to reporting. The PBCS requires only that the biennial report be provided to the company's shareholders—it does not require the report be made public. The MBCL requires that the report be made annually, that it be made public, and that it use a third-party standard.[49] Nonetheless, if a PBC chooses, it may include in its governing documents a provision that mandates that the corporation provide a report more frequently, that requires the report to be made public, or that requires the corporation to use a third-party standard in measuring its stakeholder performance.[50] The statute also authorizes provisions that require the PBC to attain third-party certification of such performance.

In requiring transparency, the PBCS departs from the standard model of Delaware corporate law. In a conventional Delaware corporation, directors have duties to promote shareholder value but no duty to report with respect to such matters. Although shareholders are entitled to information, they must make individual demands for books and records and must demonstrate the need for such documents.[51] For the most part, the PBCS operates by adapting conventional corporate governance ideas to stakeholder governance. For example, as discussed previously, the PBCS makes use of the traditional business judgment rule but expands the range of permissible considerations. Why, then, did the drafters of the PBCS add an entirely new requirement with respect to transparency?

The answer to this question is more practical than theoretical. Conventional corporations are subject to reporting obligations if they are publicly traded, and even companies that are not subject to such obligations often enter into agreements with shareholders with respect to information sharing. But all of this information is largely "financial." Thus, regardless of what may be required under corporate law, shareholders often receive reports that provide information upon which they can evaluate financial performance. This simply is not the case with respect to information relevant to other stakeholders. While many companies have begun to issue sustainability reports, these are largely reports of what management chooses to highlight, rather than being designed to provide consistent information about a corporation's impact on society and the environment.[52] This practice raises concerns about so-called greenwashing, where companies highlight certain positive practices as a distraction from general irresponsible behavior.[53] By imposing a minimal reporting standard, the PBCS may create a construct that enables both directors and shareholders to address the broad mandate for PBCs. The American Bar Association (ABA) Corporate Laws Committee reached this conclusion in its white paper, which suggested a reporting scheme similar to that of Delaware: "Some level of mandatory reporting may provide a level of transparency that will allow shareholders to use corporate governance mechanisms effectively to ensure that directors act in accordance with the public benefit provisions."[54]

OTHER SUSTAINABILITY REPORTING REQUIREMENTS IN DEVELOPMENT

Thus, the departure from conventional corporate law represents a recognition of the need for a quantum of impact reporting that does not exist in a consistent fashion in the current business environment. Nevertheless, the drafters of both the ABA white paper and the PBCS chose to depart from the third-party standard required by the MBCL. In Delaware, at least, this middle path determination may well have been influenced by a regard for the burden a regulatory-like standard might place on public companies already subject to detailed SEC reporting requirements.

In addition, as we discussed in chapter 4, standards for environmental, social, and governance reporting are developing, and it may simply be too early in the evolution of those standards to lock a rule in place in a state corporate statute. The European Union has required member states to formulate legislation that will require six thousand listed companies to report on environmental and social issues.[55] The United States government also has begun to explore this area. For example, the Small Business Administration (SBA) has proposed rules for "Impact SBICs," a new class of investment company that receives preferential financial assistance from the SBA. These entities would be required to use approved *measurement* standards.

The SBA explained the reason for proposing such standards: "The purpose of these standards is to establish a common language companies and investors can use to report the positive and negative impacts that result from their activities . . . [and to] promote the use of best practices across the [impact fund] industry." After proposing uniform measurement standards, the SBA goes on to propose uniform *assessment* standards for impact. Such a standard is necessary, the SBA explains, to reduce the risk of selective reporting: "Impact measurement standards only provide guidance on how to report impact data. . . . As with financial performance, each individual investor is empowered to reach his or her own conclusions about what constitutes 'success' with regard to impact. . . . The use of independent and transparent assessment systems not only helps reduce the risk of selective reporting, but it also promotes the use of best practices across the industry."[56]

Thus, the SBA has already begun to impose stakeholder impact reporting requirements on certain entities. The SEC, which oversees reporting for all public companies, has also begun to examine this question. In 2016, the SEC issued a concept release on periodic disclosure, which included questions addressing disclosure requirements for environmental, social, and governance matters, and received 151 responses regarding the issue.[57]

In addition to legal initiatives with respect to sustainability reporting, like those contemplated by the European Commission and the SBA, stock exchanges also may become a source of transparency regulation for environmental and social issues. Brett McDonnell of the University of Minnesota Law School has detailed several early efforts in this area. He points to the Social Stock Exchange, located in the United Kingdom, as one early experiment. The Social Stock Exchange, an "online information portal" for listed companies, is designed to provide information to interested investors and requires the preparation and annual updating of an "impact report." McDonnell also describes the Social Venture Connection, a platform for social enterprises to offer shares to "accredited investors" (i.e., investors who meet certain standards of sophistication). The Social Venture Connection requires that companies meet a strict quantitative standard—scoring at least 100 on the Global Impact Investment Rating System maintained by B Lab or achieving B Corp certification.[58]

All of the developments suggest that locking in a complex disclosure scheme at the state corporate law level may create dual sustainability reporting obligations for PBCs that go public. McDonnell also suggests that impact measurement is still developing: "At this stage, social impact measures are still evolving, and companies and investors are still learning what information really matters, as well as how to collect, measure, and report that information. Premature uniform regulation may cut short a valuable learning process."[59]

The flexible reporting provisions of the PBCS should allow PBCs to meet their statutory reporting requirements in a manner that conforms to any other reporting scheme that becomes applicable.

Supermajority Shareholder Votes

SUPERMAJORITY VOTE REQUIRED
TO OPT IN, OPT OUT, OR CHANGE PURPOSE

While a company may choose to incorporate as a PBC from the outset,[60] a conventional corporation must obtain approval from at least two-thirds (66.6 percent) of the outstanding stock of the corporation to effectuate a transition to a PBC. This enhanced voting requirement provides more protection than the simple majority vote generally required to effect a merger or amendment to the certificate of incorporation of a conventional corporation. The same high vote requirement applies for mergers of conventional corporations if their shareholders are to receive stock in a benefit corporation.[61]

The original PBCS required a conventional corporation wishing to become a public benefit corporation to obtain the approval of at least 90 percent of the outstanding shares of each class of stock, whether voting or nonvoting.[62] The amendment lowering the vote to the current two-thirds approval requirement (which became effective in August 2015) reflected a concern that the difficulty of obtaining such a high vote would preclude widespread use of the statute.[63] The two-thirds approval requirement, though still a supermajority vote, increases the ability of conventional Delaware corporations to become PBCs and for PBCs to enter into acquisition transactions with other entities. Even with the lowered vote requirement, the fiduciary duties of directors provide protection to converting or acquired corporation shareholders, because the directors of the conventional corporation must still conclude that the transaction in question is in the best interest of the shareholders.

Once an entity is organized as a PBC, there is also a supermajority approval requirement for the corporation to opt out of that status, to change its specific public benefits, or to change any specific reporting requirements, including, in each case, by merger. The vote requirement to opt out of the PBC form or to amend the corporation's stated public benefit purpose mirrors the requirements in Section 363(a) for opting in to such a corporate form.[64]

MERGERS AND ACQUISITIONS

A change in status for shareholders generally triggers a supermajority vote under Section 363. Thus, if shareholders of a conventional Delaware corporation are going to receive stock of a PBC in a merger, they will be entitled to a two-thirds vote. This provision is applicable even if the shares received are in a non-Delaware entity, as long as the entity is a benefit corporation "or similar entity."[65] It seems clear that this provision would apply if the shareholders were to receive shares in a corporation in a state that had adopted some variation of either the MBCL or the PBCS. Less clear, however, is whether a corporation with modified duties under a constituency statute, or a social purpose corporation,[66] or even just a jurisdiction outside the United States that did not impose shareholder primacy, would count as "similar."

Likewise, a PBC effectuating a merger or consolidation with a conventional corporation requires the approval of two-thirds of the outstanding stock of the corporation entitled to vote thereon if:

> as a result of the merger or consolidation, the shares in such corpo-
> ration would *become, or be converted into or exchanged for the right
> to receive* shares or other equity interests in a domestic or foreign
> corporation that is not a public benefit corporation or similar entity
> and the certificate of incorporation (or similar governing instru-
> ment) of which does not contain the identical provisions identify-
> ing the public benefit or public benefits pursuant to § 362(a) of this
> title [providing that a public benefit corporation must identify one
> or more specific public benefits in its certificate of incorporation]
> or imposing requirements pursuant to § 366(c) [providing that a
> public benefit corporation may call for more stringent reporting
> requirements in its certificate of incorporation or bylaws] of this
> title [emphasis added].[67]

Thus, a stock-for-stock merger in which shareholders were taken out of the benefit corporation structure would require a two-thirds vote. On the other hand, a cash-out merger in which the target remained a benefit corporation would not require such a vote. A cash-out merger in which the target benefit corporation loses its benefit status would trigger the high vote requirement *if* it is considered a merger in which the shares of that corporation "become" shares of a non–benefit corporation. However, the better argument seems to be that such a transaction would not require a two-thirds vote because the focus of the phrase in which the word "become" is embedded *appears focused on the consideration shareholders are forced to take*; that is, are they being moved from a benefit corporation to a conventional corporation? Had the drafters wished to address an amendment effected in a merger, they could have simply added the phrase "by merger or otherwise" to clause (c)(1), which imposes the superma-jority vote for amendments that eliminate benefit corporation status. Delaware courts have consistently found that a special vote to amend a charter that is imposed by statute or charter is not required to effect an amendment through a merger, unless the language requiring the special vote explicitly applies to amendments effected by merger.[68]

TABLE 6: TWO-THIRDS VOTE REQUIRED UNDER DELAWARE PBC PROVISIONS
1. Conventional corporation amends its charter to become a PBC.
2. PBC amends its charter to change its specific benefit.
3. PBC amends its charter to become a conventional corporation.
4. PBC amends it charter to change or delete provision requiring that its benefit report (i) be issued more frequently than biennially, (ii) be made publicly available, or (iii) use a third-party standard or include third party certification.
5. Conventional corporation merges or consolidates, if its shares become, or are converted into or exchanged for shares of PBC or similar entity.
6. PBC merges or consolidate and shares become, or are converted into or exchanged for, shares of traditional corporation or PBC with different benefit provisions.

Table 6 summarizes the situations in which corporations must obtain supermajority shareholder votes under the PBCS.

Appraisal Rights

Corporate laws grant appraisal rights (called dissenters' rights in some jurisdiction) under certain circumstances, usually including mergers. The right generally gives the shareholder the ability to go to court and engage in an adversary proceeding with the corporation in order to determine the fair value of the shares, which the shareholder is entitled to receive in exchange for the shares.

The PBCS grants appraisal rights when a corporation amends its charter to become a PBC (or to change its purpose, if it is already a PBC). These rights are extended only to shareholders who do not vote in favor of the amendment. Similarly, appraisal rights are granted to shareholders of conventional corporations who receive PBC stock in a merger.

However, the statute places limits on the circumstances in which shareholders are entitled to seek appraisal. Appraisal is generally not available if the stock is listed on a national securities exchange or is widely held. This "market-out exception" provides that shareholders are entitled to appraisal rights only if the stock is not listed on a national securities exchange and is not held of record by more than two thousand holders. But there is an exception to the market-out exception that reinstates appraisal rights if the corporation enters into a merger or consolidation that requires shareholders to accept for their stock anything other than publicly traded shares.[69] This exception mirrors the market-out exception of Delaware General Corporation Law Section 262, which governs appraisal rights for mergers of conventional Delaware corporations.[70] As a practical matter, this exception means that publicly traded companies can convert to benefit corporations without triggering appraisal rights. This provision is critical if benefit corporations are to become widely used in the public markets.

If a shareholder pursues appraisal, Section 262 requires the Court of Chancery to make an independent determination of the fair value of the shares as a going concern.[71] Appraisal rights have been granted, analyzed, and refined by the Court of Chancery in transactions by and between traditional Delaware corporations, and these transactions provide an indication of how such a valuation might occur in the public benefit corporation context.[72]

The corporation must provide shareholders entitled to appraisal with notice of their rights, the applicable statutory language granting those rights, and some instructions informing the shareholders about how to request appraisal.[73] The disclosure provided to shareholders by the corporation must disclose all material facts relevant to the shareholder's decision whether to seek appraisal.[74] The Delaware courts have adopted the meaning of materiality used under federal securities law: "A fact is considered material if there is a 'substantial likelihood that the disclosure of the omitted fact would have been viewed by the reasonable investor as having significantly altered the "total mix" of information made available.'"[75]

In a traditional appraisal situation, a shareholder is faced with the decision whether to accept the merger consideration or to seek the appraised value of the shares, two values that may be very different. Accordingly, in a traditional appraisal situation, valuation material is considered "material."[76] In contrast, the choice whether or not to seek an appraisal when a company becomes a benefit corporation may focus not on the value of the shares but rather on the change in status. Thus, "materiality" may focus on the effect of the PBC provisions rather than on the valuation of the shares. However, until there is case law addressing this question, the nature of "materiality" in this circumstance will remain uncertain.

The appraisal statute states that a "stockholder . . . shall be entitled to an appraisal by the Court of Chancery of the fair value of the stockholders' shares of stock."[77] In traditional corporations, the statute is intended to "fully compensate shareholders for whatever their loss may be, subject only to the narrow limitation that one cannot take speculative effects of the merger into account."[78] Under Delaware law, fair value is determined as of the effective date of the merger[79] and the corporation is valued as a going concern.[80] While the court considers "all relevant factors" to determine fair value,[81] the court weighs heavily the value reached by a discounted cash flow analysis, which attempts to estimate all future cash flows discounted to present value.[82]

The PBCS does not address how PBC status might affect valuation in an appraisal proceeding. The authors of one article suggest several approaches that a court might take. First, a court might simply award a petitioner the value of the shares in light of the manner in which the corporation is currently being managed, thus "essentially reduc[ing] the appraised value to the extent that the public benefit negatively affected earnings." Alternatively, the court could try to add back such lost value. This could be accomplished in two different manners. First, the court could determine the costs of pursuing public benefits and factor those into its analysis, essentially recalculating the value of the PBC if it were not pursuing the benefit. Alternatively, a court might try to value the public benefit being provided and add that to the value of the corporation.[83] Ultimately, the authors conclude that it is the first method—awarding the pecuniary value of the corporation in light of the benefits it is providing—that is most likely to prevail. Awarding additional value "would lead to an undesirable windfall and violate the appraisal mandate by awarding stockholders more than their 'proportionate interest in a going concern.'"[84]

To date, there has been no appraisal litigation involving PBCs. There are a number of practical steps that private companies that convert to PBC status can take in order to avoid appraisal. First, many companies seek waivers from their shareholders in advance to make sure that none of them plan to seek appraisal. In many cases, the corporations also make it clear that they do not intend to convert if any shareholders do perfect appraisal rights. Finally, a company can make sure that the period for perfecting appraisal right has expired before a certificate of amendment effecting a change to PBC status is filed with the secretary of state. Table 7 (on page 108) lists the circumstances in which the PBCS makes appraisal rights available. For the benefit of practitioners, appendix E provides a quick guide to appraisal for Delaware PBCs.

TABLE 7: WHEN APPRAISAL RIGHTS ARE AVAILAVLE UNDER DELAWARE PBC PROVISIONS
1. Charter amendment that changes conventional corporation to PBC unless corporation is public.
2. Merger or consolidation of conventional corporation if shares are not publicly traded and are converted into or exchanged for shares of PBC.
3. Merger or consolidation of conventional corporation if shares are converted into or exchanged for shares of PBC that is not publicly traded.

Corporate Name: Providing Notice to Investors

Notice must be provided to the public that the corporation is organized as a public benefit corporation. Such notice is achieved by including a statement that the corporation is a PBC in the heading of its certificate of incorporation, and by identifying within its statement of purpose the specific public benefits to be promoted by the corporation.[85] The statute originally required that the name of the company include the words "public benefit corporation" (or its abbreviation, PBC), but this designation is no longer required if the company follows other procedural requirements to provide notice. Under the current statute, a company may, but is not required to, include the public benefit corporation identifier within its corporate name. However, if the company chooses not to include such an identifier, the corporation must provide notice to stock purchasers that the corporation is a PBC, unless the issuance is pursuant to an offering registered under the Securities Act of 1933 or if, at the time of issuance, the corporation has a class of securities registered under the Securities Exchange Act of 1934.[86] In addition, even though the company name is no longer required to contain a "PBC" identifier, investors still receive notice that the company is organized as a public benefit corporation through the requirement that the corporation's stock certificates indicate as much.[87] All of these provisions are intended to ensure that shareholders are made aware that they are investing in a corporation that does not operate on shareholder primacy principles.

* * *

Chapters 5 and 6 have described the rules that apply to each model of the benefit corporation. Chapter 7 will address how those new legal rules become operational and how courts may interpret them.

CHAPTER SEVEN

Operating Benefit Corporations in the Normal Course

Benefit corporation statutes require directors of corporations to take the interests of a broad range of stakeholders into account, eliminating the concept of shareholder primacy. This chapter discusses how corporations operating in the normal course might operate to pursue this broader purpose, and how the business judgment rule will likely function when applied to this altered value proposition. Standards of review lie at the heart of corporate law. By examining how a court might review a shareholder challenge to an action taken by the board of a benefit corporation and contrasting that process with similar litigation involving a conventional corporation, we can gain insight into why the new statutes are important, and whether they are likely to be effective in changing corporate behavior. Chapter 8 will examine the same type of question for special situations that benefit corporations may encounter.

The Business Judgment Rule

Chapter 3 addressed the standards of review that apply in shareholder lawsuits that challenge decisions made by directors of conventional corporations. One key standard is the business judgment rule, under which courts will not interfere with a disinterested decision made by careful directors, unless the decision is irrational. This *procedural* litigation rule reflects and implements a critical *substantive* corporate law rule: business decisions are best made by or under board direction rather than by shareholders or courts. This principle is a critical element in allowing corporations to gather capital from large groups of disaggregated investors and to put that capital to work in a coherent fashion. If business decisions were subject to frequent judicial challenge, few would choose to take on the role of directors, third parties would be hesitant to contract with corporations, and capital formation would be more difficult and expensive.

By engaging in the thought experiment of asking how the business judgment will be applied or changed in litigation challenging decisions by the directors of benefit corporations, we can attain some insight into how decisions should be made by benefit corporations at the board and management level.

The benefit corporation statutes allow for-profit companies to have a purpose of "creating general public benefit"[1] or to "operate in a responsible and sustainable manner."[2] In order to function sustainably, benefit corporations are obligated to account for the interests of a broad group of stakeholders rather than narrowly focusing on shareholders.

This accounting for the interests of public beneficiaries alongside the interests of shareholders is explicitly entitled to the protection of the business judgment rule.[3] Accordingly, the general operation of the business judgment rule to protect business decisions will remain intact under the public benefit corporation statute. Under the Model Benefit Corporation Legislation, the business judgment rule will apply to fiduciary suits against directors but not to suits against the corporation for failure to meet or pursue its benefit purpose. Under the PCBS, however, any shareholder challenge will be subject to the business judgment rule. For example, a board decision to enter a new line of business will still be protected from judicial second-guessing by the broad parameters of the business judgment rule under the PBCS.[4]

However, in order to come within the ambit of business judgment rule protection, the board process should explicitly address the interests of relevant stakeholders. In order to benefit from this continued protection, directors should make a record of this balancing to establish that they have acted with requisite care.

What does this application of the business judgment rule mean from a substantive perspective? That is, how will it influence the conduct of benefit corporations, and how will it work toward accomplishing the goal of the new laws? First, it is critical to distinguish between the choices made in the MBCL and those made in the PBCS. The drafters of the Delaware model chose to hew more closely to the conventional path. If a decision does not involve a conflict, a sale of the corporation, defensive measures, or the corporate franchise, any challenge from shareholders must overcome the high hurdles of business judgment protection. This means that, in the PBC context, almost all decisions are protected by the business judgment rule. On the other hand, in the case of benefit corporations created under the MBCL, there is room for substantive review of any decision.

ORDINARY DECISIONS AND PUBLIC BENEFIT CORPORATIONS

First consider the Delaware model. The purpose of the PBC, of course, is to create corporations that affirmatively address the needs of all stakeholders. There are two important elements to creating space for this shift to occur. First, the statute must ensure that directors are *permitted* to incorporate such broad values. Second, in order to be effective, a statute should also *require* that they do so. With respect to the former, the application of business judgment review on most decisions is clearly an effective tool. As long as directors act independently and rationally, shareholders will not be able to bring legal challenges to the board's full integration of stakeholder interests into its decision making. For example, directors will be able to make rational decisions that protect the environment and workers, without fearing a lawsuit that they "cared too much" about non-shareholder issues or that those concerns were not "related" to shareholder value.[5] Although the PBCS requirement of "balancing" does impose a duty to give real weight to the stakeholder concerns, the business judgment rule means that directors have wide latitude in actually prioritizing the various interests for which they are responsible.

But does this very latitude presage ineffectiveness in the second aspect of stakeholder governance, that is, in *requiring* stakeholder interests to be considered? To put the question bluntly, is the PBCS just a dressed-up constituency statute, which gives directors the ability to consider all stakeholders when such a path serves management needs but to ignore those stakeholder concerns otherwise? There are several elements to the statutory scheme that should ameliorate this risk.

First, the business judgment rule is only applicable when the board fully informs itself. This means that directors must educate themselves on the material effects their decisions are having on the environment, on the community, and on workers throughout their supply chain. Without applying too much armchair psychology, it is not hard to believe that, by simply requiring these elements to be brought into the boardroom conversation, and by making directors legally responsible for them, the decision-making process is much more likely to give weight to those interests. Moreover, the milieu of a benefit corporation is one where the shareholders have consented to stakeholder values, so that directors will be aware that the shareholders are more likely to tolerate, or even encourage, management decisions that take responsibilities to stakeholders seriously.

Finally, there is the substantive element of the business judgment rule, under which some trade-offs may not be viewed as rational. That concept does not exist in constituency states. Under the PBCS, there will always be an awareness that if a board entirely ignores stakeholder interests, they may be approaching the zone where their conduct will be viewed as irrational for a benefit corporation.[6] In addition, the benefit reporting requirement creates an obligation to measure, assess, and report on public benefit, and this should also provide some level of accountability. As the aphorism goes, "What gets measured gets managed."[7]

ORDINARY DECISIONS AND THE MBCL

Turning to the MBCL, the business judgment rule analysis is the same: it provides all the same protections to a director who considers stakeholder interests, and the requirement of being informed, along with the larger benefit corporation milieu, contributes to enforcing some amount of concern for stakeholders. However, in contrast to the PBCS, the MBCL also allows a direct claim against the corporation for failure to pursue or create public benefit, and there is no business judgment rule protection for such a claim, even with respect to ordinary, disinterested business decisions. Thus, such a claim can succeed, even if the board is disinterested, fully informed, and rational. The plaintiffs just need to show that the company is in fact failing to pursue or achieve "a material positive impact on society and the environment."[8]

This is arguably a stronger regime for regulating corporate conduct than exists in Delaware or any other state adopting the PBCS model.[9] It presumably allows a plaintiff to take discovery as to all matters relevant to the assessment that the corporation is using, and to challenge whether the corporation has in fact endeavored to create or has created a positive effect. This question will presumably give a court much greater flexibility in litigation and make it easier for a shareholder to win such a case. The only relief available in such a case is injunctive, however, so that the court cannot award any damages. Nevertheless, the risk of lengthy litigation, and the possibility of a highly publicized loss in court, could be powerful inducements for board action that creates public benefit.[10]

Thus, with respect to ordinary business decisions, both statutory models give strong protections to directors who account for the interests of stakeholders, and both provide some inducement to do so, although the inducement is arguably stronger in the MBCL.[11]

A Longer-Term Lens?

Because many constituencies, such as employees and customers, cannot diversify in the way that shareholders can, boards taking their interests into account may need to apply longer-term horizons. One fund manager provided the following example:

> Shareholders . . . may be willing to take bigger risks with their capital in the hope of large upside returns, whereas employees may be more risk averse—being unable to take a portfolio approach to employment. This might in a particular case mean that directors [considering stakeholder concerns] decide to eschew a risky transaction involving a lot of debt, such as a new international expansion plan which could result in large gains or insolvency, as the plan may not be in the best interests of all employees.[12]

The higher risk-adjusted value to shareholders of taking the risk in this situation reflects the fact that the limited liability nature of the corporation—a state-granted privilege—allows shareholders to internalize the upside of a risky transaction in their capacity as residual risk bearers, while externalizing much of the downside risk onto others, including the employees, creditors, and communities that would be damaged by an insolvency. This differing risk calculus recalls the divergence of interest between common shareholders and preferred shareholders, discussed in the "Multiple Investor Constituencies" section of chapter 2. In any event, taking such risks may result in immediate share price increases in the public markets as the market recognizes the value of the increased risk.[13]

On the other hand, there are long-term uses of capital that may risk the capital without imposing significant insolvency risk or other costs on stakeholders, such as investing free cash flow into employee training. The benefit of such a plan, both to employees and to shareholders, is long term and subject to execution risk as well as the economic uncertainty that comes with any long-range business plan.[14] Short-term-minded shareholders might favor a return of capital as a less risky choice for themselves. This can create pressure on public companies to increase returns of capital at the expense of long-term growth. Indeed, in a January 2017 letter to the CEOs of leading companies, the chairman of the world's largest asset manager cautioned against this pressure:

> Companies have begun to devote greater attention to these issues of long-term sustainability, but despite increased rhetorical commitment, they have continued to engage in buybacks at a furious pace. In fact, for the 12 months ending in the third quarter of 2016, the value of dividends and buybacks by S&P 500 companies exceeded those companies' operating profit. While we certainly support returning excess capital to shareholders, we believe companies must balance those practices with investment in future growth. Companies should engage in buybacks only when they are confident that the return on those buybacks will ultimately exceed the cost of capital and the long-term returns of investing in future growth.[15]

Benefit corporation directors exercising their business judgment are likely to be more able to use a longer-term lens when making ordinary business decisions. This may, in turn, help to combat a short-term bias created by the intermediaries between the real economy and the ultimate beneficial owners of shares, which bias benefits the middle of the investment chain but not the top or bottom.[16] That being said, it is too simple to say that long-term values are equivalent to stakeholder interests and that short-term values favor shareholder interests. After all, some important decisions may improve the lives of stake-holders in the short run and also create long-term value for shareholders. For example, fair treatment of employees in a corporation's global supply chain will immediately improve the lives of those workers and may preserve the corporation's reputation, adding shareholder value over the long term.

Practical Implications for Ordinary Business Decisions

STARTING WITH TRANSPARENCY

The best starting point for directors considering broadened benefit corporation obligations may be the statutory transparency requirements. Both the MBCL and the PBCS impose sustainability reporting requirements.[17] Benefit corporations must distribute periodic reports. Under the PBCS, the report must include goals, objectives, standards, and an assessment and must be produced at least once every two years if the corporation has not adopted a provision requiring a more frequent report.[18] Under the MBCL, there is an annual requirement for a report made against a third-party standard. The MBCL also requires annual certification that the corporation is meeting its public benefit obligations.

In order to comply with these obligations, the board of a PBC must determine who is materially affected by the corporation's business, develop and maintain criteria for balancing the interests of those so affected and any specific benefit identified in the corporation's charter, and measure progress against those criteria. A PBC board may adopt one or more third-party standards to monitor its actions and progress.[19] For benefit corporations governed by the MBCL, the board will be required to choose and report under a third-party standard. A third-party standard is, of course, an excellent tool for a board to use to understand its stakeholders and their concerns.

Under either regime, the exercise of maintaining a credible reporting function will require the board and management to address important stakeholder issues (whether identified through a third-party standard or otherwise) and maintain a record of that work. The following are additional recommendations of procedures a benefit corporation board may adopt to ensure it is properly addressing stakeholder concerns (see appendix F for a rubric setting forth these procedures).

ESTABLISH A COMMITTEE

A committee may be tasked with responsibility for public benefit issues. Assigning this responsibility to a committee should not be viewed as isolating the benefit purposes. Instead, assigning matters to committees is generally perceived as a recognition of the importance of the delegated matters. For this reason, vital functions, such as compensation and audit, are required to be assigned to committees. Research suggests that firms that adopt effective sustainability programs are more likely to form a separate board committee to address sustainability issues.[20] The board can delegate this responsibility to an existing committee, such as audit or governance, or create a new, stand-alone committee. The committee that is responsible for sustainability issues should include in its committee charter oversight of and/or recommendations with respect to third-party standards, if any; internally generated standards; choice of certifying body or bodies, if any; the benefit report; and sustainability objectives, standards, strategies, and policies.

MANAGEMENT ROLE

Although the committee should oversee sustainability issues, management must fully integrate benefit purpose into its function. Notably, management should draft the benefit report and report to the board about progress toward the impact objectives. Additionally, management should make recommendations on the following subjects: third-party standards and internally generated standards; certification issues; and sustainability objectives, standards, strategies, and policies. Many companies already have a sustainability function, such as a chief sustainability officer. In a benefit corporation, this role will be heightened in importance, as sustainability shifts to being a primary purpose of the corporation. As we have discussed, board decisions around benefit issues will be protected by the business judgment rule, but the rule requires that directors are fully informed. Accordingly, management and sustainability officers will have a critical role in providing the board and relevant committees with the information necessary to consider and balance the interests of all relevant stakeholders.

PERIODIC ACTIVITY

Certain activities should be conducted cyclically, in accordance with the timing selected for production of the company's benefit report. Annually, sustainability objectives should be established and assessed. The committee should meet regularly and report to the board. Periodic reports to the board from the committee will allow the board significant opportunity to address stakeholder interests. Management and the committee should meet for an extended period of time, either annually or biannually, regarding these sustainability objectives. Finally, the board should review the benefit report.

NONPERIODIC ACTIVITY

Management and the committee should have different responsibilities with respect to issues that arise in a nonperiodic fashion. Management can be charged with bringing to the board significant sustainability issues that come up out of cycle and that are not covered by policies, such as the effect of a strategic change or product change on workers or customers, or the environmental impacts of significant building projects, fleet acquisitions, or other matters. Depending on magnitude, the committee should consider sustainability issues implicated by new developments, such as whether to purchase renewable energy or obtain Leadership in Energy and Environmental Design (LEED) certification for new buildings, or the effect of a transaction on workers' compensation or customers.

Of course, in larger benefit corporations, many individual decisions are made at the management level and are not brought to the directors' attention. For such delegated decisions, it is important that a corporation have adequate policies in place to guide management decisions that affect stakeholders.

With respect to director-level decisions affecting benefit purposes, the committee could make the decision or defer to the board if the particular inquiry is of great significance.[21] Regardless, the committee should report any and all decisions to the board. In general, clear policies and record keeping with respect to stakeholder concerns will preserve the protections of the business judgment rule for ordinary decisions.

PROCESS ISSUES

Good corporate governance practices can help the board effectively comply with its stakeholder obligations. Foremost, management's recommendations to the committee and the committee's recommendations to the board should be distributed well in advance of committee and board meetings in order to give directors adequate time for review.

Meeting minutes should reflect sustainability issues discussed, resolution of those issues, and any direction given to the committee or management. Additionally, if a third-party standard or internal standard has been adopted, materials and minutes should reflect consideration of how the standard maps to the interests of those affected by the corporation's conduct. Standard meeting procedure should include reviewing internal checklists to determine whether other sustainability issues should be added, and providing redline copies when materials update other materials.[22]

BOARD COMPOSITION

Another method to ensure that a benefit corporation board operates within its public benefit duty is to strategically select the board of directors. Such diversity may provide a structure that naturally addresses multiple objectives within the deliberative process. Thus, one or more directors with expertise in a particular stakeholder issue could be elected in an effort to introduce relevant interests into board discussions and prevent misunderstandings.[23] However, any such expert directors would continue to have the general duties of all directors. The PBCS does not have any requirement for a director with any specific obligations regarding the corporation's public benefit. In contrast, the MBCL does require, under certain circumstances, that a board include a "benefit director," with specified duties.[24]

CHAPTER EIGHT

Operating Benefit Corporations in Extraordinary Situations

C hapter 7 addressed the ways that courts may review ordinary course decisions of benefit corporation directors, and the implications for operations
and board decision making. This chapter will address standards of review and
board outside the ordinary course.

The analysis in chapter 7 revolved around the business judgment rule,
which leaves ordinary decision making almost entirely in the hands of directors. In extraordinary situations, however, other factors outweigh those that
favor business judgment protection. For example, when directors have a conflict
due to an interest outside of the corporation, the business judgment rule does
not apply, shareholders can challenge the substance of transactions, and courts
will review the transaction in question for "fairness." Again, this standard of
review supports an important substantive concept: directors have a trustee-like
obligation to pursue the interests of the corporation, not personal interests. If
they put themselves in a position where their personal interests and those of
the corporation conflict, then it is incumbent on the court to ensure corporate
interests are protected. Because conflict transactions are relatively rare, this

"interference" does not substantially reduce the effectiveness of the corporate structure in amassing and allocating capital.

Then there are intermediate, "grayer" areas, where the standard of review accommodates the important policy motivations underlying the business judgment rule but also incorporates concerns about intrinsic board biases. These intermediate standards are applied when a company is sold or when it takes defensive action to preclude a sale that a majority of shareholders might want to pursue. These standards reflect a concern that directors may be inclined in such situations to favor the desires of management and other insiders, who may be influential on the board, and who may have interests that diverge from the interests of shareholders.

Finally, courts apply particularly strict standards for situations where shareholder voting rights are threatened. This chapter will address how each of those heightened standards will likely be applied to benefit corporations, and what this implies for the decision-making process in those situations.

Benefit Corporations and Conflict Transactions

THE DEFINITION OF "INTEREST" IS NOT ALTERED

As with conventional corporations, decisions are not afforded the presumption of the business judgment rule if tainted by conflict. The entire fairness standard will continue to apply to decisions made by conflicted boards.[1]

Current case law defines an interested director as one who "will receive a personal financial benefit from a transaction that is not equally shared by the stockholders." Additionally, a director is interested in a transaction where the corporate decision "will have a materially detrimental impact on a director, but not on the corporation and the stockholders," because, in that situation, "a director cannot be expected to exercise his or her independent business judgment without being influenced by the adverse personal consequences resulting from the decision."[2] Thus, a disinterested director who receives the presumption of the business judgment rule is one who "neither stands to benefit financially nor suffer materially from the [board's] decision."[3] Because the language found in both statutory models matches the language of the judicially created interested director standard, courts will likely interpret the phrase "disinterested" in the same manner.[4]

It is a well-settled principle of Delaware law that "a director who is also a shareholder of the corporation is more likely to have interests that are aligned with the other shareholders of that corporation."[5] Thus, stock ownership will not generally cause a director (or a controlling shareholder) to be interested and to lose the protection of the statutory business judgment or exculpation provisions. This is also consistent with the reference in the Principles of Corporate Governance, which refers to "personal interests of directors," which presumably excludes stock ownership as a disqualifying criteria.[6] In other words, even though the directors' obligations are broader, they are still undertaken solely on behalf of the shareholders, so that stock ownership, by itself, should not be viewed as creating a conflict, except in the very limited circumstance that it might under jurisprudence for conventional corporations (as discussed in chapter 2).[7]

An argument to the contrary might be made. It could be argued that because benefit corporation directors have expanded duties that extend beyond shareholder pecuniary interests, the ownership of stock does create a conflict. That is, it might be argued, the pecuniary interest of a shareholding director may conflict with the interests of "those materially affected" by board decisions. This argument, however, misconstrues the structure of benefit corporation law. Both the PBCS and the MBCL are careful to state that no new beneficiaries are created by the new duties. Indeed, shareholders with significant levels of ownership are the only constituency that can enforce rights under the PBCS and current MBCL.[8] The logic of benefit corporation governance—from shareholders' continuing governance rights to their exclusive ability to bring derivative suits—recognizes that shareholders have a unique interest in the appropriate balancing among interests.[9] For this reason, share ownership should not be considered to create a "conflict" at the board level. Accordingly, it appears that the entire fairness test will apply to a benefit corporation transaction to the same extent, and in the same circumstances, that it would apply to a transaction entered into by a conventional corporation.

APPLICATION OF ENTIRE FAIRNESS

As we discussed in chapter 3, when a challenged transaction is subject to the entire fairness test, a court will review the transaction and determine whether it was fair to the company and its shareholders, both substantively and procedurally. Essentially, this test requires a court to determine that the conflicted directors or controlling shareholder did not use their or its position to extract an unfair amount of value, or to extract more value than they or it might have obtained in an arm's-length transaction.

An examination of entire fairness involving a benefit corporation is similarly likely to focus on any excess value received by the conflicted parties and *not* on the allocation of value among the unconflicted parties and other stakeholders. For example, if a controlling shareholder were to "squeeze out" minority shareholders in a merger in a manner that was not protected by the business judgment rule, a lawsuit would likely focus on whether the controller obtained the entity at too low a price. The "price," however, should include any value the buyer accorded to stakeholders, such as a promise to maintain or implement environmental protections or to maintain certain employment levels.

If the court did find that the price so calculated was too low, there could be a question of how to allocate damages—should they all go to shareholders, or should some value be allocated to other stakeholders? In a situation where the operation and management of a company was to continue unchanged, a court might determine that all value should go to shareholders. On the other hand, if the controller were eliminating the company's PBC status, and perhaps planning on major changes that might affect the community and workforce, it is possible that the relief could include some allocation of value to those stakeholders.

Change-in-Control and Defensive Situations

INTERMEDIATE STANDARDS: ENHANCED SCRUTINY

As we discussed in chapter 3, courts do not initially apply the business judgment rule when boards make decisions involving a sale of the corporation or defensive actions against hostile takeovers. Instead, courts review the substance of those decisions but the review is more deferential than it is in a pure conflict situation. Under conventional corporate law, the *Revlon* standard invokes a reasonableness review of the board's efforts to maximize value for shareholders in a sale transaction, while *Unocal* focuses on the reasonableness of defensive actions, again through a shareholder value lens.[10] Scholarship examining the result of expanding obligations under constituency statutes (a precursor to the benefit corporation statutes, which we will discuss in chapter 9) has found that, for the most part, courts applying constituency provisions have substituted the business judgment rule for enhanced scrutiny.[11] However, the intent of those statutes was largely focused on addressing hostile takeover and sale situations (also discussed in chapter 9).

In the case of the PBCS and the MBCL, however, *there does not appear to be any evidence of an intent to regulate standards of review, except as explicitly set forth in the statute.* Moreover, the policy rationale behind the common law imposing enhanced scrutiny involves the concern that directors have inherent conflicts in defensive and change-in-control situations (as we discussed in chapter 3), and it is clear that the drafters did not intend to alter the law with respect to conflicts. Thus, it appears likely that courts will apply enhanced scrutiny to both defensive and change-in-control situations for benefit corporations in jurisdictions where those standards would otherwise be applied, although their approach will be modified appropriately to reflect the expanded obligation of directors to consider stakeholder interests.

CHANGES IN CONTROL

The *Revlon* standard

Scholars have varying opinions on how *Revlon* will apply in a sale of a benefit corporation or change in control, but most agree that the "statute changes the board's duty in the sale of control context in a fundamental manner,"[12] and that directors will no longer have a duty to achieve the highest value for shareholders.[13] This view is not universal, however, and Haskell Murray has expressed the view that, in a *Revlon* situation, benefit corporations should be sold to the highest bidder. In Murray's view, allowing the consideration of multiple constituencies in a sale process would destroy any accountability for the sale process.[14] It seems likely, however, that because change-in-control transactions present unique risks, the heightened scrutiny applicable to such transactions will continue under the benefit corporation statutes.[15] Even so, because PBC directors have an expanded duty to consider other constituencies, satisfaction of an enhanced reasonableness standard must be measured differently than adherence to the short-term shareholder maximization requirement for conventional corporations subject to the *Revlon* standard.[16]

Although conventional corporate law prohibits directors from considering any interest that fails to lead to monetary gain for shareholders, especially in a change-in-control setting, the benefit corporation expressly allows directors to consider all constituencies. Thus, a benefit corporation board will be required to balance a multitude of interests in a sale of the company.[17] Traditional directors already balance numerous shareholder considerations when financially valuing bids for a company, and the broad stakeholder proposition of benefit corporation governance adds to the considerations benefit corporation directors should bear in mind when valuing bids.

Thus, the substantive requirement of *Revlon*—maximizing value for shareholders—is likely to change and to become an obligation to find the "best" transaction for all stakeholders as a group, but directors still may be subject to enhanced scrutiny and required to show that they pursued a reasonable path toward maximizing *collective* value for all relevant constituencies—the total value to be received by shareholders, stakeholders affected by the corporation's operations, and specific beneficiaries, if any. For both practical and conceptual reasons, this is unlikely to be enforced on a mathematical or pseudomathematical basis, in which the sum of all benefits to all stakeholders is calculated and the transaction yielding the highest sum becomes the one that must be chosen. First, such mathematical precision is not possible. Second, and more importantly, such an interpretation would run counter to the business judgment concepts inherent in the statutes with respect to balancing and considering stakeholder interests.

Instead, the court is likely to examine the same issues involved in traditional *Revlon* situations, such as market checks and deal protections, to ensure that all likely transactions emerge, and subject such provisions to *Revlon*'s reasonableness standard. On the other hand, a board's rational choice among bids that allocate value among stakeholders differently should not be subject to heightened scrutiny under Delaware's Section 365(b), which mandates the application of the business judgment rule for all allocation decisions.[18] Case law interpreting protective mechanisms involving corporations subject to constituency statutes suggests this will be the case.[19]

However, when a board does allocate value to stakeholder interests, the court could use Revlon to apply a reasonableness test to the board's actual efforts to ensure that stakeholder value is achieved. For example, the court could focus on "the extent to which, once a sale of the company occurs, any meaningful, enforceable undertaking exists that assures the seller's board and shareholders that the public benefit will be achieved once the merger is accomplished."[20] Thus, directors should understand that the courts may apply heightened scrutiny to efforts to ensure future achievement of postmerger public benefits. As with most nonconflict transactions, however, a reviewing court is still most likely to focus more on process than on substantively reviewing the board decision.[21] The next section offers guidance for selling a benefit corporation in compliance with the expanded fiduciary duties of a benefit corporation.[22]

The sale process

Because sale transactions will be subject to heightened scrutiny, and because the calculus of value will be so different, corporations will need to adopt clear procedures to reasonably address stakeholder interests. This task may be less onerous than it sounds. Presumably, a benefit corporation involved in a sale process has already established the standards by which it is addressing stakeholder concerns, including through adopting third-party standards (required under the MBCL, permitted under the PBCS) and through setting objectives and standards. The task of the board of a benefit corporation being sold may well be to make sure the sale does not unduly interfere with those objectives or negatively affect performance against the third-party standard. In this sense, the board will need to investigate the plans of the buyer, something that would be of very limited importance in a *Revlon* context for a conventional corporation.

Confidence that the buyer will maintain the status quo may well be sufficient to meet a board's public benefit obligations, but that confidence may require some combination of due diligence, contractual obligation, and corporate governance structure, as we will see in the next section on documentation. The critical concern during the sale process will be surfacing these issues, and making sure that management and outside professionals involved in the process understand the importance of addressing stakeholder concerns.

It may also be the case that simply maintaining the status quo is not sufficient. This could be because the buyer does not plan to treat the stakeholders as well or because the buyer is paying a large premium, some of which the board determines should be shared with stakeholders. An example can make this concrete: a buyer may plan to combine workforces, which will lead to extensive layoffs, and may be able to pay a large premium because of the efficiency gains from that combination. In a cash sale by a conventional corporation, all of that financial gain goes to shareholders—and the board does not even have an obligation to investigate what the transaction will mean for its workforce. In a benefit corporation, however, the board will need to determine how these stakeholders will be treated, and, when learning of the layoffs, devise a strategy that takes their interests into account. This might mean any number of things, such as negotiating severance, retraining, and similar provisions. Where a large premium results from efficiencies that do not hurt stakeholders—such as the ability to use the sales forces to sell the products from the combined companies, the board might also consider asking that some of that premium go to workers in the form of bonuses or other compensation.

Readers who have a background in mergers and acquisitions might note that many of these provisions are already included in merger negotiations for traditional corporations, often under the guise of protecting value for shareholders. For example, severance programs are often created in cash sales, because they are necessary to preserve value through the sales process. In fact, many considerations will not be different in a sale—what may be different will be the emphasis.

Documentation

Merger agreements may have to address postmerger conduct because of a need to protect stakeholder interests. In some situations, agreements will need to be drafted to ensure both the continuation of the benefit provisions in the corporation's charter and the continued implementation of the benefit principles.

One technique to accomplish these goals would be to include a provision that specifically describes how the company will operate postmerger. Still, companies will have to skillfully negotiate this point, as buyers will generally oppose any postmerger constrictions on their business management. However, the more a benefit corporation compromises on this point and offers the buyer greater postmerger flexibility, the more challenging the provision will be to enforce. Another provision that would assist PBC sellers is one that authorizes injunctive relief to enforce mission-preserving provisions. Furthermore, in order to resolve any potential standing issues, a provision could be included that expressly gives the sellers the ability to enforce the public benefit provisions, or the contract could designate certain stakeholders as third-party beneficiaries.

Another contractual provision that a benefit corporation might bargain for in a sales process would be some element of ongoing control over the acquired entity. One well-known example of this phenomenon is the terms of the transaction negotiated when Ben & Jerry's was sold to Unilever. There, although the seller was not a benefit corporation, the controlling shareholders were able to insist on an ongoing level of control.[23]

There may be alternative means to protect stakeholders. For example, a benefit corporation being sold in a transaction that will result in a loss of jobs in a community might fund a trust to provide assistance to the community, including job training and local business development. Or a company may simply favor a buyer that has a strong reputation for operating in a responsible manner.

DEFENSIVE SITUATIONS

Benefit corporations, like traditional Delaware corporations, can take defensive actions in response to a takeover threat. These defensive tactics are likely to be evaluated against the same standard that applies to conventional corporations, which requires that the defensive measures be reasonable in relation to the threat posed.[24]

Significantly, however, traditional corporations can only deploy these devices to protect shareholders from a very specific threat: a situation that jeopardizes shareholder value.[25] In contrast, because a benefit corporation board must account for a much broader range of considerations, the range of possible threats that can be addressed by defensive measures will be broader than in traditional corporations.[26] In that sense, directors will be given greater discretion to employ defensive devices in order to protect the company and its sustainable mission.[27] This is how the courts have applied *Unocal* under constituency statutes, which give directors the right, but not the obligation, to consider stakeholder interests. Additionally, because the threats PBCs face will be distinctly different than the financial threats traditional Delaware corporations often face, different defensive devices could be created, or alterations could be made to common devices. Nevertheless, any device deployed must still be reasonable in relation to the threat posed, even if the business judgment rule applies to the balancing of broad stakeholder interests.[28]

The cases applying *Unocal* to defensive action taken by conventional corporations have permitted boards to discriminate against shareholders who represent a particular threat to shareholder value. This suggests, by analogy, that the board of a benefit corporation may be able to take defensive actions directed at shareholders (or others) that pose a particular threat to other stakeholders. For example, a board might adopt a rights plan (a corporate mechanism boards can deploy to prevent acquisitions of large blocks of shares without board approval, as discussed in chapter 3) that was triggered not simply by a level of ownership but also by a level of ownership by the type of shareholder that threatens the interests of certain stakeholders.

The *Third Point, LLC v. Ruprecht* case suggests that such tactics might be permitted. In *Third Point*, a company adopted a rights plan because the board determined that share acquisitions by a hedge fund threatened the interests of shareholders. The plan operated by imposing severe economic and voting dilution on any shareholder who crossed a certain ownership threshold. In this respect, the plan operated in the same manner as any other such plan. However, the plan had one distinct feature that had not been previously litigated: it distinguished between shareholders who filed a Form 13D with the SEC from those who filed Form 13G. Each form is to be filed when a shareholder of a public company surpasses the 5 percent ownership threshold, but the latter requires a statement that the shareholder has no intent to exercise control. The plan adopted by the company in *Third Poin*t permitted 13G filers to buy up to 20 percent of the company's outstanding shares, while the cap for 13D filers was 10 percent. The hedge fund asked for a waiver of the 13D threshold, but the company refused. The company successfully defended its refusal, distinguishing between the hedge fund and 13G filers on the basis that the hedge fund principal threatened the value of the company's shares by taking certain actions that, together with its significant ownership, indicated that it could exercise negative control over the company through its stake. The court found that these actions could be reasonably perceived as threatening value, because of concern the hedge fund would be able to exercise influence sufficient to control certain important corporate actions, such as executive recruitment.[29]

The decision in *Third Point* suggests that a benefit corporation might adopt a rights plan that treats shareholders who represent a threat to stakeholder value differently from other shareholders. However, it is important to distinguish between a threat from the ownership itself and a threat from a valid exercise of voting rights. Since the advent of the rights plan, courts have been careful to ensure that imposing the plan does not interfere with the shareholder franchise. Thus, litigation over whether a rights plan is a reasonable reaction to a threat has often focused on whether ownership below the triggering threshold of a rights plan permits a shareholder to wage a proxy contest—either because the level allows the shareholder to have sufficient "skin in the game" to spend the resources a proxy contest requires or because the bloc acquired could potentially compete with an existing insider bloc. Accordingly, the triggering percentage of rights plans rarely dip below 10 percent. However, where there is a threat to value from mere ownership below that level, courts have permitted triggers as low as 5 percent.[30]

In addition to guarding the ability of shareholders to wage proxy contests, courts have also generally looked for threats other than simply losing such contests. However, courts seem to have permitted boards to treat insurgent shareholders as "threats" as long as the use of the rights plan does not make it impossible for the shareholder to run a successful contest. This background suggests that there will be considerable room for case law development with respect to benefit corporations and defensive actions. Will a board be able to adopt a rights plan that discriminates against certain holders if their mere ownership might taint the company's reputation in a way that harmed broad stakeholder interests? For example, suppose a company known for questionable environmental practices acquired a significant stake in a benefit corporation that focused on "clean energy" solutions. Could that ownership, standing alone, threaten the company's strategy to improve the environment through long-term, trust-based relationships? What if the threat were not the reputational one but merely the fact that the stake might allow the shareholder to lead a successful proxy campaign that would replace the board with directors who were not going to pursue the same environmentally friendly strategy? What if the threat of such a contest made it difficult for the company to create long-term relationships with suppliers and customers focused on environmental issues?

These questions suggest that the ability to defend the interests of all stake-holders will raise interesting questions, and it is likely to strain the distinction between the *Unocal* standard discussed in this section and the franchise standards discussed in the next section.

The foregoing discussion only addresses the legal standard that will apply in a defensive takeover situation. In addition to the alteration of the legal standard, benefit corporation status may have a second and more important effect: the status may attract shareholders who have a greater interest in long-term value creation and less focus on short-term share price: "Attracting directors and investors who believe in the corporation's mission may serve as a powerful defense against hostile corporate raiders who desire to focus more strictly on short-term profits."[31]

Proxy Contests and Franchise Rights

Courts are particularly solicitous of shareholders voting rights because they underpin the legitimacy of the directors' authority. This dynamic is not changed by the benefit corporation statutes; the directors are still elected by shareholders, and, indeed, it is only shareholders who have the right to enforce the expanded obligations of directors.[32]

It thus seems unlikely that being a benefit corporation would have a material effect on the strict standards applied in litigation involving significant threats to the shareholder franchise. This conclusion is consistent with most cases involving the shareholder franchise decided under constituency statutes.[33] That said, there are many situations in which franchise concerns are addressed under *Unocal*'s reasonableness test (as we discussed in chapter 3), and in such a situation, consideration of the interests of stakeholders may have increased legitimacy.

It should remain clear, however, that benefit corporation directors cannot act with the "primary purpose of preventing or impeding" a shareholder vote.[34] Thus, even if the board conducts a balancing of interests in accordance with their fiduciary duties, the board should not do anything to purposefully disenfranchise the shareholders.[35] Moreover, even where the vote is not "thwarted," some commentators have suggested that courts may, under *Unocal*, take an especially hard look at board actions affecting the franchise in the context of benefit corporations, because of the subjective nature of the board's balancing task: "It could be argued that since the balancing required for PBCs is inherently subjective, the shareholders' vote on a merger (expressing their judgment on the balance) is as, if not more, important than the directors' decision. Thus there should be little or no hindrance to the stockholders of a PBC making the ultimate balancing decision by their votes on a proposed merger."[36]

All of the foregoing suggests that actual conduct in proxy contests—scheduling meetings, setting record dates, and all the other board powers related to voting—will be subject to the same limitations as they are in proxy contests involving conventional corporations. Of course, board considerations and the arguments that directors make to convince shareholders may be very different for a benefit corporation. For example, in a situation where shareholder activists seek to replace some or all board members, because they believe that a company is overinvesting in capital expenditures, a conventional corporation can only respond by arguing that it will produce a greater shareholder return over time by making such investments. Although a benefit corporation board may well make the same argument, it is also free to point out that the capital expenditures will create jobs, reduce toxic emissions, or have other positive effects on the community. And these arguments may actually be persuasive for universal owners (discussed in chapter 4), who conceive of themselves as stewards not only of individual companies but also of the systems in which those companies—and the shareholders—are embedded and invested.

Decisions Affecting Security Holders of Different Classes Differently

As we noted in "Multiple Investor Constituencies" (chapter 2), Delaware courts have extended the ideas of shareholder primacy to encompass the relationship between common shareholders and investors with greater priority, such as preferred shareholders and lenders. This is indeed the logical extension of the idea that common shareholders have no contract rights and are merely the residual risk bearers, entitled to what remains after others (including creditors and preferred shareholders) get what they bargained for. This idea, however, can lead to results that seem irrational from a broad perspective.

Robert Bartlett notes that a company with a deteriorating cash position might undertake a risky plan with a risk-adjusted value well below what the assets of the company would be worth in a sale, if, in that sale, most of the proceeds were to go to the creditors and preferred shareholders. The rationale behind such a perverse decision would be that the common shareholders are the beneficiaries of all the upside but share little of the downside risk in such a situation. As Bartlett says:

> That directors might be forced to pursue socially suboptimal invest-
> ments in these situations is peculiar to say the least. Those familiar
> with corporate finance theory no doubt find this outcome especially
> perplexing. . . . More generally, this approach would also seem to
> require as a matter of complying with the directors' fiduciary duties
> the type of reckless go-for-broke gambles known to plague lever-
> aged firms nearing financial distress and commonly associated with
> the lead up to the financial crisis.[37]

However, by eliminating shareholder primacy and allowing boards to con-sider the interests of all their stakeholders, including preferred shareholders and lenders, directors will be freed from the obligation to take risks that look par-ticularly unappealing from the point of view of the firm as an entirety. Benefit corporation directors may be able to weigh the interests of all investors in their decision processes, returning the law to that described in the *Credit Lyonnais Bank Nederland, N.V. v. Pathe Commc'ns Corp.* decision, which we mentioned in chapter 2.

* * *

We have now completed our survey of the new law of benefit corporations. Part 3 addresses alternative methods that businesses might use to achieve stake-holder governance.

PART III

Other Paths

STAKEHOLDER GOVERNANCE BY OTHER MEANS

Curiosity keeps leading us down new paths.

Walt Disney

CHAPTER NINE

Constituency Statutes

A VIABLE ALTERNATIVE
FOR STAKEHOLDER GOVERNANCE?

Prior to the advent of benefit corporation legislation across the United States, many legislatures responded to the rise of shareholder primacy by adopting "constituency statutes." These laws permit a board of directors to consider the interests of non-shareholders ("constituencies") in making certain decisions.

This chapter examines the content of those statutes, as well as the treatment of the statutes in litigation and in the academic literature. The terms of the statutes should provide a useful contrast to the operative provisions of benefit corporation statutes, and the treatment by courts of constituency statutes may provide guidance as to how courts will interpret benefit corporation laws.

Adoption of Constituency Statutes

States began adopting constituency just over thirty years ago, and thirty-three states have now adopted a constituency statute (although Delaware has not).[1] These statutes have not caused the expected increase in litigation, significantly deterred institutional investment, or affected stock values.[2] Constituency statutes represent attempts by legislatures to change the common law rule of shareholder primacy. Specifically, a constituency statute permits a board of directors to consider non-shareholder interests when making decisions, rather than focusing solely on the interests of shareholders.[3] Through this grant of authority, boards are given significant discretion to consider the interests of stakeholders, regardless of the relation of those interests to stockholder value.[4]

Some jurisdictions also used their constituency statute to explicitly reject enhanced scrutiny in change-in-control transactions. As a historical matter, adoption of constituency statutes was initiated in the 1980s as a tool for directors to use in fighting hostile takeovers.[5] Many were concerned that the real purpose of constituency provisions was to protect incumbent management rather than stakeholders. This concern was fueled by the fact that the provisions were generally permissive; that is, that there was no *requirement* to consider the interests of stakeholders.[6]

Each state's constituency statute permits directors to consider one or more of the following non-stockholder interests:

1. employees, customers, creditors, suppliers, and communities in which the corporation has facilities;

2. national and state economies and other community and societal considerations;

3. the long-term and short-term interests of the corporation and its stockholders;

4. the desirability of remaining independent, and the resources, intent, conduct (past, stated, and potential) of a person seeking to acquire control of the corporation; and

5. the corporation's officers.[7]

The statutes often are silent as to how a director may weigh these various considerations. Some states, such as Indiana and Pennsylvania, explicitly state that no one interest may prevail in the directors' considerations.[8]

Operation of Constituency Statutes

CONSTITUENCY STATUTES PERMIT, BUT DO NOT REQUIRE, CONSIDERATION OF STAKEHOLDER INTERESTS

Presently, all jurisdictions with constituency statutes permit, but do not *require*, directors to consider non-shareholder interests. This is a critical distinction from benefit corporation statutes, which obligate boards to consider the interests of stakeholders in their decisions. Connecticut originally had a mandatory statute, which required director consideration of non-shareholder interests, but the statute was amended in 2010 to make it permissive.[9]

Thus, corporations seeking a governance model that is conducive to social responsibility should recognize that incorporation in a jurisdiction with a constituency statute does not, in fact, create any responsibility or accountability to stakeholders—it only *decreases* responsibility to shareholders.[10] For example, the Indiana code provides: "A director *may*, in considering the best interests of a corporation, consider the effects of any action on shareholders, employees, suppliers, and customers of the corporation, and communities in which offices or other facilities of the corporation are located, and any other factors the director considers pertinent" [emphasis added].[11]

In contrast, when Connecticut first adopted its constituency provision in 1988, it required directors of corporations with registered securities to consider other constituencies in making decisions.[12] As enacted, the statute "impose[d] a strict obligation on directors," mandating consideration of non-shareholder interests.[13] In 2010, Connecticut amended its code, making it a permissive grant of authority that allows, but does not require, directors to consider other interests.[14]

Idaho has a hybrid form, mandating consideration of *shareholder* interests while permitting consideration of other constituencies.[15] The Idaho code provides:

> In discharging the duties of the position of director of an issuing public corporation, a director, in considering the best interests of the corporation, *shall* consider the long-term as well as the short-term interests of the corporation and its shareholders, including the possibility that these interests may be best served by the continued independence of the corporation. In addition, a director *may* consider the interests of Idaho employees, suppliers, customers and communities in discharging his duties [emphases added].[16]

The permissive nature of constituency statutes seems counter to the claim that shareholder primacy does not exist in corporate law—one of the arguments made against benefit corporation statutes (as outlined in chapter 4). It is not clear why thirty-three states would have thought it necessary to adopt a law that eliminated shareholder primacy if it did not exist in the first place.

Indeed, Chief Justice Strine cites Delaware's failure to adopt such a provision in his academic work explaining why Delaware must be viewed as a shareholder primacy jurisdiction.[17]

More importantly, however, even if constituency statutes only confirmed what the law already was in one or more jurisdictions, that law is completely permissive as to stakeholder interests. The current law under all constituency statutes creates no obligations or accountability with respect to those interests.

UNIFORM, OPT-IN, AND OPT-OUT CONSTITUENCY PROVISIONS
Constituency statutes are typically uniform in application, reaching all corporations incorporated within a given jurisdiction. However, one state, Pennsylvania, allows a company to opt out of its constituency statute. In addition, a few states have opt-in statutes that permit a corporation to include a constituency provision in its articles of incorporation if it so chooses.[18] For example, Georgia's constituency statute permits a Georgia corporation to include a provision in its articles of incorporation that allows its board of directors to consider constituencies other than stockholders when making decisions.[19]

Reaction to Constituency Statutes

Although thirty-three U.S. jurisdictions adopted the constituency model, the reaction to the concept was not positive among a large segment of the legal community. Delaware, the primary jurisdiction for incorporation in the United States, did not adopt a constituency statute. Nor was such a provision included in the influential Model Business Corporation Act (MBCA). In addition, many commentators questioned the motivation behind the provisions. As we will discuss, benefit corporation law may address the concerns that led to a lack of acceptance of the constituency model.

THE AMERICAN BAR ASSOCIATION AND DELAWARE
REJECT CONSTITUENCY PROVISIONS
In 1990, the ABA's Committee on Corporate Laws considered amending the MBCA to include a constituency provision.[20] The committee ultimately rejected such an amendment:

> In conclusion, the Committee believes that other constituencies stat-
> utes are not an appropriate way to regulate corporate relationships
> or to respond to unwanted takeovers and that an expansive inter-
> pretation of the other constituencies statutes cast in the permissive
> mode is both unnecessary and unwise. Those statutes that merely
> empower directors to consider the interests of other constituencies
> [in the course of managing the corporation in the shareholders'
> interests] are best taken as a legislative affirmation of what courts
> would be expected to hold, in the absence of a statute. Interpreting
> the statutes to have the same force as the express Indiana provision
> [which clarified that stakeholder interests could be primary] would
> accomplish a change in traditional corporate law so radical that
> it should be undertaken only after there has been extensive and
> broad-based deliberation on the effects of reshuffling of fundamen-
> tal relationships among shareholders and other persons who may be
> affected by the affairs of an incorporated business.[21]

The committee cited with approval Delaware's case law that allows consideration of other interests when those interests are reasonably related to the
long-term interests of shareholders, unless the decision concerns the sale of the
company.[22] Overall, the committee believed that constituency statutes "may
have ramifications that go far beyond a simple enumeration of the other interests directors may recognize in discharging their duties."[23]

Similarly, Delaware did not adopt constituency provisions. Although there
is no legislative history explaining the absence of a change, it is likely that the
members of the Delaware State Bar Association responsible for drafting changes
to the Delaware General Corporation Law had the same concerns as the drafters
of the Model Business Corporation Act. Moreover, at the height of the hostile
takeover era that engendered constituency statute adoption, the law in Delaware
was evolving rapidly, and, in the view of many, was evolving toward a stakeholder model, alleviating any need for a statutory change.[24] Equally important,
because of the large number of public companies incorporated in Delaware, the
effect of a mandatory change in director responsibility would be enormous and
sudden. In that environment, it is likely that the Delaware bar felt that changing
the statute would do more harm than good.

CRITICISMS OF CONSTITUENCY STATUTES

Early on, constituency statutes were criticized for conflicting with the share-holder primacy norm. As we discussed in chapter 2, the shareholder primacy model views shareholders as the owners of the corporation, which is to be managed solely in their interests.[25] Anticonstituency scholars argued that con-stituency statutes would destroy shareholder value: "Opponents' greatest fear is that constituency statutes will upset the shareholder primacy norm by changing the fiduciary duties that directors owe to shareholders. Specifically, they fear that constituency statutes allow constituency interests to compete with share-holder interests in corporate decision-making, thereby jeopardizing corporate profitability and shareholder value."[26]

The Committee on Corporate Laws based much of its criticism of constit-uency statutes on their apparent conflict with the shareholder primacy model. The committee found that consideration of non-shareholder interests without relation to shareholder interests "would conflict with the directors' responsibil-ity to shareholders and could undermine the effectiveness of the system that has made the corporation an efficient device for the creation of jobs and wealth," and that allowing directors to engage in this balancing of interests would likely yield poorer decisions. The committee emphasized that "courts have consis-tently avowed the legal primacy of shareholder interests when management and directors make decisions."[27]

Another, related concern about constituency statutes was the lack of accountability and the potential for director abuse at the expense of sharehold-ers.[28] Because the statutes are generally permissive, directors have complete discretion as to whether to use the expanded considerations in making deci-sions. Directors can easily justify any decision, depending on how they weigh the considerations, thus harming a plaintiff's ability to meaningfully challenge board action. One law professor posed the following hypothetical:

> What if management simply uses the constituency provision to negotiate a better deal for itself without regard to the constituency at issue. For example, if a rust belt company is approached with an offer to go private at $21, it could well respond, "I'm sorry, but at $21, this deal is not good for our employees, the local community or the environment." Imagine the surprise of constituencies when,

at $25, the board changes its mind, and takes the offer. In the end, the only constituency with standing is the shareholder community. Consequently, one shouldn't be surprised if/when directors use these statutes as little more than bargaining levers at the expense of the communities they were meant to protect.[29]

Commentators were concerned that, because the courts will largely defer to the directors' determination whether to consider permitted constituency interests, there would be little accountability. Others have echoed concerns that these statutes serve to protect directors at the expense of shareholders and other constituencies.[30]

In addition, and perhaps most importantly, there is the retrospective criticism that constituency statutes simply are ineffective with respect to their primary purpose of countering shareholder primacy:

> Constituency statutes, however, do not seem to have been very effective in combating the shareholder wealth maximization norm. Perhaps this lack of effectiveness stems from the fact that the typical constituency statute is permissive and does not give non-shareholder stakeholders standing to sue. While constituency statutes undoubtedly provide some protections for directors seeking to further the social or environmental mission of the corporation, the constituency statutes do not seem to motivate the average director to move beyond the shareholder wealth maximization norm.[31]

BENEFIT CORPORATION LAWS ARE A BETTER ANSWER TO STOCKHOLDER PRIMACY THAN CONSTITUENCY STATUTES

Those states that have adopted uniform constituency provisions have made a public policy decision to reject the shareholder primacy model for all corporations. In light of the modern view that corporate statutes should be "enabling" rather than prescriptive, this may be viewed as an unusual choice. However, the choice may be consistent with the policy considerations that drive the stakeholder model discussed in chapter 2. In this view, the privileges of corporate personality, perpetual existence, and limited liability should not be granted to an entity that will only act selfishly for the benefit of its shareholders and ignore its effect on other stakeholders. However, if this is in fact the justification for the uniform application of many constituency provisions, it seems inconsistent with the permissive nature of the provisions, since the statutes do not create any obligation or accountability for broad stakeholder interests. Public policy making truly guided by the stakeholder model should create corporate governance rules that include accountability for stakeholder interests, like Connecticut's original constituency statute, or like benefit corporation provisions.

The benefit corporation governance model addresses the concern that constituency statutes lack accountability; under the benefit corporation model, directors must balance the interests of all stakeholders and must be transparent about such balancing. However, even if a provision is mandatory, there may be significant policy objections were its operation uniform, because a uniform statute would mandate a change from shareholder primacy to the benefit corporation model for all corporations.

A mandatory provision, in contrast to an enabling provision, may simply be too much, too quickly, for the markets, particularly in a jurisdiction such as Delaware, where thousands of publicly traded companies are incorporated. Given the competition for corporate charters among states, such a mandatory change in the U.S. corporate system seems like an unlikely first step toward stakeholder governance.[32] It should be noted that this circumstance differs from the usual idea that states are "too friendly" to management in an effort to attract charters. In this case, the initial objections would come from shareholders as well as management, because they might perceive the change as taking away their supremacy. The move from shareholder primacy to stakeholder governance is likely to succeed broadly only with considerable investor support, and a broad imposition of change is unlikely to engender such support. An enabling provision, like Georgia's constituency provision or Delaware's benefit corporation statute, allows companies to test the stakeholder model waters without mandating wholesale change in the public equity markets.

Constituency Statute Litigation

A study by Christopher Geczy and colleagues identified forty-seven relevant cases in the thirty-year period from 1983 through 2013.[33] Examination of that case law should provide guidance for corporations opting into benefit corporation status because, although the statutory schemes have differences, they both reject the doctrine of stockholder primacy. The case law addresses constituency statutes from thirteen jurisdictions, and most cases occurred during the last fifteen years. The study categorized cases into one of five categories (Positive, Neutral/Positive, Neutral, Neutral/Negative, Negative) based on the court's treatment of the constituency statute. Forty of the cases involved claims for breach of fiduciary duty.[34]

Enforcement was positive overall: twenty-nine of forty-seven cases fell into the Positive and Neutral/Positive categories. Seventeen of these cases recognized expanded director discretion, and twelve recognized that there was no enforceable right for non-stockholders.[35] In Positive cases, the statute was a determining factor in the decision and the court recognized the legitimacy of stakeholder consideration, or declined to create enforcement rights in stakeholder constituents. In Neutral/Positive cases, there was a substantive discussion that recognized the expanded scope of director decision making or the limits on stakeholder rights, but such factors were not essential to the holding. In Neutral cases, the court cited or referenced constituency statutes but did not include substantive discussions. Only four out of the forty-seven cases were coded Neutral/Negative and no cases fell under the Negative category. In Neutral/Negative cases, the court addressed constituency statutes but did not recognize expanded director authority or decline to apply *Revlon*, or declined to permit expanded discretion in situations affecting franchise rights. Negative cases (of which there were none) would have declined to apply expanded director authority where the reasoning would have been a factor in the holding.[36] These results suggest that benefit corporation statutes will be enforced, and will provide directors with additional discretion, without creating rights in non-shareholders.

EXPANDED INTERESTS FOR DIRECTORS TO CONSIDER
Much of the case law recognized the expanded interests that directors could consider under constituency statutes. Frequently, constituency statutes were successfully invoked by directors seeking to uphold their decisions. Courts rarely found that directors went too far in considering other constituencies, only finding an abuse of discretion when a decision conflicted with voting rights. Constituency provisions have not been successfully used offensively by plaintiffs claiming that directors failed to consider non-stockholder constituents. However, the constituency statutes have not prevented shareholders from bringing claims that directors either completely ignored shareholders' interests

or acted in a manner that would not advance the interests of any stakeholders. These cases should provide guidance in litigation involving benefit corporations, and three of them are discussed briefly here.

Kloha v. Duda is an example of directors successfully using a constituency statute to uphold a decision.[37] In *Kloha*, the plaintiff alleged that the defendant directors breached their fiduciary duties by, among other things, considering family employment concerns in their decision making. The court determined that the board could consider the impact of its decisions on employees, including family members.[38]

Similarly, in *Safety-Kleen Corp. v. Laidlaw Envtl. Servs. Inc.*, the court declined to grant a preliminary injunction, finding that the Safety-Kleen board did not breach its fiduciary duties in recommending one proposal to stockholders and keeping defensive measures in place, where the directors' decision involved the consideration of non-shareholder interests that the Wisconsin statute expressly endorsed. However, the *Safety-Kleen* court also suggested some limits on director discretion in considering other constituencies, noting that the board might be prevented from ignoring a clearly superior proposal solely due to the interests of other constituencies.[39]

Moreover, plaintiffs may still allege breaches of duty that do not involve questions of allocating value among different stakeholders and simply reflect breaches to the combined class of constituencies. In *Shepard v. Humke*, the court found the plaintiff's fiduciary duty claim sufficient to survive the defendants' motion to dismiss. The court explained that allegations of involving misrepresentations and a breakup fee could involve a claim that the directors failed to act in the best interests of all of the corporation's constituencies.[40]

APPLICATION TO VOTING RIGHTS

Although courts have acknowledged the expanded discretion afforded to directors by constituency statutes, that discretion is not without limits, particularly where voting rights are concerned. Those cases may provide important guidance for benefit corporations, because it is likely that the same concern for the corporate franchise will be applicable.

In *Warehime v. Warehime*, the defendant directors cited the Pennsylvania constituency statute, justifying their actions based on permissive consideration of constituents other than stakeholders. While the court acknowledged the broad discretion granted by the business judgment rule, and the ability of directors to consider non-stockholder constituencies, it concluded that those provisions could not validate actions intended to interfere with voting rights.[41] However, in one case, a Georgia court refused to apply the *Blasius* test because a constituency statute was in effect.[42]

IMPACT ON ENHANCED SCRUTINY

The Barzuza study examined the question of whether other constituency statutes affect the judicial standard of review. In some states, the constituency statute explicitly rejects the enhanced scrutiny standards of *Revlon* and *Unocal*, and the cases follow the legislative mandate. In other jurisdictions, however, the statute does not explicitly address the standard of review. In some of those states, courts have nevertheless interpreted constituency statutes to mandate business judgment rule treatment of cases that might otherwise be subject to enhanced scrutiny. In other states, the courts continued to apply enhanced scrutiny.[43] These cases raise issues that will also be raised when benefit corporations are in situations that involve enhanced scrutiny for traditional corporations.

Although some jurisdictions have interpreted constituency statutes as eliminating enhanced scrutiny in defensive and sale situations, even where the statues did not expressly do so, it seems unlikely that the benefit corporation statutes would be interpreted in that fashion. Although there is a key similarity between benefit corporation legislation and constituency statutes (i.e., the rejection of shareholder primacy), the statutes are largely driven by different motivations. In many cases, constituency statutes were a response to the courts' use of the *Revlon* and *Unocal* standards to limit board discretion, which raised a concern that the important policies behind the business judgment rule were being ignored. It is thus understandable that courts would read a rejection of those doctrines into constituency statutes. In contrast, benefit corporation law is not driven by a concern that directors have too little discretion—rather it is driven by the concern that the space in which they are allowed to exercise that discretion is circumscribed incorrectly, from a policy perspective. Accordingly, there is little reason to believe that courts will not continue to apply enhanced scrutiny to benefit corporations in situations involving defensive tactics and company sales, as predicted in chapter 8.

STANDING FOR NON-STOCKHOLDERS

The Geczy study found that none of the constituency statute cases recognized an enforceable right for non-stockholders, with twelve explicitly declining to do so.[44] Because constituency statutes are permissive in nature, no fiduciary duty runs to non-stockholders.[45] For example, in *Official Comm. of Unsecured Creditors of PHD, Inc. v. Bank One*, the court relied on the permissive nature of the constituency statute to deny fiduciary duties to creditors.[46] Similarly, the court in *In re I.E. Liquidation*, Inc. dismissed breach of fiduciary duty claims based on the directors' failure to consider creditors' interests.[47] Thus, the courts have consistently interpreted the permissive language of constituency statutes as creating neither an affirmative duty to consider non-stockholders' interests nor an attendant right of action for failure to do so.

Although benefit corporation legislation, including the Delaware statute, is mandatory, the statutes expressly provide that no right of action is created other than the right of stockholders to bring a derivative suit.[48] Similarly, the MBCL provides no right of action for non-stockholders.[49] Thus, benefit corporation legislation provides greater clarity than many constituency statutes, where a lack of enforcement right for third parties is only implied by the permissive nature of the statutes.[50]

CONCLUSIONS

Overall, the Geczy study found that constituency statutes truly expanded the authority of directors, as opposed to simply codifying earlier common law.[51] In some jurisdictions, the language permitting directors to consider other constituencies was found to reinstate the business judgment rule where enhanced scrutiny might otherwise apply.[52] However, with the exception of one case, no courts found that such language altered the standard of review applicable to decisions affecting the stockholder franchise. The case law also shows constituency statutes did not create a concurrent expansion of non-stockholder constituent rights.[53] Each of these outcomes is likely to resonate in the interpretation of benefit corporation statutes.

Economic Impact of Constituency Statutes

A 1993 event study determined that the adoption of constituency statutes did not have a statistically significant impact on stock prices.[54] Nearly twenty years later, the Geczy study was conducted to determine the impact of constituency statutes on investment by high-fiduciary-duty institutions, defined as pension funds and endowments, which share similar, strict fiduciary duties with respect to investing.[55] Ultimately, the study found no significant adverse impact on investment by high-fiduciary-duty institutions when corporations in which they are invested become subject to constituency legislation:

> The empirical findings show that constituency statutes were not a roadblock to institutional investment with especially high fiduciary duties. We cannot rule out that constituency statutes had *some* effect on HFDI [high-fiduciary-duty institution] investment, but we can rule out that these investors significantly altered investment behavior after the passage of the statutes, as one might expect if these institutions perceived material conflicts with their fiduciary duties. We consider these findings promising for new legislations such as the benefit corporation laws, insofar as constituency laws expanded management prerogatives to consider nonshareholder interests.[56]

At least two other papers have found that the adoption of constituency statutes is linked to increased innovation.[57] Although the research is limited, it does suggest that eliminating shareholder primacy did not adversely impact corporations or their stockholders. Stock prices were not affected, and investor fiduciaries did not flee based on a perception that investments in companies without shareholder primacy regimes violated their own fiduciary duties. Although the benefit corporation regime provides greater accountability and transparency than does the constituency statute regime, there is no reason to believe that the results for benefit corporations and their stockholders will be radically different.

* * *

The present chapter shows that, although there are important lessons from the experience of a quarter century of constituency statutes, these statutes are not a good alternative for imposing stakeholder governance principles. Chapter 10 will examine whether conventional corporations can modify their own charters in order to take on stakeholder governance without using benefit corporation provisions.

CHAPTER TEN

Could a Conventional Corporation Adopt Stakeholder Values?

Some readers may understand the benefits of stakeholder governance but wonder why an entirely new statute is really needed. Most corporation laws are fairly flexible, after all. This chapter examines whether it would be possible for a conventional corporation to simply add language to its charter in order to adopt a stakeholder form of governance. The conclusion is that it is very questionable whether such provisions would be enforceable (especially in a state like Delaware, which has not adopted a constituency statute) and that, in any event, there is little reason to resort to such private ordering when there are so many clear alternatives provided under the entity laws in a variety of U.S. jurisdictions.

The Statutory Framework in Delaware

Although shareholder wealth maximization is the default law for Delaware corporations, there are no statutes that explicitly forbid a corporation from altering the duties of directors so that they are not bound to act solely in the interests of shareholders. Accordingly, potential users of the public benefit corporation provisions might question whether they could modify directors' fiduciary duties to include duties to stakeholders by "private ordering"—by simply writing such provisions into a corporation's certificate of incorporation (and thus without becoming a benefit corporation). Indeed, some scholars have posited that fiduciary duties to shareholders may be contracted away via the certificate of incorporation.[1] However, as we will see, there would be substantial uncertainty around the enforceability of such a provision.

Delaware law has various statutes that enable corporations to modify the default corporation law.[2] In addition, there are specific provisions in the Delaware General Corporation Law that permit the modification of fiduciary law applicable to a corporation. Specifically, Section 102(b)(7) permits a Delaware corporation to limit the personal liability of directors for certain fiduciary duty breaches,[3] and Section 122(17) permits a corporation to limit the effect of the "corporate opportunity doctrine."[4] (The corporate opportunity doctrine is a subset of the duty of loyalty that limits the ability of a fiduciary to take advantage of business opportunities that are deemed to belong to the corporation.) Furthermore, Delaware statutes that govern noncorporate entities (such as LLCs) expressly permit broad modifications of fiduciary duty.[5] Finally, Section 102(b)(1) expressly permits a company's certificate of incorporation to contain "any provision for the management of the business and for the conduct of the affairs of the corporation, and any provision creating, defining, limiting and regulating the powers of the corporation, the directors, and the stockholders, or any class of the stockholders ... if such provisions are not contrary to the laws of this State."[6]

Delaware Law Does Not Authorize Private Ordering of Fiduciary Duties

The viability of altering fiduciary duties through a provision in the certificate of incorporation adopted pursuant to Section 102(b)(1) would likely turn on the question of whether such a provision were "contrary to the laws of this state." This phrase has been interpreted as encompassing the Delaware corporate common law as well as statutory law.[7] However, the Delaware Court of Chancery has held that it may strike down a provision in the certificate of incorporation only if it "contravenes Delaware public policy."[8] Therefore, it seems likely that if litigation arose concerning a conventional corporation's alteration of shareholder primacy in its certificate of incorporation, the Delaware courts would have to determine whether the common law precedents such as *eBay* and *Revlon* represent the type of public policy that cannot be overridden under Section 102(b)(1).

It seems likely that such a provision would be considered contrary to public policy and thus contrary to Delaware law and precluded under Section 102(b)(1). The fundamental nature of the duty that directors owe to shareholders, as well as the fact that the legislature has thought it necessary to authorize certain fiduciary duty modifications in both the DGCL and the statutes governing limited partnerships and limited liability companies, support this conclusion. Indeed, in one Court of Chancery case, the court specifically found that Section 102(b)(7), by negative implication, precluded charter provisions that limited director liability for breaching the duty of loyalty by usurping corporate opportunities.[9] The case was decided after the adoption of Section 102(b)(7), which allows charter provisions that limit liability for breach of the duty of care, but not for breaches of the duty of loyalty, and before the adoption of Section 122(17), which authorizes limitations on liability for one category of loyalty claims: usurpation of corporate opportunities.

In addition, some scholars have posited that fiduciary principles stand separate from contract principles and serve as a protective measure for shareholders who have no bargained-for contractual rights in the corporation.[10] This line of reasoning suggests that fiduciary duties should not be subject to contractual alteration, except where authorized by statute. This result is consistent with the idea that, despite the benefits of flexible corporate statutes, too much flexibility may be counterproductive.[11]

A final argument against permitting a corporation to limit directors' fiduciary duties in the same manner permitted by the Delaware benefit corporation statute is that such an interpretation would allow corporations to amend their charters to make the changes contemplated by the PBCS by simple majority vote, and without triggering appraisal rights. This would allow corporations to easily evade the statutory protections that the legislature thought were necessary in connection with such changes.

Other Jurisdictions and Practicalities

The foregoing analysis has only addressed Delaware law. Of course, one might ask a similar question with respect to any jurisdiction. The question becomes more interesting, perhaps, in states that have constituency statutes; are they less likely to find that there is a public policy that would be violated by mandatory stakeholder obligations? It would seem so, but ultimately, this question would require a close review of the relevant corporate statute and applicable case law.

As a practical matter, however, private ordering with respect to this issue does not seem to be advisable without clear authority. It risks having directors make stakeholder-based decisions, only to discover that, in fact, the charter provisions authorizing such consideration are void. On the other hand, to the extent such provisions are valid, there may be a risk that they create rights in stakeholders, since, unlike the situation that exists for benefit corporations, there is no statutory protection from stakeholder suits, nor statutory exculpation and business judgment rule protection. In light of these uncertainties, businesses that want to form with stakeholder governance would be well advised to use a benefit corporation statute in one of the states where it has been authorized, or to use an alternative entity, or social purpose corporation, as described in the next chapter.

* * *

Now that we have established that conventional corporations are not good vehicles for establishing stakeholder governance, we turn to the next chapter, which discusses some more viable alternatives to the benefit corporation.

CHAPTER ELEVEN

Limited Liability Companies and Social Purpose Corporations

Having determined that conventional corporations, whether located in states with constituency statutes or not, are not viable alternatives for imposing stakeholder governance, we can ask one final question. Are there any other alternatives? The answer is yes, and this chapter discusses the use of limited liability companies, benefit LLCs, and social purpose corporations to do so.

Ordinary Limited Liability Companies

Benefit corporations are increasingly popular structures for entrepreneurs looking to achieve both profit and social benefit, but similar goals can be accomplished with a limited liability company. For ease of reference, this chapter will focus on Delaware LLC law, as the statutory provisions permitting fiduciary modification differ among U.S. jurisdictions. LLCs may present an attractive alternative for entrepreneurs who want to incorporate a social purpose into their companies. Forming as an LLC can bring many benefits, including pass-through taxation and a flexible management structure.

The founder of an LLC may contract around default fiduciary duties to create a company with managers who have the same obligations as the directors of a benefit corporation. Delaware cases have addressed the issue of default fiduciary duties in the LLC context,[1] and recent amendments to Delaware's Limited Liability Company Act clarified that managers of LLCs have default fiduciary duties.[2] Nevertheless, the managers' duties may be "expanded or restricted or eliminated by provisions in the limited liability company agreement."[3] LLC founders are free to choose the terms of the agreement because courts will enforce explicit contractual provisions, even if they may appear onerous or one-sided.[4]

The LLC Act imposes one limit on private ordering when it states that an LLC agreement "may not eliminate the implied contractual covenant of good faith and fair dealing."[5] The implied covenant of good faith and fair dealing has been described in two potentially conflicting ways. First, courts have explained it as a limited "gap filler" requiring the court to arrive at an answer for a situation not explicitly accounted for in the contract.[6] According to this view, "one generally cannot base a claim for breach of the implied covenant on conduct authorized by the agreement."[7] Second, courts have identified the implied covenant as a broader method for a court to "refrain from arbitrary or unreasonable conduct which has the effect of preventing the other party to the contract from receiving" the benefit of the bargain.[8]

Despite this limit, the LLC structure is sufficiently flexible to create a benefit corporation–like arrangement through private ordering. In fact, many LLCs (e.g., Urban Green Development LLC, Blue Earth Consultants LLC, and Good Capital LLC) are already certified as B Corps by B Lab, a nonprofit entity that certifies socially conscious business entities and that requires a legal structure that creates broad accountability.[9] B Lab requires certain language in the operating agreement to ensure that the LLC's mission is aligned with its stakeholders. That language is reproduced in appendix G.

There also are significant drawbacks to using an LLC structure. First, many investors strongly favor investing in a corporation rather than an LLC. While there is a well-developed body of case law for corporations, LLC case law is much less developed. Additionally, LLC operating agreements are more varied than their corporate counterparts (charters and bylaws), which are relatively "standard-form." For these reasons, many investors avoid investing in LLCs.[10] If founders anticipate raising capital, they should be wary of forming an LLC. Second, writing benefit corporation provisions into an LLC agreement does not allow companies to differentiate themselves from the competition with a recognizable entity form. In a marketplace where "greenwashing" is common, a legal change of structure from LLC to public benefit corporation can signal the company's commitment to its core values.[11]

Several states have adopted specific provisions for the "low-profit limited liability company." This form was adopted for social enterprises that want to encourage investments from foundations that are allowed to invest in "program-related investments." For a number of reasons, low-profit limited liability companies have not been a particularly successful experiment.[12] Although the form can be used for entities that intend to be governed by stakeholder values, there are probably few advantages to using them in the place of standard LLCs.

Benefit Limited Liability Companies

In addition, despite the flexibility inherent in LLC law, three states have moved to authorize a "Benefit LLC."[13] Such a provision locks in LLC managers' broad obligations to all stakeholders, along with broad purpose and transparency requirements. Although such a provision might not be necessary, it addresses some of the problems mentioned in the previous section. It provides a measure of uniformity, so that investors, workers, customers, and other interested stakeholders can recognize the benefit "brand." It also saves cash-strapped start-ups from the need to have legal counsel draft bespoke provisions. Finally, because the purpose, accountability, and transparency elements are mandatory, the provisions help to avoid the greenwashing concern.

Social Purpose Corporations

Concurrent with the movement to adopt benefit corporation statutes, a number of states have adopted a form known generally as the social purpose corporation, although the name varies from state to state.[14] These statutes permit a departure from shareholder primacy by allowing corporations to select one or more stakeholder interests that directors are required to consider. Unlike benefit corporations, however, they are not required to consider their general effect on society and the environment. As a result, they do not mandate the broad stakeholder governance envisioned by the benefit corporation statutes.

However, corporations that are formed under social purpose corporation provisions can choose a general public benefit and, in doing so, attain benefit corporation–like governance. B Lab has prepared language that social purpose corporations can use in their charters to adopt such a structure.[15]

* * *

Table 8 lists which forms of stakeholder governance exist in each of the fifty U.S. states and the District of Columbia.

TABLE 8: STAKEHOLDER GOVERNANCE STATE-BY-STATE				
	Benefit Corp	Constituency Statute	Social Purpose Corporation	Benefit LLC
AL	NO	NO	NO	NO
AK	NO	NO	NO	NO
AZ	YES	NO	NO	NO
AR	YES	YES	NO	NO
CA	YES	NO	YES	NO
CO	YES	NO	NO	NO
CT	YES	YES	NO	NO
DC	YES	YES	NO	NO
DE	YES	NO	NO	NO
FL	YES	YES	YES	NO
GA	NO	YES	NO	NO
HI	YES	YES	NO	NO
ID	YES	YES	NO	NO
IL	YES	YES	NO	NO
IN	YES	YES	NO	NO
IA	NO	YES	NO	NO
KS	YES	NO	NO	NO
KY	YES	YES	NO	NO
LA	YES	YES	NO	NO
ME	NO	YES	NO	NO
MD	YES	YES	NO	YES

	Benefit Corp	Constituency Statute	Social Purpose Corporation	Benefit LLC
MA	YES	YES	NO	NO
MI	NO	NO	NO	NO
MN	YES	YES	YES	NO
MS	NO	YES	NO	NO
MO	NO	YES	NO	NO
MT	YES	NO	NO	NO
NE	YES	NO	NO	NO
NV	YES	YES	NO	NO
NH	YES	NO	NO	NO
NJ	YES	YES	NO	NO
NM	NO	YES	NO	NO
NY	YES	YES	NO	NO
NC	NO	NO	NO	NO
ND	NO	YES	NO	NO
OH	NO	YES	NO	NO
OK	NO	NO	NO	NO
OR	YES	YES	NO	YES
PA	YES	YES	NO	YES
RI	YES	YES	NO	NO
SC	YES	NO	NO	NO
SD	NO	YES	NO	NO
TN	YES	NO	YES	NO
TX	YES	NO	YES	NO
UT	YES	NO	NO	NO
VT	YES	YES	NO	NO
VA	YES	NO	NO	NO
WA	NO	NO	YES	NO
WV	YES	NO	NO	NO
WI	NO	YES	NO	NO
WY	NO	YES	NO	NO

Epilogue

I wrote this book because of my belief that the incredible gains of modern civilization that have lifted billions out of poverty are threatened by some of the very elements that brought those gains. The atmosphere's carrying capacity for greenhouse gas is limited; society's carrying capacity for inequality is limited; the financial system's capacity for risk is limited. The monocapitalist system that evolved as a means for allocating economic resources simply does not adequately address these limitations. Continuing to rely on a legal and financial system that answers only to financial capital is untenable.

Attempts to address the threats to our rapidly diminishing stocks of human, social, and natural capital through regulation and repair cannot overcome the overwhelming momentum of an economy run solely on financial principles. The power of financial capital—hundreds of trillions of dollars—is too powerful for governments and nongovernmental organizations to overcome. If we are to address these threats before the system reaches a tragic overload—and if we are to address the inequality that leaves so many in poverty—we must establish an economic system that accounts for the value of all forms of capital.

The global economic system is not the result of a grand design, any more than human beings are. Both evolved haphazardly in response to a constantly changing environment, and both have many elements that just don't work well in the modern world. Our sweet tooth was great on the savanna, when ripe fruit was a rare but critical source of calories and nutrition. Not so much in an era when drugstores, grocery stores, and vending machines are full of cookies, cakes, and candy, as our epidemic of obesity-related illness shows. By the same token, the idea of shareholder primacy might have worked well to combat the

agency problem discussed in chapter 2, but as our economic system has global-
ized and become more interdependent, and as the earth's population has grown,
the financial system's "short-term-profit tooth" has become a similar liability,
with corporations consuming social and environmental resources at an unsustainable pace.

This book is not simply about corporate law. It is really about public policy
and the need to insist that the professionals responsible for managing our stores
of financial wealth use tools that manage all of the capitals they impact, and not
just the money. This applies to asset allocators, such as pension funds, and to
managers, such as mutual fund complexes and their advisers, and finally to the
corporate directors and managers that apply that capital in the real economy.

The simplest and most direct way to accomplish that change is to begin
at the level of the real economy. Every time a corporation becomes a benefit
corporation, all of the assets under its control are reoriented to respect all of the
limited resources we share. Such corporations must be mindful of the environment, their workforces, and all the communities they impact. If not, they will
have to find a trajectory that takes them there. Such determinations will not be
easy; there are many complicated questions about what sort of consumption is
sustainable and what any one company's fair share of that consumption is. But
being approximately right is better than being precisely wrong, especially when
the questions are existential.

The benefit corporation structure relies on shareholders understanding the
need to value systems—if they remain in share-value mode, they will not use
their power to enforce the new obligations. And while some institutional shareholders are beginning to recognize that value, it is not yet the norm. Although
there certainly is increased understanding of the need to manage systems, institutions struggle to find tools to do so, and they worry about free riding and
problems of collective action. Benefit corporations are one way to address those
concerns. By encouraging corporations in their portfolios to change governance
focus, investors can work together to make these changes.

There will certainly be objections. Some will say that corporations can
already do well by doing good and that creating this distinction just gives other
companies further license to exploit resources. The fact is, they are already

doing that. The stronger objection, perhaps, is that there is just no way to make this work. There is too much opportunity for free riding and commons grazing, and there will always be non–benefit corporations that rush in to profit from unsustainable behavior.

I am more optimistic. There are many companies for whom benefit corporation adoption is actually a way to implement their business plan. For these companies, the ability to make authentic commitments to their stakeholders is a way to induce those stakeholders to commit back, so that benefit corporation law represents a new opportunity. As these companies introduce responsible governance into the market, more workers and customers will look for businesses that have stakeholder values in their DNA, and investors can contribute to this pressure. Eventually, there will be a tipping point and the paradigm will shift.

And shift it must. I opened this book with a dedication to the memory of the more than one thousand individuals who died in a garment factory in 2012. Business behavior had signaled that corporations and their shareholders cared more about profits than about the safety of those workers. We can put a stop to these signals by changing the question from *"Why are you a benefit corporation?"* to *"Why aren't you?"*

Model Benefit Corporation Legislation (with Explanatory Comments)

Version of September 16, 2016

[*Chapter*] __

Benefit Corporations

[*Subchapter*]
1. Preliminary Provisions
2. Corporate Purposes
3. Accountability
4. Transparency

[*Subchapter*] 1

Preliminary Provisions

Section

101. Application and effect of [chapter].

102. Definitions.

103. Incorporation of benefit corporation.

104. Election of benefit corporation status.

105. Termination of benefit corporation status.

§ 101. Application and effect of [*chapter*].

(a) **General rule.** – This [*chapter*] shall be applicable to all benefit corporations.

(b) **Application of business corporation law generally.** – The existence of a provision of this [*chapter*] shall not of itself create an implication that a contrary or different rule of law is applicable to a business corporation that is not a benefit corporation. This [*chapter*] shall not affect a statute or rule of law that is applicable to a business corporation that is not a benefit corporation.

(c) **Laws applicable.** – Except as otherwise provided in this [*chapter*], [*the enacting state's business corporation law*] shall be generally applicable to all benefit corporations. A benefit corporation may be subject simultaneously to this [*chapter*] and [*cite any statutes that provide for the incorporation of a specific type of business corporation, such as a professional corporation or for-profit cooperative corporation*]. The provisions of this [*chapter*] shall control over the provisions of [*cite the business corporation law*] [*and*] [*cite the professional corporation, cooperative corporation and other relevant laws*].

(d) **Organic records.** – A provision of the articles of incorporation or bylaws of a benefit corporation may not limit, be inconsistent with, or supersede a provision of this [*chapter*].

Comment:

This chapter authorizes the organization of a form of business corporation that offers entrepreneurs and investors the option to build, and invest in, a business that operates with a corporate purpose broader than maximizing shareholder value and that consciously undertakes a responsibility to maximize the benefits of its operations for all stakeholders, not just shareholders. Enforcement of that purpose and responsibility comes not from governmental oversight, but rather from new provisions on transparency and accountability included in this chapter.

The second sentence of subsection (c) makes clear that if a state provides for the incorporation of specialized types of business corporations, such as statutory close corporations, insurance corporations, for-profit cooperative corporations, or professional corporations, those corporations may also be benefit corporations. In the case of a professional corporation, section 201(e) provides a special rule that eliminates any conflict between this chapter and the requirement found in many professional corporation laws that limits the purposes or business of a professional corporation to providing a particular type of professional service.

As a result of subsection (d), a corporation that elects to be subject to this chapter will be subject to all of the provisions of the chapter and will not be able to vary their application to the corporation.

The term "benefit corporation" used in this section is defined in section 102.

§ 102. Definitions.

The following words and phrases when used in this [*chapter*] shall have the meanings given to them in this section unless the context clearly indicates otherwise:

"Benefit corporation." A business corporation:

(1) that has elected to become subject to this [*chapter*]; and

(2) the status of which as a benefit 81 corporation has not been terminated.

"Benefit director." The director, if any, designated as the benefit director of a benefit corporation under section 302.

"Benefit enforcement proceeding." A claim, action, or proceeding for:

(1) failure of a benefit corporation to pursue or create general public benefit or a specific public benefit purpose set forth in its articles; or

(2) violation of any obligation, duty, or standard of conduct under this [*chapter*].

"Benefit officer." The individual, if any, designated as the benefit officer of a benefit corporation under section 304.

"General public benefit." A material positive impact on society and the environment, taken as a whole, from the business and operations of a benefit corporation assessed taking into account the impacts of the benefit corporation as reported against a third-party standard.

"Independent." Having no material relationship with a benefit corporation or a subsidiary of the benefit corporation. Serving as a benefit director or benefit officer does not make an individual not independent. A material relationship between an individual and a benefit corporation or any of its subsidiaries will be conclusively presumed to exist if any of the following apply:

(1) The individual is, or has been within the last three years, an employee other than a benefit officer of the benefit corporation or a subsidiary.

(2) An immediate family member of the individual is, or has been within the last three years, an executive officer other than a benefit officer of the benefit corporation or a subsidiary.

(3) There is beneficial or record ownership of 5% or more of the outstanding shares of the benefit corporation, calculated as if all outstanding rights to acquire equity interests in the benefit corporation had been exercised, by:

(i) the individual; or

(ii) an entity:

(A) of which the individual is a director, an officer, or a manager; or

(B) in which the individual 126 owns beneficially or of record 5% or more of the outstanding equity interests, calculated as if all outstanding rights to acquire equity interests in the entity had been exercised.

"Minimum status vote."

(1) In the case of a business corporation, in addition to any other required approval or vote, the satisfaction of the following conditions:

(i) The shareholders of every class or series shall be entitled to vote as a [*separate voting group*] [*class*] on the corporate action regardless of a limitation stated in the articles of incorporation or bylaws on the voting rights of any class or series.

(ii) The corporate action must be approved by the affirmative vote of the shareholders of each class or series entitled to cast at least two-thirds of the votes that all shareholders of the class or series are entitled to cast on the action.

[*(2) In the case of a domestic entity other than a business corporation, in addition to any other required approval, vote, or consent, the satisfaction of the following conditions:*

(i) The holders of every class or series of equity interest in the entity that are entitled to receive a distribution of any kind from the entity shall be entitled to vote on or consent to the action regardless of any otherwise applicable limitation on the voting or consent rights of any class or series.

(ii) The action must be approved by the affirmative vote or consent of the holders described in subparagraph (i) entitled to cast at least two-thirds of the votes or consents that all of those holders are entitled to cast on the action.]

"Specific public benefit." Includes:

(1) providing low-income or underserved individuals or communities with beneficial products or services;

(2) promoting economic opportunity for individuals or communities beyond the creation of jobs in the normal course of business;

(3) protecting or restoring the environment;

(4) improving human health;

(5) promoting the arts, sciences, or advancement of knowledge;

(6) increasing the flow of capital to entities with a purpose to benefit society or the environment; and

(7) conferring any other particular benefit on society or the environment.

"Subsidiary." In relation to a person, an entity in which the person owns beneficially or of record 50% or more of the outstanding equity interests, calculated as if all outstanding rights to acquire equity interests in the entity had been exercised.

"Third-party standard." A recognized standard for reporting overall social and environmental performance of a business that is:

(1) Comprehensive because it assesses the effects of the business and its operations upon the interests listed in section 301(a)(1)(ii), (iii), (iv) and (v)

(2) Developed by an entity that is not controlled by the benefit corporation.

(3) Credible because it is developed by an entity that both:

(i) has access to necessary expertise to assess overall corporate social and environmental performance; and

(ii) uses a balanced multistakeholder approach to develop the standard, including a reasonable public comment period.

(4) Transparent because the following information is publicly available:

(i) About the standard:

(A) The criteria considered when measuring the overall social and environmental performance of a business.

(B) The relative weightings, if any, of those criteria.

(ii) About the development and revision of the standard:

(A) The identity of the directors, officers, material owners, and the governing body of the entity that developed and controls revisions to the standard.

(B) The process by which revisions to the standard and changes to the membership of the governing body are made.

(C) An accounting of the revenue and sources of financial support for the entity, with sufficient detail to disclose any relationships that could reasonably be considered to present a potential conflict of interest.

Comment:

"Benefit corporation." The provisions of this chapter apply to a business corporation while it has the status of a benefit corporation because its articles contain a statement that it is a benefit corporation. If that statement is deleted as provided in section 105, the corporation will cease to be a benefit corporation immediately upon the effectiveness of the deletion.

"Benefit enforcement proceeding." This definition not only describes the action that may be brought under section 305, but it also has the effect of excluding other actions against a benefit corporation and its directors and officers because section 305(a) provides that no person may bring an action or assert a claim with respect to violation of the provisions of this chapter except in a benefit enforcement proceeding.

The obligations that may be enforced through a benefit enforcement proceeding include the obligations of a benefit corporation under section 402(b) to post its benefit reports on its Internet website and to supply copies of its benefit report if it does not have an Internet website. In the case of a failure to provide a copy of a benefit report, a benefit enforcement proceeding to enforce that obligation may only be brought by the persons listed in section 305 and not by the person requesting the copy of the report unless the person otherwise has standing under section 305.

"General public benefit." By requiring that the impact of a business on society and the environment be looked at "as a whole," the concept of general public benefit requires consideration of all of the effects of the business on society and the environment. What is involved in creating general public benefit is informed by section 301(a) which lists the specific interests and factors that the directors of a benefit corporation are required to consider.

"Minimum status vote." An amendment of the articles or a fundamental change that has the effect of changing the status of a corporation so that it either becomes a benefit corporation or ceases to be a benefit corporation must be approved by the minimum status vote. *See* sections 104 and 105. The purpose of requiring a two-thirds vote under this chapter is to ensure that there is broad shareholder support for an action. This definition will not be needed in states that require a supermajority vote of two-thirds or more for amendments of the articles or fundamental changes.

The second paragraph of the definition extends its policy to other forms of entities so that, for example, a merger of a limited liability company into a benefit corporation must be approved by the members of the limited liability company by at least a two-thirds vote. The second paragraph should be omitted by those states that require a supermajority vote of two-thirds or more by the owners of an unincorporated entity to approve a fundamental change. *See, e.g.,* Uniform Limited Liability Company Act (2006) (Last Amended 2013) § 1023, which requires a unanimous vote by the members of a limited liability company to approve a merger.

The two-thirds vote required by the definition is in addition to any other vote required in the case of any particular corporation or other form of entity. If the articles of a corporation were to require, for example, an 80% supermajority vote to approve a merger, a 70% vote to approve a merger of the corporation into a benefit corporation would be sufficient to satisfy the requirement that the merger be approved by the minimum status vote but would not be sufficient for valid approval of the merger.

"Specific public benefit." Every benefit corporation has the purpose under section 201(a) of creating general public benefit. A benefit corporation may also elect to pursue one or more specific public benefit purposes. Since the creation of specific public benefit is optional, paragraph (7) of this definition permits a benefit corporation to identify a specific public benefit that is different from those listed in paragraphs (1) through (6)

"Third-party standard." The requirement in section 401 that a benefit corporation prepare an annual benefit report that assesses its performance in creating general public benefit against a third-party standard provides an important protection against the abuse of benefit corporation status. The performance of a regular business corporation is measured by the financial statements that the corporation prepares. But the performance of a benefit corporation in creating general or specific public benefit will not be readily apparent from those financial statements. The annual benefit report is intended to permit an evaluation of that performance so that the shareholders can judge how the directors have discharged their responsibility to manage the corporation and thus whether the directors should be retained in office or the shareholders should take other action to change the way the corporation is managed. The annual benefit report is also intended to reduce "greenwashing" (the phenomenon of businesses seeking to portray themselves as being more environmentally and socially responsible than they actually are) by giving consumers and the general public a means of judging whether a business is living up to its claimed status as a benefit corporation.

The financial support that must be disclosed by an organization if it wishes to make available a third party standard should include investment income, grants, and other types of support in addition to revenue it receives from its operations.

§ 103. Incorporation of benefit corporation.

A benefit corporation shall be incorporated in accordance with [*cite incorporation provisions of the business corporation law*], but its articles of incorporation must also state that it is a benefit corporation.

Comment:

This section provides for how a corporation that is being newly formed may elect to be a benefit corporation. Existing corporations may become benefit corporations in the manner provided in section 104.

This chapter only applies to domestic business corporations. A foreign business corporation that has a status in its home jurisdiction similar to the status of a benefit corporation under this chapter is not subject to this chapter and has the status simply of a foreign business corporation for purposes of the state's business corporation law.

The term "benefit corporation" used in this section is defined in section 102.

§ 104. Election of benefit corporation status.

(a) Amendment. – An existing business corporation may become a benefit corporation under this [*chapter*] by amending its articles of incorporation so that they contain, in addition to the requirements of [*cite section of the business corporation law on the required contents of articles of incorporation*], a statement that the corporation is a benefit corporation. In order to be effective, the amendment must be adopted by at least the minimum status vote.

(b) Fundamental transactions. –

(1) Except as provided in paragraph (2), if a domestic entity that is not a benefit corporation is a party to a merger[, *consolidation, or conversion*] [*or the exchanging entity in a share exchange*] and the

surviving[, *new, or resulting*] entity in the merger, [*consolidation, conversion, or share exchange*] is to be a benefit corporation, the [*plan of*] merger[, *consolidation, conversion, or share exchange*] must be [*adopted*] [*approved*] by the domestic entity by at least the minimum status vote.

(2) Paragraph (1) does not apply in the case of a corporation that is a party to a merger if the shareholders of the corporation are not entitled to vote on the merger pursuant to [*cite section of the business corporation law authorizing "short form" mergers*].

Comment:

This section provides the procedures for an existing corporation to become a benefit corporation. A corporation that is being newly formed may become a benefit corporation in the manner provided in section 103. Subsection (a) applies to a business corporation that is directly electing to be a benefit corporation by amending its articles of incorporation. Subsection (b) applies when a corporation is becoming a benefit corporation indirectly in the context of a fundamental transaction. In both cases, the change to benefit corporation status must be approved by at least the minimum status vote.

Subsection (b) also applies to a domestic entity that is not a corporation when the

Entity is a party to a transaction that will result in a benefit corporation. In those situations, a supermajority vote of the owners of the entity is required by subsection (b).

See section 201(d) with respect to changing the identification of a specific public benefit that it is the purpose of a benefit corporation to pursue.

The following terms used in this section are defined in section 102:

"benefit corporation"
"minimum status vote"

§ 105. Termination of benefit corporation status.

(a) **Amendment.** – A benefit corporation may terminate its status as such and cease to be subject to this [*chapter*] by amending its articles of incorporation to delete the provision required by section 103 or 104 to be stated in the articles of a benefit corporation. In order to be effective, the amendment must be adopted by at least the minimum status vote.

(b) **Fundamental transactions.** –

(1) Except as provided in paragraph (2), if a [*plan of*] merger[*, consolidation, conversion, or share exchange*] would have the effect of terminating the status of a business corporation as a benefit corporation, the [*plan*] [*transaction*] must be adopted by at least the minimum status vote in order to be effective.

(2) Paragraph (1) does not apply in the case of a corporation that is a party to a merger if the shareholders of the corporation are not entitled to vote on the merger pursuant to [*cite section of the business corporation law authorizing "short form" mergers*].

(3) Any sale, lease, exchange, or other disposition of all or substantially all of the assets of a benefit corporation, unless the transaction is in the usual and regular course of business, shall not be effective unless the transaction is approved by at least the minimum status vote.

Comment:

This section provides the procedures for a benefit corporation to terminate voluntarily its status as a benefit corporation. As with an election of benefit corporation status under section 104, the termination may be accomplished either directly by an amendment of the articles or indirectly through a fundamental transaction.

Subsection (b)(3) provides a special rule for a sale of all or substantially all of the assets of a benefit corporation. Such a transaction will not result in a termination of the status of the corporation as a benefit corporation, but will have effectively the same result since it will terminate the operations of the business. Thus it was considered appropriate to require approval of a sale of assets by the minimum status vote. Whether a sale of assets is in the usual and regular course will be determined under the same standards as apply to that question under the state's business corporation law. *See, e.g.,* Model Business Corporation Act §§ 12.01 and 12.02.

The following terms used in this section are defined in section 102:

"benefit corporation"

"minimum status vote"

Subchapter 2

Corporate Purposes

Section

201. Corporate purposes.

§ 201. Corporate purposes.

(a) **General public benefit purpose.** – A benefit corporation shall have a purpose of creating general public benefit. This purpose is in addition to its purpose under [*cite section of the business corporation law on the purpose of business corporations*].

(b) **Optional specific public benefit purpose.** – The articles of incorporation of a benefit corporation may identify one or more specific public benefits that it is the purpose of the benefit corporation to create in addition to its purposes under [*cite section of the business corporation law on the purpose of business corporations*] and subsection (a). The identification of a specific public benefit under this subsection does not limit the purpose of a benefit corporation to create general public benefit under subsection (a).

(c) **Effect of purposes.** – The creation of general public benefit and specific public benefit under subsections (a) and (b) is in the best interests of the benefit corporation.

(d) Amendment. – A benefit corporation may amend its articles of incorporation to add, amend, or delete the identification of a specific public benefit that it is the purpose of the benefit corporation to create. In order to be effective, the amendment must be adopted by at least the minimum status vote.

(e) Professional corporations. – A professional corporation that is a benefit corporation does not violate [*cite section of professional corporation law, if any, that restricts the business in which a professional corporation may engage*] by having the purpose to create general public benefit or a specific public benefit.

Comment:

Every benefit corporation has the corporate purpose of creating general public benefit. A benefit corporation may also elect to pursue specific public benefits under subsection (b).

Subsection (c) confirms that pursuing general and specific public benefit is in the best interests of the benefit corporation. Because the basic duty of a director is to act in a manner that the director reasonably believes to be in the best interests of the corporation, decisions by the board of directors that promote the creation of general or specific public benefit will satisfy the requirement to act in the best interests of the corporation. If an ordinary business corporation includes in its articles of incorporation a statement of a specific purpose, it is by definition in the best interests of the corporation for the directors to pursue that purpose. Thus the rule in subsection (c) would be the case in any event with respect to specific public benefit purposes, but specific public benefits have been referred to expressly in subsection (c) to avoid the confusion that might result if subsection (c) only referred to the creation of general public benefit.

Some professional corporation statutes provide that a professional corporation may not engage in any business other than rendering the professional service for which it was specifically incorporated. Subsection (e) makes clear that such a limitation will not interfere with a professional corporation electing to be a benefit corporation. In such a case, the professional corporation (such as a law firm, accounting firm, or medical practice) will be limited to providing the professional services for which it was incorporated, but it will be able to provide those services in a manner that creates general public benefit or a specific public benefit (for example, a medical practice that focuses on providing care for low-income individuals).

The following terms used in this section are defined in section 102:

"benefit corporation"
"general public benefit"
"minimum status vote"
specific public benefit"

Subchapter 3

Accountability

Section
301. Standard of conduct for directors.
302. Benefit director.
303. Standard of conduct for officers.
304. Benefit officer.
305. Right of action.

§ 301. Standard of conduct for directors.

(a) Consideration of interests. – In discharging the duties of their respective positions and in considering the best interests of the benefit corporation, the board of directors, committees of the board, and individual directors of a benefit corporation:

(1) shall consider the effects of any action or inaction upon:

(i) the shareholders of the benefit corporation;

(ii) the employees and work force of the benefit corporation, its subsidiaries, and its suppliers;

(iii) the interests of customers as beneficiaries of the general public benefit or a specific public benefit purpose of the benefit corporation;

(iv) community and societal factors, including those of each community in which offices or facilities of the benefit corporation, its subsidiaries, or its suppliers are located;

(v) the local and global environment;

(vi) the short-term and long-term interests of the benefit corporation, including benefits that may accrue to the benefit corporation from its long-term plans and the possibility that these interests may be best served by the continued independence of the benefit corporation; and

(vii) the ability of the benefit corporation to accomplish its general public benefit purpose and any specific public benefit purpose; and

(2)   may consider:

[(i)   *the interests referred to in [cite constituencies provision of the business corporation law if it refers to constituencies not listed above]; and*

(ii)] other pertinent factors or the interests of any other group that they deem appropriate; but

(3) need not give priority to a particular interest or factor referred to in paragraph (1) or (2) over any other interest or factor unless the benefit corporation has stated in its articles of incorporation its intention to give priority to certain interests or factors related to the accomplishment of its general public benefit purpose or of a specific public benefit purpose identified in its articles.

(b) Coordination with other provisions of law. 531 –The consideration of interests and factors in the manner provided by subsection (a)[:

(1)] does not constitute a violation of [*cite provision of the business corporation law on the duties of directors generally*] [*; and*

(2) is in addition to the ability of directors to consider interests and factors as provided in [cite constituencies provision of the business corporation law]].

(c) **Exoneration from personal liability.** – Except as provided in the [*articles of incorporation*] [*bylaws*], a director is not personally liable for monetary damages for:

(1) any action or inaction in the course of performing the duties of a director under subsection (a) if the director was not interested with respect to the action or inaction; or

(2) failure of the benefit corporation to pursue or create general public benefit or specific public benefit.

(d) **Limitation on standing.** – A director does not have a duty to a person that is a beneficiary of the general public benefit purpose or a specific public benefit purpose of a benefit corporation arising from the status of the person as a beneficiary.

(e) **Business judgments.** – A director who makes a business judgment in good faith fulfills the duty under this section if the director:

(1) is not interested in the subject of the business judgment;

(2) is informed with respect to the subject of the business judgment to the extent the director reasonably believes to be appropriate under the circumstances; and

(3) rationally believes that the business judgment is in the best interests of the benefit corporation.

Comment:

This section is at the heart of what it means to be a benefit corporation. By requiring the consideration of interests of constituencies other than the shareholders, the section rejects the holdings in *Dodge v. Ford*, 170 N.W. 668 (Mich. 1919), and *eBay Domestic Holdings, Inc. v. Newmark*, 16 A.3d

1 (Del. Ch. 2010), that directors must maximize the financial value of a corporation.

In a state that has adopted a "constituency statute," directors are authorized to consider the interests of corporate constituencies other than the shareholders, but the directors are not *required* to do so. Subsection (a) makes it mandatory for the directors of a benefit corporation to consider the interests and factors that they would otherwise simply be permitted to consider in their discretion under the typical constituency statute.

Subsection (d) negates any enforceable duty of directors to non-shareholder constituents. *But see* section 305(b) which permits a benefit corporation to provide in its articles that an identified category of persons may bring a benefit enforcement proceeding. If a benefit corporation were to do so, the identified non-shareholder constituents would be able to allege a breach of duty by the directors under this chapter for failing to pursue or create general or specific public benefit, but subsection (d) would prevent those constituents from alleging a breach of duty to them.

Subsection (e) confirms that the business judgment rule applies to actions by directors under this section. The formulation of the rule is patterned after American Law

Institute, Principles of Corporate Governance: Analysis and Recommendations § 4.01(c). If the law of the enacting state is not clear that the business judgment rule applies generally to actions by directors of corporations that are not business corporations, consideration should be given to confirming that the rule applies more broadly than just under this chapter. The best interests of the corporation referred to in subsection (e) (3) include the creation of general public benefit and specific public benefit as provided in section 201(c) and the determination of what is in the best interests of the benefit corporation requires consideration of the interests and factors listed in subsection (a).

The following terms used in this section are defined in section 102:

"benefit corporation"
"general public benefit"

"specific public benefit"

"subsidiary"

§ 302. Benefit director.

(a) **General rule.** – The board of directors of a benefit corporation may include a director who:

(1) is designated the benefit director; and

(2) has, in addition to the powers, duties, rights, and immunities of the other directors of the benefit corporation, the powers, duties, rights, and immunities provided in this [*chapter*].

(b) **Election, removal, and qualifications.** – A benefit director shall be elected, and may be removed, in the manner provided by [*cite provisions of the business corporation law on the election and removal of directors generally*]. [*Except as provided in subsection (f),*] a benefit director shall be an individual who is independent. A benefit director may serve as the benefit officer at the same time as serving as the benefit director. The articles of incorporation or bylaws of a benefit corporation may prescribe additional qualifications of a benefit director not inconsistent with this subsection.

(c) **Annual compliance statement.** – The benefit director shall prepare, and the benefit corporation shall include in the annual benefit report to shareholders required by section 401, a report from the benefit director on all of the following:

(1) Whether the benefit corporation acted in accordance with its general public benefit purpose and any specific public benefit purpose in all material respects during the period covered by the report.

(2) Whether the directors and officers complied with sections 301(a) and 303(a), respectively.

(3) If the benefit director believes that the benefit corporation or its directors or officers failed to act or comply in the manner described in paragraphs (1) and (2), a description of the ways in which the benefit corporation or its directors or officers failed to act or comply.

(d) **Status of actions.** – The act or inaction of an individual in the capacity of a benefit director shall constitute for all purposes an act or inaction of that individual in the capacity of a director of the benefit corporation.

(e) **Exoneration from personal liability.** – Regardless of whether the articles of incorporation or bylaws of a benefit corporation include a provision eliminating or limiting the personal liability of directors authorized by [*cite section of the business corporation law permitting exoneration of directors*], a benefit director shall not be personally liable for an act or omission in the capacity of a benefit director unless the act or omission constitutes self-dealing, willful misconduct, or a knowing violation of law.

[*(f) Professional Corporations. – The benefit director of a professional corporation does not need to be independent.*]

Comment:

The designation of a benefit director is optional. But if a benefit director is designated, one of the duties of that director will be to prepare the annual compliance statement required by subsection (c). The statement of the benefit director required by subsection (c) is an important part of the transparency required under this chapter. The perspective of the benefit director on whether the corporation has been successful in pursuing its general and any named specific public benefit purpose will be an important source of information for the shareholders as to whether the directors have adequately discharged their stewardship of the benefit corporation and its resources.

Subsection (d) makes clear that the actions of a benefit director are actions of a director of the benefit corporation and are subject to the same standards as actions of directors generally.

The wording of subsection (e) should be conformed to the provision of the state's business corporation law that permits the shareholders to adopt a provision of the articles of incorporation or bylaws exonerating directors from liability for breach of duty. But unlike existing exoneration provisions, subsection (e) does not require the benefit corporation to adopt an implementing provision in the articles or bylaws. Instead the liability shield provided by subsection (e) automatically applies to all benefit directors.

The following terms used in this section are defined in section 102:

"benefit corporation"

"benefit director"

"benefit officer"

"general public benefit"

"independent"

"publicly traded corporation"

"specific public benefit"

§ 303. Standard of conduct for officers.

(a) **General rule.** – Each officer of a benefit corporation shall consider the interests and factors described in section 301(a)(1) in the manner provided in section 301(a)(3) if:

(1) the officer has discretion to act with respect to a matter; and

(2) it reasonably appears to the officer that the matter may have a material effect on the creation by the benefit corporation of general public benefit or a specific public benefit identified in the articles of incorporation of the benefit corporation.

(b) **Coordination with other provisions of law.** – The consideration of interests and factors in the manner provided in subsection (a) shall not constitute a violation of [*cite provision, if any, of the business corporation law on the duties of officers*] [*the duties of an officer*].

(c) **Exoneration from personal liability.** – Except as provided in the [*articles of incorporation*] [*bylaws*], an officer is not personally liable for monetary damages for:

(1) an action or inaction as an officer in the course of performing the duties of an officer under subsection (a) if the officer was not interested with respect to the action or inaction; or

(2) failure of the benefit corporation to pursue or create general public benefit or specific public benefit.

(d) Limitation on standing. – An officer does not have a duty to a person that is a beneficiary of the general public benefit purpose or a specific public benefit purpose of a benefit corporation arising from the status of the person as a beneficiary.

(e) Business judgments. – An officer who makes a business judgment in good faith fulfills the duty under this section if the officer:

(1) is not interested in the subject of the business judgment;

(2) is informed with respect to the subject of the business judgment to the extent the officer reasonably believes to be appropriate under the circumstances; and

(3) rationally believes that the business judgment is in the best interests of the benefit corporation.

Comment:

As an agent of the corporation, an officer is generally required to follow the instructions of his or her principal. But in those instances where an officer has discretion to act with a respect to a matter, subsection (a) requires the officer to consider the interests of the benefit corporation's constituencies in the same manner as required of the directors by section 301.

This section applies to all of the officers of a benefit corporation and is not limited just to the benefit officer, if any, of the benefit corporation.

Subsection (c) provides an exoneration from personal liability for officers similar to the exoneration provided for directors. If the law of the enacting state is not clear that officers can be exonerated in the same manner as directors, consideration should be given to confirming that officers of business corporations that are not benefit corporations may be exonerated. *See also* the Comment to section 301(d) with respect to subsection (d).

Subsection (e) confirms that the business judgment rule applies to actions by officers under this section. The formulation of the rule is patterned after American Law Institute, Principles of Corporate Governance: Analysis and Recommendations § 4.01(c). If the law of the enacting state is not clear that the business judgment rule applies generally to actions by officers of corporations, consideration should be given to confirming that the rule applies more broadly than just under this chapter. The best interests of the corporation referred to in subsection (e)(3) include the creation of general public benefit and specific public benefit under section 201(c) and the determination of what is in the best interests of the benefit corporation requires consideration of the interests and factors listed in section 301(a) (as provided by subsection (a)).

The following terms used in this section are defined in section 102:

"benefit corporation"
"benefit officer"
"general public benefit"
"specific public benefit"

§ 304. Benefit officer.

(a) **Designation.** – A benefit corporation may have an officer designated the benefit officer.

(b) **Functions.** – A benefit officer shall have:

(1) the powers and duties relating to the purpose of the corporation to create general public benefit or specific public benefit provided:

(i) by the bylaws; or

(ii) absent controlling provisions in the bylaws, by resolution or order of the board of directors.

(2) the duty to prepare the benefit report required by section 401.

Comment:

The designation of a benefit officer is optional. But if a benefit officer is designated, one of the duties of that officer will be to prepare the annual benefit report required by section 401.

The following terms used in this section are defined in section 102:

"benefit corporation"
"benefit officer"
"general public benefit"
"specific public benefit"

§ 305. Right of action.

(a) General rule. – Except in a benefit enforcement proceeding, no person may bring an action or assert a claim with respect to:

(1) failure of a benefit corporation to pursue or create general public benefit or a specific public benefit set forth in its articles of incorporation; or

(2) violation of an obligation, duty, or standard of conduct under this [*chapter*].

(b) Standing. – A benefit enforcement proceeding may be commenced or maintained only:

(1) directly by the benefit corporation; or

(2) derivatively [*in accordance with [cite sections of business corporation law on derivative suits]*] by:

(i) a person or group of persons that owned beneficially or of record at least 2% of the total number of shares of a class or series outstanding at the time of the act or omission complained of; or

(ii) a person or group of persons that owned beneficially or of record 5% or more of the outstanding equity interests in an entity of which the benefit corporation is a subsidiary at the time of the act or omission complained of.

(c) Beneficial ownership. – For purposes of this section, a person is the beneficial owner of shares or equity interests if the shares or equity interests are held in a voting trust or by a nominee on behalf of the beneficial owner.

Comment:

This section limits actions to enforce this chapter just to suits against the directors, but it broadens the categories of persons that can bring a derivative suit to include 5% owners of a parent entity of a benefit corporation. To reduce the possibility of nuisance suits, a shareholder or group of shareholders bringing a derivative suit must own at least 2% of the outstanding shares of the benefit corporation.

This section only applies to actions or claims arising under this chapter. Lawsuits for breaches of duty arising outside of this chapter, or for breach of contract by directors, officers, or the benefit corporation are not subject to this section.

The following terms used in this section are defined in section 102:

"benefit corporation"
"benefit enforcement proceeding"
"general public benefit"
"specific public benefit"
"subsidiary"

Subchapter 4

Transparency

Section

401. Preparation of annual benefit report.

402. Availability of annual benefit report.

§ 401. Preparation of annual benefit report.

(a) Contents. – A benefit corporation shall prepare an annual benefit report including all of the following:

(1) A narrative description of:

(i) The ways in which the benefit corporation pursued general public benefit during the year and the extent to which general public benefit was created.

(ii) Both:

(A) the ways in which the benefit corporation pursued a specific public benefit that the articles of incorporation state it is the purpose of the benefit corporation to create; and

(B) the extent to which that specific public benefit was created.

(iii) Any circumstances that have hindered the creation by the benefit corporation of general public benefit or specific public benefit.

(iv) The process and rationale for selecting or changing the third-party standard used to prepare the benefit report.

(2) An assessment of the overall social and environmental performance of the benefit corporation determined taking into account the impacts of the benefit corporation reported against a third-party standard:

(i) applied consistently with any application of that standard in prior benefit reports; or

(ii) accompanied by an explanation of the reasons for:

(A) any inconsistent application; or

(B) the change to that standard from the one used in the immediately prior report

(3) The name of the benefit director and the benefit officer, if any, and the address to which correspondence to each of them may be directed.

(4) The compensation paid by the benefit corporation during the year to each director in the capacity of a director.

(5) The statement of the benefit director described in section 302(c).

(6) A statement of any connection between the organization that established the third-party standard, or its directors, officers or any holder of 5% or more of the governance interests in the organization, and the benefit corporation or its directors, officers or any holder of 5% or more of the outstanding shares of the benefit corporation, including any financial or governance relationship which might materially affect the credibility of the use of the third-party standard.

(b) **Change of benefit director.** – If, during the year covered by a benefit report, a benefit director resigned from or refused to stand for reelection to the position of benefit director, or was removed from the position of benefit director, and the benefit director furnished the benefit corporation with any written correspondence concerning the circumstances surrounding the resignation, refusal, or removal, the benefit report shall include that correspondence as an exhibit.

(c) **Audit not required.** – Neither the benefit report nor the assessment of the performance of the benefit corporation in the benefit report required by subsection (a)(2) needs to be audited or certified by a third party.

Comment:

A benefit corporation may change from year to year the standard it uses under subsection (a)(2) for assessing its performance. But if a benefit corporation uses the same standard for assessing its performance in more than one year, the standard must either be applied consistently or the benefit corporation must provide an explanation of the reasons for any inconsistent use of the standard.

Subsection (b) is patterned after Item 5.02(a)(2) of Form 8-K under the Securities Exchange Act of 1934.

The following terms used in this section are defined in section 102:

"benefit corporation"
"benefit director"
"general public benefit"
"specific public benefit"
"third-party standard"

§ 402. Availability of annual benefit report.

(a) **Timing of report.** – A benefit corporation shall send its annual benefit report to each shareholder on the earlier of:

    (1) 120 days following the end of the fiscal year of the benefit corporation; or

    (2) the same time that the benefit corporation delivers any other annual report to its shareholders.

(b) **Internet website posting.** – A benefit corporation shall post all of its benefit reports on the public portion of its Internet website, if any; but the compensation paid to directors and financial or proprietary information included in the benefit reports may be omitted from the benefit reports as posted.

(c) **Availability of copies.** – If a benefit corporation does not have an Internet website, the benefit corporation shall provide a copy of its most recent benefit report, without charge, to any person that requests a copy, but the compensation paid to directors and financial or proprietary information included in the benefit report may be omitted from the copy of the benefit report provided.

(d) **Filing of report.** – Concurrently with the delivery of the benefit report to shareholders under subsection (a), the benefit corporation shall deliver a copy of the benefit report to the [*Secretary of State*] for filing, but the compensation paid to directors and financial or proprietary information included in the benefit report may be omitted from the benefit report as delivered to the [*Secretary of State*]. The [*Secretary of State*] shall charge a fee of $__ for filing a benefit report.

Comment:

Subsection (b) requires a benefit corporation to post all of its annual benefit reports on its website, but subsection (c) only requires that the most recent benefit report be supplied if the benefit corporation does not have a website.

The term "benefit corporation" used in this section is defined in section 102.

"benefit corporation"
"benefit director"

Delaware General Corporation Law Subchapter XV

PUBLIC BENEFIT CORPORATIONS

§ 361 Law applicable to public benefit corporations; how formed.

This subchapter applies to all public benefit corporations, as defined in § 362 of this title. If a corporation elects to become a public benefit corporation under this subchapter in the manner prescribed in this subchapter, it shall be subject in all respects to the provisions of this chapter, except to the extent this subchapter imposes additional or different requirements, in which case such requirements shall apply.

§ 362 Public benefit corporation defined; contents of certificate of incorporation.

(a) A "public benefit corporation" is a for-profit corporation organized under and subject to the requirements of this chapter that is intended to produce a public benefit or public benefits and to operate in a responsible and sustainable manner. To that end, a public benefit corporation shall be managed in a manner that balances the stockholders' pecuniary interests, the best interests of those materially affected by the corporation's conduct, and the public benefit or public benefits identified in its certificate of incorporation. In the certificate of incorporation, a public benefit corporation shall:

(1) Identify within its statement of business or purpose pursuant to § 102(a)(3) of this title 1 or more specific public benefits to be promoted by the corporation; and

(2) State within its heading that it is a public benefit corporation.

(b) "Public benefit" means a positive effect (or reduction of negative effects) on 1 or more categories of persons, entities, communities or interests (other than stockholders in their capacities as stockholders) including, but not limited to, effects of an artistic, charitable, cultural, economic, educational, environmental, literary, medical, religious, scientific or technological nature. "Public benefit provisions" means the provisions of a certificate of incorporation contemplated by this subchapter.

(c) The name of the public benefit corporation may contain the words "public benefit corporation," or the abbreviation "P.B.C.," or the designation "PBC," which shall be deemed to satisfy the requirements of § 102(a)(l)(i) of this title. If the name does not contain such language, the corporation shall, prior to issuing unissued shares of stock or disposing of treasury shares, provide notice to any person to whom such stock is issued or who acquires such treasury shares that it is a public benefit corporation; provided that such notice need not be provided if the issuance or disposal is pursuant to an offering registered under the Securities Act of 1933 [15 U.S.C. § 77r et seq.] or if, at the time of issuance or disposal, the corporation has a class of securities that is registered under the Securities Exchange Act of 1934 [15 U.S.C. § 78a et seq.].

§ 363 Certain amendments and mergers; votes required; appraisal rights

(a) Notwithstanding any other provisions of this chapter, a corporation that is not a public benefit corporation, may not, without the approval of 2/3 of the outstanding stock of the corporation entitled to vote thereon:

    (1) Amend its certificate of incorporation to include a provision authorized by § 362(a)(1) of this title; or

    (2) Merge or consolidate with or into another entity if, as a result of such merger or consolidation, the shares in such corporation would become, or be converted into or exchanged for the right to receive, shares or other equity interests in a domestic or foreign public benefit corporation or similar entity.

    The restrictions of this section shall not apply prior to the time that the corporation has received payment for any of its capital stock, or in the case of a nonstock corporation, prior to the time that it has members.

(b) Any stockholder of a corporation that is not a public benefit corporation that holds shares of stock of such corporation immediately prior to the effective time of:

    (1) An amendment to the corporation's certificate of incorporation to include a provision authorized by § 362(a)(1) of this title; or

    (2) A merger or consolidation that would result in the conversion of the corporation's stock into or exchange of the corporation's stock for the right to receive shares or other equity interests in a domestic or foreign public benefit corporation or similar entity; and has neither voted in favor of such amendment or such merger or consolidation nor consented thereto in writing pursuant to § 228 of this title, shall be entitled to an appraisal by the Court of Chancery of the fair value of the stockholder's shares of stock; provided, however, that no appraisal rights under this section shall be available for the shares of any class or series of stock, which stock, or depository receipts in respect thereof, at the record date fixed to determine

the stockholders entitled to receive notice of the meeting of stockholders to act upon the agreement of merger or consolidation, or
amendment, were either: (i) listed on a national securities exchange
or (ii) held of record by more than 2,000 holders, unless, in the case
of a merger or consolidation, the holders thereof are required by the
terms of an agreement of merger or consolidation to accept for such
stock anything except (A) shares of stock of any other corporation,
or depository receipts in respect thereof, which shares of stock (or
depository receipts in respect thereof) or depository receipts at the
effective date of the merger or consolidation will be either listed on
a national securities exchange or held of record by more than 2,000
holders; (B) cash in lieu of fractional shares or fractional depository
receipts described in the foregoing clause (A); or (C) any combination of the shares of stock, depository receipts and cash in lieu of
fractional shares or fractional depository receipts described in the
foregoing clauses (A) and (B).

(c) Notwithstanding any other provisions of this chapter, a corporation
that is a public benefit corporation may not, without the approval of
2/3 of the outstanding stock of the corporation entitled to vote thereon:

(1) Amend its certificate of incorporation to delete or amend a provision
authorized by § 362(a)(1) or § 366(c) of this title; or

(2) Merge or consolidate with or into another entity if, as a result of
such merger or consolidation, the shares in such corporation would
become, or be converted into or exchanged for the right to receive,
shares or other equity interests in a domestic or foreign corporation that is not a public benefit corporation or similar entity and
the certificate of incorporation (or similar governing instrument)
of which does not contain the identical provisions identifying the
public benefit or public benefits pursuant to § 362(a) of this title or
imposing requirements pursuant to § 366(c) of this title.

(d) Notwithstanding the foregoing, a nonprofit nonstock corporation may
not be a constituent corporation to any merger or consolidation governed by this section.

§ 364 Stock certificates; notices regarding uncertificated stock.

Any stock certificate issued by a public benefit corporation shall note conspicuously that the corporation is a public benefit corporation formed pursuant to this subchapter. Any notice given by a public benefit corporation pursuant to § 151(f) of this title shall state conspicuously that the corporation is a public benefit corporation formed pursuant to this subchapter.

§ 365 Duties of directors.

(a) The board of directors shall manage or direct the business and affairs of the public benefit corporation in a manner that balances the pecuniary interests of the stockholders, the best interests of those materially affected by the corporation's conduct, and the specific public benefit or public benefits identified in its certificate of incorporation.

(b) A director of a public benefit corporation shall not, by virtue of the public benefit provisions or § 362(a) of this title, have any duty to any person on account of any interest of such person in the public benefit or public benefits identified in the certificate of incorporation or on account of any interest materially affected by the corporation's conduct and, with respect to a decision implicating the balance requirement in subsection (a) of this section, will be deemed to satisfy such director's fiduciary duties to stockholders and the corporation if such director's decision is both informed and disinterested and not such that no person of ordinary, sound judgment would approve.

(c) The certificate of incorporation of a public benefit corporation may include a provision that any disinterested failure to satisfy this section shall not, for the purposes of § 102(b)(7) or § 145 of this title, constitute an act or omission not in good faith, or a breach of the duty of loyalty.

§ 366 Periodic statements and third-party certification.

(a) A public benefit corporation shall include in every notice of a meeting of stockholders a statement to the effect that it is a public benefit corporation formed pursuant to this subchapter.

(b) A public benefit corporation shall no less than biennially provide its stockholders with a statement as to the corporation's promotion of the public benefit or public benefits identified in the certificate of incorporation and of the best interests of those materially affected by the corporation's conduct. The statement shall include:

   (1) The objectives the board of directors has established to promote such public benefit or public benefits and interests;

   (2) The standards the board of directors has adopted to measure the corporation's progress in promoting such public benefit or public benefits and interests;

   (3) Objective factual information based on those standards regarding the corporation's success in meeting the objectives for promoting such public benefit or public benefits and interests; and

   (4) An assessment of the corporation's success in meeting the objectives and promoting such public benefit or public benefits and interests.

(c) The certificate of incorporation or bylaws of a public benefit corporation may require that the corporation:

   (1) Provide the statement described in subsection (b) of this section more frequently than biennially;

   (2) Make the statement described in subsection (b) of this section available to the public; and/or

   (3) Use a third-party standard in connection with and/or attain a periodic third-party certification addressing the corporation's promotion of the public benefit or public benefits identified in the certificate of incorporation and/or the best interests of those materially affected by the corporation's conduct.

§ 367 Derivative suits.

Stockholders of a public benefit corporation owning individually or collectively, as of the date of instituting such derivative suit, at least 2% of the corporation's outstanding shares or, in the case of a corporation with shares listed on a national securities exchange, the lesser of such percentage or shares of at least $2,000,000 in market value, may maintain a derivative lawsuit to enforce the requirements set forth in § 365(a) of this title.

§ 368 No effect on other corporations.

This subchapter shall not affect a statute or rule of law that is applicable to a corporation that is not a public benefit corporation, except as provided in § 363 of this title.

Quick Guide to Becoming a Delaware PBC

This outline describes the major steps required for an existing Delaware corporation to become a Delaware public benefit corporation.

1. Summary. In order to become a public benefit corporation (PBC), a traditional Delaware corporation must draft an amendment to its certificate of incorporation. The amendment must be approved by the board of directors and then by the shareholders. Once approved, the amendment must be filed with the Secretary of State of Delaware. Under certain circumstances, the corporation must provide its shareholders who do not approve the amendment with the right to cash out their stock for fair value (known as appraisal rights). Once the amendment is filed, the corporation should include a legend on its stock certificates, stating that the corporation is a PBC. A newly forming corporation may simply file its initial certificate of incorporation as a PBC.

2. Contents of Amendment. The following certificate provisions are either required or should be considered:

   2.1. The heading of the certificate must state that the corporation is a public benefit corporation.

2.2. The name of the corporation may be changed to include the words "public benefit corporation," the abbreviation "P.B.C.," or the designation "PBC." If the name does not include such indicators, then if the PBC is not publicly traded, the PBC must notify anyone who purchases stock that the corporation is a PBC.

2.3. The certificate must identify one or more specific public benefits to be promoted by the corporation.

2.4. Delaware gives a PBC the option of committing, in the certificate of incorporation or bylaws, to make its statement about its efforts to create public benefit either (1) available to the public (as opposed to its shareholders only); (2) annually (as opposed to biennially); or (3) in accordance with a third-party standard (as opposed to using its own methodology).

2.5. Delaware permits a PBC to include in its certificate a provision that a disinterested failure by a director to satisfy the requirements applicable to directors of a public benefit corporation will not constitute an act or omission not in good faith or a breach of the duty of loyalty. The purpose of such a provision is to protect directors and should be considered by any corporation considering an election to be a public benefit corporation. See the sample language in appendix D.

Note: The Delaware statute will permit the provisions described in 2.4 to be placed in the bylaws instead of the certificate. Placing them in the certificate of incorporation will make them more difficult to change.

3. Board approval. The board of directors must approve the amendment and recommend that the amendment be submitted to the shareholders for approval. The certificate of incorporation and bylaws should be reviewed to determine the vote required.

4. Shareholder approval. The shareholders must approve the amendment. The statute requires a two-thirds affirmative vote of the outstanding shares of the corporation. The certificate of incorporation and bylaws should be reviewed to determine whether any additional vote is required.

5. Appraisal rights. If the corporation is not publicly traded, shareholders who did not vote for an amendment are entitled to a Delaware Court of Chancery appraisal of the fair market value of the shareholders' stock. The corporation is required to provide its shareholders with notice of their right to an appraisal. See appendix D for details regarding the process and requirements for appraisal rights in Delaware.

6. File Amendment. After the board and shareholders approve the amendment, the amendment must be prepared and filed with the secretary of state.

7. Print and issue new stock certificates. Delaware law requires that a stock certificate issued by a PBC note conspicuously that the corporation is a PBC. It is unclear whether that requirement applies to stock certificates issued before a corporation becomes a PBC. To avoid a later challenge by a person that acquires shares represented by a stock certificate without that notation, the corporation should consider printing new stock certificates with the required notation and issuing the new stock certificates to its existing shareholders.

8. Name change. If the PBC has adopted a new name, it should make the necessary changes to reflect the new name. The corporation should update, for example, bank accounts, business cards, registrations, and so forth. There is no set timing for completion of these changes; however, a corporation should aim to complete them within a commercially reasonable time following the PBC election.

Public Benefit Corporation Charter Provisions

Purpose Clause

Public Benefit Corporation. The Corporation shall be a public benefit corporation as contemplated by subchapter XV of the Delaware General Corporation Law (the "DGCL"), or any successor provisions, that it is intended to operate in a responsible and sustainable manner and to produce a public benefit or benefits, and is to be managed in a manner that balances the stockholders' pecuniary interests, the best interests of those materially affected by the corporation's conduct and the public benefit or benefits identified in this certificate of incorporation. If the DGCL is amended to alter or further define the management and operation of public benefit corporations, then the corporation shall be managed and operated in accordance with the DGCL, as so amended.

The purposes of the Corporation are (a) to engage in any lawful act or activity for which a corporation may be organized under the Delaware General Corporation Law and (b) to promote a positive effect (or reduce negative effects) [state affected persons, entities, communities or interests and effects constituting the corporation's specific public benefit(s), which may include (without limitation) effects of an artistic, charitable, cultural, economic, educational, environmental, literary, medical, religious, scientific or technological nature].

Liability Limitation*

To the fullest extent permitted by law, a director of the Corporation shall not be personally liable to the Corporation or its stockholders for monetary damages for breach of fiduciary duty as a director. If the Delaware General Corporation Law is amended to authorize corporate action further eliminating or limiting the personal liability of directors, then the liability of a director of the Corporation shall be eliminated or limited to the fullest extent permitted by the Delaware General Corporation Law, as so amended.

Any disinterested failure to satisfy DGCL § 365 shall not, for the purposes of Sections 102(b)(7) or 145 of the DGCL, or for the purposes of any use of the term "good faith" in this certificate of incorporation or the bylaws in regard to the indemnification or advancement of expenses of officers, directors, employees and agents, constitute an act or omission not in good faith, or a breach of the duty of loyalty. Any repeal or modification of this ARTICLE [_____] shall not adversely affect any right or protection of a director of the Corporation existing at the time of such repeal or modification.

*When adding this provision, indemnification contracts with directors and officers should be reviewed to ensure that any use of the term "good faith" is appropriately modified to include the broadened concept of Section 365.

Quick Guide to Appraisal for Public Benefit Corporations

A ppraisal rights are a statutory remedy available to shareholders who object to certain extraordinary actions taken by a corporation (such as mergers, and now, under the PBCS, charter amendments to elect PBC status or similar events). This remedy allows shareholders to require the corporation to buy their stock at a price equal to its fair market value (plus interest) as of the time immediately before the extraordinary corporate action is taken.

The Corporation's Obligations Relating to Appraisal Rights

Vote at a shareholder meeting. If the event is to be submitted for approval at a meeting of the shareholders, the corporation must:

- ▶ notify all of the shareholders (as of the record date for notice) at least 20 days prior to the meeting that appraisal rights are available;

- ▶ include in the notice a copy of Section 262 of the DGCL; and

- ▶ include in the notice all information material to the shareholders' decision whether to seek appraisal.

Approval by written consent. If the event is approved by written consent of the shareholders (in accordance with DGCL § 228), the corporation must:

- ► before the effective date of the event or within 10 days thereafter, notify each shareholder of the approval of the event and that appraisal rights are available;

- ► include in the notice a copy of Section 262 of the DGCL;

- ► include in the notice all information material to the shareholders' decision whether to seek appraisal; and

- ► notify such shareholders of the effective date of the event if given on or after the effective date.

How a Shareholder Perfects Appraisal Rights

To perfect appraisal rights in Delaware, a shareholder must comply with all of the following procedures:

- ► *Demand appraisal.* The shareholder must file a written demand for appraisal with the corporation before the shareholder vote on the event (or, if the event is approved by written consent, within 20 days of the appraisal notice).

- ► *Not vote in favor of or consent to the event.* The shareholder must either vote against the event or abstain from the vote.

- ► *Maintain continuous record ownership.* The shareholder making the demand must be the record (registered) holder of the stock from the date of the demand for appraisal through the effective date of the event.

- ► *File a petition with the Delaware Court of Chancery and serve a copy of the petition on the corporation.* Within 120 days after the effective date of the event, the shareholder must file a petition with the Court of Chancery and demand that it determine the value of the stock of all shareholders. It is not necessary for all dissenting shareholders to file the petition, but one shareholder (or the corporation) must file to start the proceeding to determine the fair value of the corporation's stock (DGCL § 262[e]). All dissenting shareholders share in the cost of the proceeding.

How a Corporation Must Respond to a Demand for Appraisal Rights

The corporation must follow certain procedures set out in the statute when responding to a demand for appraisal. These requirements include:

▶ Providing a statement stating the aggregate number of shares for which demands for appraisal have been received if requested by a shareholder who has perfected the right to an appraisal. This statement must be provided within ten days of the request (DGCL § 262[e]).

▶ Filing a verified list of shareholders who have demanded appraisal with the office of the Register in Chancery within 20 days from receiving service of the appraisal petition (DGCL § 262[f]).

Rubric for Board Decision Making of a Delaware Public Benefit Corporation

Summary

In 2013, Delaware adopted legislation authorizing a corporation created in Delaware to become a public benefit corporation (PBC). The new law (like its counterparts, now adopted in more than thirty U.S. jurisdictions) allows for-profit companies to operate in a manner that sustainably creates long-term value for its stakeholders and others. Specifically, the Delaware law defines a PBC as a for-profit corporation that is intended to produce a public benefit or benefits and to operate in a responsible and sustainable manner.

The statute does not define "responsible and sustainable," but instead mandates that the directors must balance the interests of its stockholders with the public benefits it has identified in its charter, and the interests of those materially affected by the corporation's conduct. The Delaware law gives directors broad discretion with respect to such balancing, and allows corporations to eliminate monetary liability for disinterested directors making such balancing decisions.

The statute also requires that the corporation provide its stockholders with a "benefit report" at least once every two years. The report must include:

- the sustainability objectives established by the board;

- standards adopted to measure progress in promoting those objectives;

- factual information based on those standards, regarding the corporation's success in meeting the standards; and

- an assessment of the corporation's success in meeting the standards.

Thus, in order to operate in a responsible and sustainable manner and meet its reporting requirements, the board of a PBC should engage in a continuing process of (1) determining who is materially affected by the corporation's business, (2) developing and maintaining criteria for balancing both the interests of those so affected, as well as any specific benefit identified in the corporation's charter, and (3) measuring progress against those criteria. The board may determine that some or all of the balancing obligations may be met by adopting one or more third-party standards, and engaging in a continuing process of measuring against those standards.

The list below is an example of procedures a board may adopt to ensure that it is properly attending to the balancing question. There is no requirement that these particular procedures be followed.

Committee

Establish a stand-alone committee or delegate sustainability issues to audit, governance, or other committee. Include in committee charter oversight of and/or recommendation with respect to:

- third-party standards, if any;

- internally generated standards;

- choice of certifying body or bodies, if any;

- benefit report;

- sustainability objectives and standards; and

- sustainability strategies and policies.

Management Role

- ▶ Recommendations on third-party standards and internally generated standards
- ▶ Recommendations on certification issues
- ▶ Recommendation of sustainability objectives and standards
- ▶ Recommendation of sustainability strategies and policies
- ▶ Report on progress toward impact objectives
- ▶ Draft benefit report

Periodic Activity

- ▶ Cycle should be synchronized with benefit reporting period
- ▶ Sustainability objectives to be established and assessed on an annual basis
- ▶ Quarterly committee meetings
- ▶ Quarterly report to board, with longer session once or twice a year, giving board significant opportunity to balance public benefits and stockholders' pecuniary interests
- ▶ Board to approve benefit report and impact objectives

Non-Periodic Activity

- ▶ Management charged with bringing significant sustainability issues to the board that come up out of cycle and that are not covered by policies (e.g., negotiation of energy contract; significant building projects)
- ▶ Committee should consider sustainability issues implicated by new developments (e.g., whether to purchase renewable energy or obtain LEED certification for new buildings)
- ▶ Committee may make balance decision or decide to take balance question to board based on significance; should report any decision to board

Process Issues

- ▶ Management recommendations to committee and committee recommendations to board should be distributed well in advance of committee and board meetings in order to give directors adequate time to review

- ▶ Where materials update prior materials, directors should be provided with redline copies, so that they can focus on changes

- ▶ Minutes should reflect sustainability issues discussed, resolution of those issues, and any direction given to the committee or management

- ▶ Internal checklists should be reviewed to determine whether sustainability issues should be added

- ▶ Where third-party or internal standard is adopted, materials and minutes should reflect consideration of how standard maps to interests of those affected by the corporation's conduct

Rubric for Individual Decisions

- ▶ Identify materially affected constituencies (including specific benefits)

- ▶ Identify any standards or certifications that company uses that are implicated by decision

- ▶ Determine how different options would be assessed under such standards

- ▶ Determine whether there are any third-party standards not being used by the company that should be used to assess the various options

- ▶ If so, determine how each option will be assessed under such standards

- ▶ Determine whether any outside expertise should be brought in

- ▶ Use relevant standards, certifications, management input and outside expertise, as applicable, to determine the effects of different options on shareholders and other relevant constituencies

- ▶ If the different choices the board faces have better implications for shareholders or one or more constituencies, board should acknowledge the necessity of making trade-offs, and make what it believes to be a reasonable decision

- ▶ A record should be made of the standards used, and how they were applied, as well as reports from management and outside experts
- ▶ The minutes should reflect the board's acknowledgment and consideration of the trade-offs at issue

Stakeholder Governance Provisions for a Delaware LLC

PURPOSE CLAUSE:

The purpose of the Company shall include creating a material positive impact on society and the environment, taken as a whole, from the business and operations of the Company.

DIRECTORS CLAUSE:

a) In discharging the duties of their positions and in considering the best interests of the Company, a [manager] [managing member] shall consider the effects of any action or inaction on:

   i) the members of the Company;

   ii) the employees and work force of the Company, its subsidiaries, and its suppliers;

   iii) the interests of its customers as beneficiaries of the purpose of the Company to have a material positive impact on society and the environment;

iv) community and societal factors, including those of each community in which offices or facilities of the Company, its subsidiaries, or its suppliers are located;

v) the local and global environment;

vi) the short-term and long-term interests of the Company, including benefits that may accrue to the Company from its long-term plans and the possibility that these interests may be best served by the continued independence of the Company; and

vii) the ability of the Company to create a material positive impact on society and the environment, taken as a whole.

b) In discharging his or her duties, and in determining what is in the best interests of the Company and its members, a [manager] [managing member] shall not be required to regard any interest, or the interests of any particular group affected by an action or inaction, including the members, as a dominant or controlling interest or factor. A [manager] [managing member] shall not be personally liable for monetary damages for: (i) any action or inaction in the course of performing the duties of a [manager] [managing member] under this paragraph if the [manager] [managing member] was not interested with respect to the action or inaction; or (ii) failure of the Company to create a material positive impact on society and the environment, taken as a whole.

c) A [manager] [managing member] does not have a duty to any person other than a member in its capacity as a member with respect to the purpose of the Company or the obligations set forth in this Article, and nothing in this Article express or implied, is intended to create or shall create or grant any right in or for any person other than a member or any cause of action by or for any person other than a member or the Company.

d) Notwithstanding anything set forth herein, a [manager] [managing member] is entitled to rely on the provisions regarding "best interests" set forth above in enforcing his or her rights hereunder and under state law, and such reliance shall not, absent another breach, be construed as a breach of a [manager's] [managing member's] duty of care, even in the context of a Change in Control Transaction where, as a result of weighing the interests set forth in subsection (a)(i)-(vii) above, a managing member determines to accept an offer, between two competing offers, with a lower price per unit.

e) A [manager] [managing member] who makes a business judgment in good faith fulfills the duty under this section if the [manager] [managing member]: (i) is not interested in the subject of the business judgment; (ii) is informed with respect to the subject of the business judgment to the extent the director reasonably believes to be appropriate under the circumstances; and (iii) rationally believes that the business judgment is in the best interests of the Company.

The process of amending your Membership Agreement or Partnership Agreement is typically outlined in your governing documents. You should consult with your counsel as to the necessary procedures and documentation to effect such amendments.

Notes

Introduction: A Corporate Lawyer's Journey

1. Lynn Stout, *The Shareholder Value Myth: How Putting Shareholders First Harms Investors, Corporations, and the Public* (San Francisco: Berrett-Koehler, 2012).

2. Simon Deakin, "Corporate Governance and Financial Crisis in the Long Run," in *The Embedded Firm: Corporate Governance, Labor, and Finance Capitalism*, ed. Cynthia A. Williams and Peer Zumbansen (Cambridge: Cambridge University Press, 2011), 15.

3. Colin Mayer, *Firm Commitment: Why the Corporation Is Failing Us and How to Restore Trust In It* (Oxford: Oxford University Press, 2013).

Chapter 1. Corporations and Investors: Setting The Stage

1. I use the term "entities" rather than "corporation" because several jurisdictions now permit the formation of limited liability companies (LLCs) with benefit corporation characteristics. See chapter 11, present volume.

2. For ease of reference, this book will generally refer to "corporations" and "benefit corporations." However, depending on jurisdiction and circumstance, other entities may take on the essential characteristics of corporations. In the United States, for example, publicly traded master limited partnerships play the same economic role as corporations but receive beneficial tax treatment not available to widely held corporations. Many enterprises that are not publicly traded are formed as limited liability companies, which also share the essential characteristics of corporations but are subject to a more flexible legal regime than are corporations. See David McBride, General Corporation Laws: History and Economics, *Law and Contemporary Problems* 74 (Winter 2011): 5, noting the proliferation of forms of entity.

3. Cary Krosinsky, "Overcoming Distractions on the Road to Increased Levels of ESG Integration," in *The Routledge Handbook of Responsible Investment*, ed. Tessa Hebb et al. (New York: Routledge, 2016), 614.

4. Henry W. Ballantine, *Ballantine on Corporations* (Chicago: Callaghan and Company, 1946), 1.

5. Colin Mayer, Reinventing the Corporation, *Journal British Acad.* 4 (2015): 59.

6. Ballantine, *Ballantine on Corporations*, 31–32; Mayer, "Reinventing the Corporation," 53.

7. Mayer, "Reinventing the Corporation," 54. Alongside the development of special charters granting the important privileges of limited liability, English business developed nonchartered "joint-stock companies" that permitted investment in transferable shares, but this did not adequately address the issue of liability for the company's debts. See also Ballantine, *Ballantine on Corporations*, 33.

8. McBride, "General Corporation Laws," 3; Ballantine, *Ballantine on Corporations,* 31–41.

9. Adolf Berle and Gardner Means, *The Modern Corporation and Private Property* (1932; reprint, New Brunswick: Transaction Publishers, 2010), 313: "The modern corporation may be regarded not simply as one form of social organization but potentially (if not actually) as the dominant institution of the modern world." McBride,

221

"General Corporation Laws," 4: "By the end of the nineteenth century, the laws governing incorporation had evolved to respond to the needs of the economy and the objectives of the business and financial worlds. No longer a privilege, incorporation became a right."

10. Will Hutton, Colin Mayer, and Philippe Schneider, The Rights and Wrongs of Shareholder Rights, *Seattle Univ. L. Rev.* 40 (2017): 376: "It was with freedom of incorporation in the middle of the nineteenth century that the focus on public purpose gave way to private interest."

11. J. Haskell Murray, An Early Report on Benefit Corporations, *W. Va. L. Rev.* 118 (2015): 38: "Concession theory focuses on the grants of limited liability, transferability of ownership, and potentially permanent legal existence by the state to the corporation. Due to these grants by the state, concession theory assumes that the state may regulate the corporation and that the corporation should benefit society. Concession theory was most popular between the 17th and 19th centuries, and the theory stems from a time when the state granted charters individually and based on some social benefit."

12. Krosinsky, "Overcoming Distractions," 614, cites $10 trillion invested in private equity and venture capital backed entities. The vital corporate characteristics are possessed by a number of alternative entities that have proliferated in the United States, such as limited liability corporations and limited partnerships.

13. Bespoke Investment Group, "US Stock Market Tops $25 Trillion—Up $1.9 Trillion Since Election" (January 26, 2017), https://www.bespokepremium.com/think-big-blog/us-stock-market-tops-25-trillion-up-1-9-trillion-since-election.

14. See Hugues Letourneau, "The Responsible Investment Practices of the World's Largest Government-Sponsored Investment Funds," in *The Routledge Handbook of Responsible Investment*, ed. Tessa Hebb et al. (New York: Routledge, 2016), 446–447. As of 2012, worldwide assets under management at pension funds equaled $33.9 trillion, at insurance funds $26.5 trillion, at mutual funds $26.1 trillion, and at sovereign wealth funds $5.2 trillion.

15. See Anne Tucker, The Citizen Shareholder: Modernizing the Agency Paradigm to Reflect How and Why a Majority of Americans Invest in the Market, *Seattle Univ. L. Rev.* 35 (2012): 1302.

16. As of 2011, 90 million Americans and 54 percent of American households invested in mutual funds (Tucker, "The Citizen Shareholder," 1315).

17. Sebastien Pouget, "Financial Markets' Inefficiencies and Long-Term Investments," in *The Routledge Handbook of Responsible Investment*, ed. Tessa Hebb et al. (New York: Routledge, 2016), 700.

18. See John Kay, *Other People's Money: The Real Business of Finance* (New York: PublicAffairs, 2015), 193: "The economic functions of the investment channel are: to search for good investments for new savings; to secure the effective management of assets through stewardship; and to do these things while helping households transfer wealth across their lifetime and between generations."

19. James Gifford, "The Changing Role of Asset Owners in Responsible Investment: Reflections on the Principles for Responsible Investment—The Last Decade and the Next," in *The Routledge Handbook of Responsible Investment*, ed. Tessa Hebb et al. (New York: Routledge, 2016), 435–436.

20. See "Universal Owners: Making Concessions to Preserve the Commons" (chapter 4, present volume).

21. Leo E. Strine Jr., Who Bleeds When the Wolves Bite? A Flesh-and-Blood Perspective on Hedge Fund Activism and Our Strange Corporate Governance System, *Yale L. J.* 126 (2017): 1912.

22. Raj Thamotheram and Aidan Ward, "Whose Risk Counts?," in *Cambridge Handbook of Institutional Investment and Fiduciary Duty*, ed. James P. Hawley et al. (Cambridge: Cambridge University Press, 2014), 210. Many believe that this situation is aggravated by the finance industry itself. See Gifford, "The Changing Role of Asset Owners," 441: "Citizens are realizing that their savings are being invested in ways that are not representing their interests. They are realizing that the status quo of Wall Street and the City of London has failed them. The agency chain is broken, and it is becoming clear that the finance sector is primarily there to serve itself, and not the function for which it exists; that is, to efficiently allocate capital to productive enterprises. See, generally, Stephen Davis, Jan Lukomnik, and David Pitt-Watson, *What They Do with Your Money: How the Financial System Fails Us and How to Fix It* (New Haven, CT: Yale University Press, 2016).

23. See Strine, "Who Bleeds," 1927: "The alignment between the interest of fund managers and human investors is, at best, imperfect, and at worst, out of sync. . . . Nothing close to a serious attempt to subject fund managers to the risks of truly stuck-in 401(k) investors has been made"; Principles for Responsible Investment, *Sustainable Financial System, Principles, Impact: Literature Review* (June 2016), https://www.unpri.org/download_report/17907 (summarizing Aviva, *A Roadmap for Sustainable Capital Markets*, https://www.aviva.com/media/thought-leadership/roadmap-sustainable-capital-markets, which recommended that governments "incorporate sustainable development into the duties (e.g., fiduciary duty, duty of care) of asset owners, asset managers and investment consultants"; Rory Sullivan et al., *Fiduciary Duty in the 21st Century* (2015), http://www.unepfi.org/fileadmin/documents/fiduciary_duty_21st_century.pdf, page 18, reporting suggestions that "investors need to encourage the adoption of policy measures to correct market failures and to require companies and investors to internalize externalities as an integral part of their fiduciary duties."

24. See FairPensions, "Protecting Our Best Interests: Rediscovering Fiduciary Obligation" (2015), http://shareaction.org/wp-content/uploads/2016/01/BestInterests.pdf., 5: "The key issue that arises here, both legally and practically, is the 'remoteness problem': individual investors may be too small to have a material impact on a given macroeconomic issue. This creates a serious collective action problem if—as with climate change—the optimal outcome for all beneficiaries would be universal action which *could* have a material effect on the problem."

25. Judith Rodin and Margot Brandenburg, *The Power of Impact Investing* (Philadelphia, PA: Wharton Digital Press, 2014), xii.

Chapter 2. Fiduciary Duties for Conventional Corporations: Enforcing Shareholder Primacy

1. See, e.g., 8 Del. C. §§ 141(a) and 211; § 141(k); § 242 (charter amendments); § 251 and forward (mergers); § 271 (sales of substantially all assets); § 275 (dissolution); and § 220.

2. 8 Del. C. § 141(a). In the United States, corporate law is a state law question, so that a corporation's internal affairs are guided by the law of the jurisdiction in which it is incorporated. Regardless of physical location, most corporations can freely choose their state of incorporation under the U.S. federal system. Delaware has come to hold the leading position among states, both in the number of significant businesses incorporated there and in the influence of its jurisprudence. See David Yosifon, The Law of Corporate Purpose, *Berkeley Bus. L. J.* 10 (2013): 184: "Delaware dominates the corporate law landscape in the United States"; Omari Simmons, Branding the Small Wonder: Delaware's Dominance and the Market for Corporate Law, *U. Rich. L. Rev.* 42 (2008): 1129. Although only a few states actually follow Delaware's statute, in many ways, Delaware corporate law is American corporate law. However, thirty-three jurisdictions follow the Model Business Corporation Act (MBCA), a model statute maintained by the influential Committee on Corporate Laws of the American Bar Association. Other states, including New York and California, follow neither the Delaware General Corporation Law nor the MBCA.

3. Section 8.01(b) of the MBCA contains a similar rule: "All corporate powers shall be exercised by or under the authority of the board of directors of the corporation, and the business and affairs of the corporation shall be managed by or under the direction, and subject to the oversight, of its board of directors, subject to any limitation set forth in the articles of incorporation or in an agreement authorized under section 7.32."

4. *Mills Acq. Co. v. Macmillan, Inc.*, 559 A.2d 1261, 1280 (Del. 1989): "Directors owe fiduciary duties of care and loyalty to the corporation and its shareholders"; *Polk v. Good*, 507 A.2d 531, 536 (Del. 1986): "In performing their duties the directors owe fundamental fiduciary duties of loyalty and care to the corporation and its shareholders."

5. *Aronson v. Lewis*, 473 A.2d 805, 812 (Del. 1984): "Directors have a duty to inform themselves, prior to making a business decision, of all material information reasonably available to them. Having become so informed, they must then act with requisite care in the discharge of their duties"; *Cede & Co. v. Technicolor, Inc.*, 634 A.2d 345, 368 (Del. 1993): "We have defined a board's duty of care in a variety of settings. For example, we have stated that a director's duty of care

requires a director to take an active and direct role in the context of a sale of a company from beginning to end. In a merger or sale, we have stated that the director's duty of care requires a director, before voting on a proposed plan of merger or sale, to inform himself . . . of all material information that is reasonably available to them"; Cede & Co., 634 A.2d at 368: "Directors individually and the board collectively failed to inform themselves fully and in a deliberate manner before voting on a board upon a transaction" (citing Smith v. Van Gorkom, 488 A.2d 858, 873 [Del. 1985]); Aronson, 473 A.2d at 812).

6. Cede & Co., 634 A.2d at 361: "The best interest of the corporation and its shareholders takes precedence over any interest possessed by a director, officer or controlling shareholder and not shared by the stockholders generally"; Guth v. Loft, 5 A.2d 503, 510 (Del. 1939), holding that the duty of loyalty requires a director or officer not "to use their position of trust and confidence to further their private interests" and, therefore, a director or officer is required "to refrain from doing anything that would work injury to the corporation, or to deprive it of profit or advantage which his [or her] skill and ability might properly bring to it, or to enable it to make in the reasonable and lawful exercise of its powers"; Aronson, 473 A.2d at 812: "Directors can neither appear on both sides of a transaction nor expect to derive any personal financial benefit from it in the sense of self-dealing, as opposed to a benefit which devolves upon the corporation or all stockholders generally"; Ivanhoe Partners v. Newmont Min. Corp., 535 A.2d 1334, 1345 (Del. 1987), stating that the duty of loyalty "embodies not only an affirmative duty to protect the interests of the corporation, but also an obligation to refrain from conduct which would injure the *corporation and its stockholders* [emphasis added] or deprive them of profit or advantage."

7. Stone ex rel. AmSouth Bancorporation v. Ritter, 911 A.2d 362, 370 (Del. 2006): good faith is "a subsidiary element, i.e., a condition, of the fundamental duty of loyalty." Thus, "the obligation to act in good faith does not establish an independent fiduciary duty that stands on the same footing as the duties of care and loyalty. Only the latter two duties, where violated, may directly result in liability, whereas a failure to act in good faith may do so, but indirectly." However, "a director cannot act loyally towards the corporation unless she acts in the good faith belief that her actions are in the corporation's best interest" (Guttman v. Huang, 823 A.2d 492, 506 n. 34 [Del. Ch. 2003]). The Delaware Supreme Court in In re Walt Disney Co. Derivative Litig., 906 A.2d 27, 67 (Del. 2006) described conduct that would violate a director's obligation to act in good faith: "A failure to act in good faith may be shown, for instance, where the fiduciary intentionally acts with a purpose other than that of advancing the best interests of the corporation, where the fiduciary acts with the intent to violate applicable positive law, or where the fiduciary intentionally fails to act in the face of a known duty to act, demonstrating a conscious disregard for his duties. There may be other examples of bad faith yet to be proven or alleged, but these three are the most salient."

8. In re Orchard Enters., Inc. S'holder Litig., 88 A.3d 1, 33 (Del. Ch. 2014).

9. Of course, these two models are not the only possibilities. Corporations might be managed for the benefit of some other subset of stakeholders as well, and, as discussed in chapter 11 of the present volume, the social purpose corporation, a little-used alternative corporate form, does authorize governance that favors some other stakeholder group. But for purposes of the present discussion it is sufficient to contrast these two models.

10. Compare to William T. Allen, Our Schizophrenic Conception of the Business Corporation, Cardozo L. Rev. 14 (1992): 264: "I suggest that at least over the course of this century there have been, in our public life and in our law, two quite different and inconsistent ways to conceptualize the public corporation and legitimate its power. I will call them the property conception and the social entity conception."

11. A. A. Berle Jr., Corporate Powers as Powers in Trust, Harv. L. Rev. 44 (1931): 1049, asserted that "all powers granted to a corporation or to the management of a corporation, or to any group within the corporation, whether derived from statute or charter or both, are necessarily and at all times be exercisable only for the ratable benefit of all the shareholders as their interest appears." See also Leo E. Strine Jr., The Dangers of Denial: The Need for a Clear-Eyed Understanding of the Power and Accountability Structure Established by the Delaware General

Corporation Law, *Wake Forest L. Rev.* 50 (2015): *10: "Despite attempts to muddy the doctrinal waters, a clear-eyed look at the law of corporations in Delaware reveals that, within the limits of their discretion, directors must make stockholder welfare their sole end, and that other interests may be taken into consideration only as a means of promoting stockholder welfare."

12. In response to Berle's *Harvard Law Review* article ("Corporate Powers"), Dodd, in the same publication, argued for "a view of the business corporation as an economic institution which has a social service as well as a profit-making function." See E. Merrick Dodd Jr., For Whom are Corporate Managers Trustees?, *Harv. L. Rev.* 45 (1932): 1148. See also Allen, "Our Schizophrenic Conception," 265, describing the "social entity" conception of the corporation as encompassing the idea that "corporate purpose can be seen as including the advancement of the general welfare. The board of directors' duties extend beyond assuring investors a fair return, to include a duty of loyalty, in some sense, to all those interested in or affected by the corporation."

13. See also *Hale v. Henkel*, 201 U.S. 43, 74 (1906): "The corporation is a creature of the state. It is presumed to be incorporated for the benefit of the public. It receives certain special privileges and franchises, and holds them subject to the laws of the state and the limitations of its charter. Its powers are limited by law"; Allen, "Our Schizophrenic Conception," 265: "The corporation comes into being and continues as a legal entity only with governmental concurrence. The legal institutions of government grant a corporation its juridical personality, its characteristic limited liability, and its perpetual life. This conception sees this public facilitation as justified by the state's interest in promoting the general welfare. Thus, corporate purpose can be seen as including the advancement of the general welfare."

14. *Dodge v. Ford Motor Co.*, 170 N.W. 668 (Mich. 1919) at 671, 684.

15. Michael C. Jensen and William H. Meckling, Theory of the Firm: Managerial Behavior, Agency Costs, and Ownership Structure, *J. Fin. Econ.* 3 (1976): 305.

16. Allen, "Our Schizophrenic Conception," 265.

17. See Lynn A. Stout, Bad and Not-So-Bad Arguments for Shareholder Primacy, *S. Cal. L. Rev.* 75 (2002): 1192–93, discussing Frank Easterbrook and Daniel Fischel of the Chicago school and their conceptions of shareholders as the residual risk bearers of the corporation; David Min, Corporate Political Activity and Non-Shareholder Costs, *Yale J. on Reg.* 33 (2016): 439, discussing the "canonical" work of Michael Jensen and William Meckling that described corporation as "nexus of contracts" in which shareholder bargain for control and economic residue.

18. James J. Hanks Jr., Playing with Fire: Nonshareholder Constituency Statutes in the 1990s, *Stetson L. Rev.* 21 [1991]: 115, has made the nexus of contracts argument for primacy: "The economic interests of employees, for example, are protected by minimum wage, safety, health, and plant-closing laws, and in many cases, collective bargaining agreements. Creditors are protected by fraudulent conveyance, preference, and bulk transfer statutes, as well as by contract. In recent years, after being battered by the increased debt burdens taken on by corporations acquired in leveraged buyouts, many lenders now include in their loan documents so-called 'event risk' provisions protecting them in the event of a restructuring that substantially increases debt or otherwise depresses the value of the lenders' debt securities."

19. Stout, "Bad and Not-So-Bad Arguments," 1193, note 19, quoting Frank H. Easterbrook and Daniel R. Fischel, *The Economic Structure of Corporate Law* (Cambridge, MA: Harvard University Press, 1991), 36–39.

20. This theoretical framework uses the term "agency," but it is important to note that the concept does not involve legal agency, wherein an agent is subject to the direct command of her principal; the corporation law itself is quite clear that although management decisions are made on behalf of shareholders, the directors retain broad discretion over those decisions.

21. See Lawrence Mitchell, "Financialism: A (Very) Brief History," in *The Embedded Firm: Corporate Governance, Labor, and Finance Capitalism*, ed. Cynthia A. Williams and Peer Zumbansen (Cambridge: Cambridge University Press, 2011), 42, 55: "Agency costs are the losses that result when corporate managers favor their own interest over that of the shareholders together with the expense of preventing this."

22. See Eric D. Beinhocker, *The Origin of Wealth* (Boston, MA: Harvard Business Review Press, 2006), 406: "Shareholders want the company they own to be managed for the maximum value of their shares. . . . The CEO and the management team, if left to their own devices, might manage the company to maximize other things, like their salaries, the fancy artwork in the lobby, and the size of the corporate jet."

23. E. Merrick Dodd Jr., For Whom are Corporate Managers Trustees?, *Harv. L. Rev.* 45 (1932): 1148.

24. Allen, "Our Schizophrenic Conception," 271: "The corporation has other purposes of perhaps equal dignity [to shareholder wealth maximization]: satisfaction of consumer wants, the provision of meaningful employment opportunities, and the making of a contribution to the public life of its communities."

25. Margaret M. Blair and Lynn A. Stout, A Team Production Theory of Corporate Law, *Va. L. Rev.* 85 (1999): 280–281; see also Allen, "Our Schizophrenic Conception," 271: "Resolving the often conflicting claims of these various corporate constituencies calls for judgment, indeed calls for wisdom, by the board of directors of the corporation."

26. Frank Abrams, chairman of Standard Oil of New Jersey, in a 1951 address, quoted in *Fortune* (October 1951).

27. "Business: The New Conservatism," *Time*, November 26, 1956; see also Allen, "Our Schizophrenic Conception," 271–72, writing in 1992 that the stakeholder model "appears to have been the dominant view among business lenders for at least the last fifty years"; David J. Berger, "In Search of Lost Time: What if Delaware Had Not Adopted Shareholder Primacy?," https://ssrn.com/abstract=2916960, page 11: "The dominant view of corporate law for most of the 20th century eschewed the notion of 'shareholder primacy,' and still the modern corporation managed to exist quite nicely."

28. Robert Reich, *Saving Capitalism: For The Many, Not The Few* (New York: Vintage, 2016), 18. See also Simon Deakin, "Corporate Governance and Financial Crisis in the Long Run," in *The Embedded Firm: Corporate Governance, Labor, and Finance Capitalism*, ed. Cynthia A. Williams and Peer Zumbansen (Cambridge: Cambridge University Press, 2011), 18: "As recently as the

1960s, the mission statement of large companies and the public declarations of industry bodies such as the Confederation of British Industry ('CBI') in Britain and the U.S. Business Roundtable referred to companies in entirely different terms. Companies should, it was suggested, be providing secure jobs and good working conditions; they should minimize environmental damage; and they should seek close ties with local communities. . . . These corporate mission statements usually did not mention shareholders at all. This was deliberate. Shareholders were not seem just as passive, but as *irrelevant* to the running of the company" (emphasis in original).

29. Adolf Berle and Gardner Means, *The Modern Corporation and Private Property* (1932; reprint, New Brunswick: Transaction Publishers, 2010), 312–313. See Fenner Stewart Jr., Berle's Conception of Shareholder Primacy: A Forgotten Perspective for Reconsideration During the Rise of Finance, *Seattle Univ. L. Rev.* 34 (2011): 1458, contrasting Berle's view of shareholder primacy, which "would make the corporation a tool for the wider polity," with modern shareholder primacy, and its focus on shareholder wealth maximization.

30. Lynn Stout, *The Shareholder Value Myth: How Putting Shareholders First Harms Investors, Corporations, and the Public* (San Francisco, CA: Berrett-Koehler, 2012), quoting Michael C. Jensen, Value Maximization, Stakeholder Theory, and the Corporate Objective Function, *Business Ethics Quarterly* 12 (2002): 238.

31. Stout, *The Shareholder Value Myth*, 108: "Balancing interests—decently satisfying several sometimes compelling objectives, rather than trying to maximize only one—is the rule and not the exception in human affairs." See also Colin Mayer, *Firm Commitment: Why the Corporation Is Failing Us and How to Restore Trust In It* (Oxford: Oxford University Press, 2013), 193: "The condemnation of multiple targets confuses simplicity of execution with completeness of principles. . . . The corporation should have a simple set of objectives but a broad set of values by which it judges their implementation."

32. See, e.g., U.K. Companies Act of 2006, § 172: directors must "have regard" to multiple stakeholders, but only in service of the interests of "members" (shareholders); Will Hutton, Colin

Mayer, and Philippe Schneider, The Rights and Wrongs of Shareholder Rights, *Seattle Univ. L. Rev.* 40 (2017): 391: "Derivative responsibilities" to stakeholders under § 172 "subordinate to those of the owners of the company; they are not primary obligations in their own right."

33. Pavlos E. Masouros, *Corporate Law and Economic Stagnation* (The Hague: Eleven International, 2013).

34. Joan MacLeod Heminway, Corporate Purpose and Litigation Risk in Publicly Held U.S. Benefit Corporations, *Seattle Univ. L. Rev.* 40 (2017): 613: "Delaware decisional law is arguably particularly unfriendly to for-profit corporate boards that fail to place shareholder financial wealth maximization first in every decision they make."

35. *Revlon, Inc. v. MacAndrews & Forbes Holdings, Inc.,* 506 A.2d 173 (Del. 1986), holding that when a corporation is to be sold in a cash-out merger, the directors' duty is to maximize the short-term value to shareholders, regardless of the interests of other constituencies.

36. See Berger, "In Search of Lost Time," 20: "Revlon planted the Delaware flag firmly in the ground of stockholder primacy."

37. See *Katz v. Oak Indus. Inc.,* 508 A.2d 873, 879 (Del. Ch. 1986): "It is the obligation of directors to attempt, within the law, to maximize the long-run interests of the corporation's stockholders; that they may sometimes do so 'at the expense' of others [e.g., debtholders] . . . does not . . . constitute a breach of duty"; Leo E. Strine Jr., The Social Responsibility of Boards of Directors and Stockholders in Change of Control Transactions: Is There Any "There" There?, *S. Cal. L. Rev.* 75 (2002): 1170: "The predominant academic answer is that corporations exist primarily to generate stockholder wealth, and that the interests of other constituencies are incidental and subordinate to that primary concern."

38. 8 Del. C. § 101(b); 8 Del. C. § 102(a)(3): "It shall be sufficient to state [in the corporate charter] . . . that the purpose of the corporation is to engage in any lawful act or activity."

39. *eBay Domestic Holdings, Inc. v. Newmark,* 16 A.3d 1 (Del. Ch. 2010) at 15–16, 32; quote at 34–35.

40. See Alicia Plerhoples, *Nonprofit Displacement and the Pursuit of Charity Through Public Benefit Corporations* (Washington, DC: Georgetown University Law Center, 2016), 17: "[eBay] makes

absolutely clear that Delaware corporate law espouses shareholder wealth maximization norm as the central corporate purpose."

41. See, for example, Stout, *The Shareholder Value Myth.*

42. J. Haskell Murray, Defending Patagonia: Mergers & Acquisitions with Benefit Corporations, *Hastings Bus. L. J.* 9 (2013): 493 (footnotes omitted). See also William Clark and Elizabeth Babson, How Benefit Corporations Are Redefining the Purpose of Business Corporations, *Wm. Mitchell L. Rev.* 38 (2012): 825–826, acknowledging commentary denying precedential support for shareholder primacy, but concluding weight of precedent clearly favors primacy.

43. Leo E. Strine Jr., Our Continuing Struggle with the Idea that For-Profit Corporations Seek Profit, *Wake Forest L. Rev.* 47 (2012): 151.

44. American Bar Association, "Sustainable Development Task Force," http://www.americanbar.org/groups/leadership/office_of_the_president/sustainable_development_task_force.html; American Bar Association, *Information for the United States Concerning Legal Perspectives on an Annual Board "Statement of Significant Audiences and Materiality,"* http://www.americanbar.org/content/dam/aba/administrative/environment_energy_resources/resources/usa_legal_memo.authcheckdam.pdf (United States response).

45. Milton Friedman, "The Social Responsibility of Business Is to Increase Its Profits," *New York Times Magazine* (September 13, 1970). See George A. Akerlof and Robert J. Shiller, *Phishing For Phools: The Economics of Manipulation and Deception* (Princeton, NJ: Princeton University Press, 2015), 150: "In contrast, the prominent economic story in the United States (and quite possibly the dominant one) since the 1950s has been that free markets . . . are always good for us; just so long as we are free to choose." It should be noted that Akerlof and Shiller, both winners of the Nobel Prize in economics, were contrasting that "story" with the actual, very different, functioning of markets.

46. See Masouros, *Corporate Law,* 73; Berger, "In Search of Lost Time, "15–18, discussing economic and political factors leading to growth of shareholder primacy in the late twentieth century.

47. Ben Hubbard, Dionne Searcey, and Nicholas Casey, "Under Rex Tillerson, Exxon Mobil Forged Its Own Path Abroad," *New York Times* (December 13, 2016).

48. Some commentators point to the breadth of discretion under the business judgment rule as evidence that directors are not bound by shareholder primacy. Blair and Stout, "A Team Production Theory," 299–303. However, as the cases cited in the text make clear, that discretion must be used with the intent to create shareholder value. For a discussion regarding the breadth of the business judgment rule, see "The Business Judgment Rule" (chapter 3, present volume).

49. According to *TW Servs., Inc. v. SWT Acquisition Corp.*, 14 Del. J. Corp. L. 1169, 1183–84 (Del. Ch. 1989): "Directors, in managing the business and affairs of the corporation, may find it prudent (and are authorized) to make decisions that are expected to promote corporate (and shareholder) long run interests, even if short run share value can be expected to be negatively affected, and thus directors in pursuit of long run corporate (and shareholder) value may be sensitive to the claims of other 'corporate constituencies.'" See also *Revlon, Inc. v. MacAndrews & Forbes Holdings, Inc.*, 506 A.2d 173, 182 (Del. 1986): "A board may have regard for various constituencies in discharging its responsibilities, provided there are rationally related benefits accruing to the stockholders"; *Mills Acq. Co. v. MacMillan, Inc.*, 449 A.2d 1261, 1282 n. 29 (Del. 1989), permitting a board to consider "the impact of both the bid and the potential acquisition on other constituencies, provided that it bears some reasonable relationship to general shareholder interests"; William B. Chandler III, Hostile M&A and the Poison Pill in Japan: A Judicial Perspective, *Colum. Bus. L. Rev.* 2004 (2004): 56: "Directors are permitted to consider the interests of other constituencies (such as creditors, employees, and the local community in which the company operates), but Delaware law emphasizes that they should consider these other interests only to the extent that they affect stockholder interest. This position obviously aligns the Delaware courts with the school of thought *holding that the corporation's sole purpose is to achieve the best financial return for the present group of stockholders*" (emphasis added).

50. *Unocal v. Mesa Petroleum Co.*, 493 A.2d 946 (Del. 1985).

51. See Leo E. Strine Jr., Who Bleeds When the Wolves Bite? A Flesh-and-Blood Perspective on Hedge Fund Activism and Our Strange Corporate Governance System, *Yale L. J.* 126 (2017).

52. *Unocal*, 493 A.2d 946 (Del. 1985) at 955.

53. Lynn A. Stout, Why We Should Stop Teaching *Dodge v. Ford*, *Va. L. & Bus. Rev.* 3 (2008): 170.

54. See Strine, "Dangers of Denial." Compare Stout, "Bad and Not-So-Bad Arguments," 1203–04 ("In *Revlon*, the Delaware Supreme Court held that in an 'end-game' situation where the directors of a publicly traded firm had decided to sell the firm to a company with a controlling shareholder— in brief, had decided to turn their publicly held company into a privately held one—the board had a duty to maximize shareholder wealth by getting the best possible price for the firm's shares. *Revlon* thus defines the one context in which Delaware law mandates shareholder primacy") with Yosifon, "Law of Corporate Purpose," 199–200: "Stout does discuss *Revlon*, but, like many scholars, she misconstrues its point. Stout argues that *Revlon* stands for the proposition that directors are only obligated to maximize shareholder value when a firm is about to be sold. . . . In terms of formal logic, Stout has committed the fallacy of 'denying the antecedent.' For the logical statement, 'if A, then B' it is a fallacy to conclude 'not A, therefore not B.' In *Revlon*, the Delaware Supreme Court held that if [A] the firm is for sale, then [B] directors must maximize profits. Stout concludes from this that if the firm is not for sale, directors do not have to maximize profits. But this does not follow as a matter of logic, and it is not *Revlon*'s teaching. . . . *Revlon* . . . holds that so long as a business is a going concern Delaware will defer to the directors' discretion in determining how to maximize shareholder value. This, the *Unocal* and *Revlon* courts recognize, may often include being good to non-shareholders. However, in the last period, where the shareholders will have no continuing interest in the firm, directorial attention to the interests of non-shareholders cannot possibly bear on shareholder interests, and, therefore, at the moment, attention to non-shareholder interests would necessarily violate the one duty that is always in place: the duty to the shareholders." See also Clark and Babson, "How Benefit Corporations Are Redefining," 833: "Delaware has addressed the issue of consideration of other constituencies, but only in the

context of takeovers, and even then courts still require a connection to shareholder value maximization" (citing *Unocal*).

55. Strine, "Dangers of Denial," 11–12. The historical implication of this anecdote should not be lost: before 1985, it was not clear, even to prominent Delaware practicing lawyers, that Delaware followed shareholder primacy. See Berger, "In Search of Lost Time," 21, noting that Supreme Court acknowledged in the *Revlon* case that it had not previously addressed the issue.

56. *Revlon*, 506 A.2d 173, at 182, holding that "The rights of the [noteholders] were fixed by contract" and therefore the noteholders "required no further protection" from Revlon's board of directors.

57. 8 Del. C. § 122(9).

58. *Theodora Holding Corp. v. Henderson*, 257 A.2d 398, 405 (Del. Ch. 1969). See Strine, "Dangers of Denial," 24: "When approving contested charitable gifts, Delaware courts have emphasized that the stockholders would ultimately benefit from the gift in the long run"; also (20): "Of course, it is true that the business judgment rule provides directors with wide discretion, and that it enables directors to justify by reference to long run stockholder interests a number of decisions that may in fact be motivated more by a concern for a charity the CEO cares about, or the community in which the corporate headquarters is located, or once in a while, even the company's ordinary workers, than long run stockholder wealth. But that does not alter the reality of what the law is. *Dodge v. Ford* and *eBay* are hornbook law because they make clear that if a fiduciary admits that he is treating an interest other than stockholder wealth as an end in itself, rather than an instrument to stockholder wealth, he is committing a breach of fiduciary duty."

59. N. Am. Catholic Educ. Programming Found., Inc. v. Gheewalla, 930 A.2d 92, 99 (Del. 2007), citing Prod. Res. Grp. v. NCT Grp., Inc., 863 A.2d 772, 790 (Del. Ch. 2004).

60. See, e.g., *Simons v. Cogan*, 549 A.2d 300, 304 (Del. 1988); *Katz v. Oak Indus. Inc.*, 508 A.2d 873, 879 (Del. Ch. 1986); *Geyer v. Ingersoll Publ'ns Co.*, 621 A.2d 784, 787 (Del. Ch. 1992); *Prod. Res. Grp.*, 863 A.2d at 787.

61. *N. Am. Catholic*, 930 A.2d at 101: "The need for providing directors with definitive guidance compels us to hold that no direct claim for

breach of fiduciary duties may be asserted by the creditors of a solvent corporation that is operating in the zone of insolvency. When a solvent corporation is navigating in the zone of insolvency, the focus for Delaware directors does not change: directors must continue to discharge their fiduciary duties to the corporation and its shareholders by exercising their business judgment in the best interests of the corporation for the benefit of its shareholder owners."

62. *Prod. Res. Grp.*, 863 A.2d at 794, note 67.

63. *N. Am. Catholic*, 930 A.2d at 103: "We hold that individual *creditors* of an *insolvent* corporation have *no right to assert direct* claims for breach of fiduciary duty against corporate directors. Creditors may nonetheless protect their interest by bringing derivative claims on behalf of the insolvent corporation or any other direct nonfiduciary claim . . . that may be available for individual creditors."

64. *In re Trados Inc. S'holder Litig.*, No. 1512-CC, 2009 WL 2225958, at *7 (Del. Ch. July 24, 2009); see also *Jedwab v. MGM Grand Hotels, Inc.*, 509 A.2d 584, 594 (Del. Ch. 1986): "With respect to matters relating to preferences or limitations that distinguish preferred stock from common, the duty of the corporation and its directors is essentially contractual and the scope of the duty is appropriately defined by reference to the specific words evidencing that contract."

65. *Jedwab*, 509 A.2d at 594, holding that preferred shareholders may be owed fiduciary where the right claimed is "a right shared equally with the common [stockholders]."

66. *Trados*, 2009 WL 2225958, at *7, note 42, quoting *Equity-Linked Investors, L.P. v. Adams*, 705 A.2d 1040, 1042 (Del. Ch. 1997).

67. *LC Capital Master Fund, Ltd. v. James*, 990 A.2d 435, 447 (Del. Ch. 2010): "The only protection for the preferred is if the directors, as the back-stop fiduciaries managing the corporation that sold them their shares, figure out a fair way to fill the gap left by incomplete contracting."

68. See *Credit Lyonnais Bank Nederland, N.V. v. Pathe Commc'ns Corp.*, No. 12150, 1991 WL 277613, at *34 (Del. Ch. Dec. 30, 1991): "At least where a corporation is operating in the vicinity of insolvency, a board of directors is not merely the agent of the residue risk bearers, but owes its duty to the corporate enterprise." In footnote 55 of that decision, Chancellor Allen poses a

hypothetical in which a corporation's sole asset is a judgment against a solvent debtor. With the case on appeal, the corporation's directors must consider offers to settle for significantly less than the value of the judgment sought. Chancellor Allen discusses the differing incentives of shareholders, who would be likely to reject a settlement offer as the residual owners of the corporation entitled to any upside of a large judgment, and debtholders, who would likely be in favor of accepting a smaller settlement to avoid risk that the judgment would be overturned, so long as the settlement was enough to satisfy the corporation's liabilities. Chancellor Allen speculated that a court should reject the shareholder primacy model where a corporation is in the "vicinity of insolvency," indicating that in that situation directors could "consider the community of interests that the corporation represents," and that "the right (both the efficient and the fair) course to follow for the corporation may diverge from the choice that the stockholders (or the creditors, or the employees, or any single group interested in the corporation) would make if given the opportunity to act."

69. See, e.g., *In re Answers Corp. S'holders Litig.*, No. 6170-VCN, 2012 WL 1253072, at *8, note 48 (Del. Ch. Apr. 11, 2012), finding that plaintiffs' complaint adequately alleged facts sufficient to infer that (1) two directors appointed by a 30 percent shareholder were interested in a merger where the 30 percent shareholder desired to exit its otherwise illiquid investment, and (2) otherwise disinterested and independent directors acted in bad faith by consciously failing to seek the highest value reasonably available for all shareholders based on allegations that, against their own financial advisor's advice, those directors acquiesced in an expedited sale process in order to accommodate the 30 percent shareholder; noting that the court "wonder[ed] if an explanation will emerge [for the independent directors' decision to conduct an expedited market check] because disinterested and independent directors do not usually act in bad faith."

70. *In re Synthes, Inc. S'holder Litig.*, 50 A.3d 1022, 1036 (Del. Ch. 2012): "It may be that there are very narrow circumstances in which a controlling stockholder's immediate need for liquidity could constitute a disabling conflict of interest irrespective of pro rata treatment. Those circumstances would have to involve a

crisis, fire sale where the controller, in order to satisfy an exigent need (such as a margin call or default in a larger investment) agreed to a sale of the corporation without any effort to make logical buyers aware of the chance to sell, give them a chance to do due diligence, and to raise the financing necessary to make a bid that would reflect the genuine fair market value of the corporation." *Synthes* also states: "The world is diverse enough that it is conceivable that a mogul who needed to address an urgent debt situation at one of his coolest companies (say a sports team or entertainment or fashion business), would sell a smaller, less sexy, but fully solvent and healthy company in a finger snap (say two months) at 75% of what could be achieved if the company sought out a wider variety of possible buyers." See also *In re Trados Inc. S'holder Litig.*, 73 A.3d 17, 38 (Del. Ch. 2013): "Stockholders may have idiosyncratic reasons for preferring decisions that misallocate capital. Directors must exercise their independent fiduciary judgment; they need not cater to stockholder whim."

71. See *Walt Disney Co.*, 906 A.2d 27, 67 (Del. 2006).

Chapter 3. Standards of Review: How Judges Decide Whether Directors Are Putting Shareholders First

1. See William T. Allen, Jack B. Jacobs, and Leo E. Strine Jr., Function Over Form: A Reassessment of Standards of Review in Delaware Corporation Law, *Del. J. Corp. L.* 26 (2001): 867: "The standard of review defines the freedom of action (or, if you will, deference in the form of freedom from intrusion) that will be accorded to the persons who are subject to its reach."

2. *In re Trados Inc. S'holder Litig.*, 73 A.3d 17, 36 (Del. Ch. 2013): "The standard of review depends initially on whether the board members (i) were disinterested and independent (the business judgment rule), (ii) faced potential conflicts of interest because of the decision dynamics present in particular recurring and recognizable situations (enhanced scrutiny), or (iii) confronted actual conflicts of interest such that the directors making the decision did not comprise a disinterested and independent board majority (entire fairness). The standard of review may change further depending on whether the directors took steps to address the potential or

actual conflict, such as by creating an independent committee, conditioning the transaction on approval by disinterested shareholders, or both."

3. David Yosifon, *The Law of Corporate Purpose*, *Berkeley Bus. L. J.* 10 (2013): 223, note 155.

4. *Aronson*, 473 A.2d at 812: "The business judgment rule is . . . a presumption that in making a business decision the directors of a corporation acted on an informed basis, in good faith and in the honest belief that the action taken was in the best interests of the company. Absent an abuse of discretion, that judgment will be respected by the courts. The burden is on the party challenging the decision to establish facts rebutting the presumption"; *Gagliardi v. Trifoods Int'l, Inc.*, 683 A.2d 1049, 1052–53 (Del. Ch. 1996), holding that the business judgment rule "provides that where a director is independent and disinterested, there can be no liability for corporate loss, unless the facts are such that no person could possibly authorize such a transaction if he or she were attempting in good faith to meet their duty." The business judgment rule "posits a powerful presumption in favor of actions taken by . . . directors." See also *Cede & Co. v. Technicolor, Inc.*, 634 A.2d 345, 361 (Del. 1993); *McMullin v. Beran*, 765 A.2d 910, 916 (Del. 2000), holding that the business judgment rule "combines a judicial acknowledgement of the managerial prerogatives that are vested in the directors of a Delaware corporation by statute with a judicial recognition that the directors are acting as fiduciaries in discharging their statutory responsibilities to the corporation and its shareholders"; *In re RJR Nabisco, Inc. S'holders Litig.*, No. 10389, 1989 WL 7036, at *1156 (Del. Ch. Jan. 31, 1989): In order to determine whether a transaction is entitled to the business judgment rule, the court will undertake "a threshold review of the objective financial interests of the board whose decision is under attack (i.e., independence), a review of the board's subjective motivation (i.e., good faith), and an objective review of the process by which it reached the decision under review (i.e., due care)."

5. *Brazen v. Bell Atlantic Corp.*, 695 A.2d 43, 49 (Del. 1997), stating that under the business judgment rule, "courts give deference to directors' decisions reached by a proper process, and do not apply an objective reasonableness test in such a case to examine the wisdom of the decision itself"; *In re Caremark Int'l Inc. Derivative Litig.*, 698 A.2d 959, 967–68 (Del. Ch. 1996):

"Compliance with a director's duty of care can never appropriately be judicially determined by reference to *the content of the board decision* that leads to a corporate loss, apart from consideration of the good faith or rationality of the process employed. That is, whether a judge or jury considering the matter after the fact, believes a decision substantively wrong, or degrees of wrong extending through 'stupid' to 'egregious' or 'irrational,' provides no ground for director liability, so long as the court determines that the process employed was either rational or employed in a *good faith* effort to advance corporate interests. To employ a different rule—one that permitted an 'objective' evaluation of the decision—would expose directors to substantive second guessing by ill-equipped judges or juries, which would, in the long-run, be injurious to investor interests. Thus, the business judgment rule is process oriented and informed by a deep respect for all *good faith* board decisions."

6. See, e.g., *Aronson v. Lewis*, 473 A.2d 805, 812 (Del. 1984); *Kaplan v. Centex Corp.*, 284 A.2d 119, 124 (Del. Ch. 1971).

7. *Sinclair Oil Corp. v. Levien*, 280 A.2d 717, 720 (Del. 1971): Decision not to be disturbed if "attributed to any rational business purpose"; *Unitrin, Inc. v. Am. Gen. Corp.*, 651 A.2d 1361, 1373 (Del. 1995), holding that a decision made by a loyal and informed board will not be overturned by the courts unless it cannot be attributed to same; *Gagliardi*, 1052–53, holding that the business judgment rule "provides that where a director is independent and disinterested, there can be no liability for corporate loss, unless the facts are such that no person could possibly authorize such a transaction if he or she were attempting in good faith to meet their duty."

8. In re *RJR Nabisco, Inc. S'holders Litig.*, No. 10389, 1989 WL 7036, note 13: "As I conceptualize the matter, such limited review as the rule contemplates (i.e., is the judgment under review "egregious" or "irrational" or "so beyond reason," etc.) really is a way of inferring bad faith."

9. Compare chapter 5 of the present volume (discussing Model Benefit Corporation Legislation, which allows purely substantive challenges to trade off decisions) with chapter 6 (describing the Delaware model of benefit corporation law, which fully preserves the business judgment rule).

10. *Paramount Commc'ns, Inc. v. Time Inc.*, 571 A.2d 1140, 1150 (Del. 1989): "Absent a limited set of circumstances as defined under *Revlon*, a board of directors, while always required to act in an informed manner, is not under any *per se* duty to maximize shareholder value in the short term, even in the context of a takeover"; and 1154: "The fiduciary duty to manage a corporate enterprise includes the selection of a time frame for achievement of corporate goals. . . . Directors are not obliged to abandon a deliberately conceived corporate plan for a short-term shareholder profit unless there is clearly no basis to sustain the corporate strategy." See also Corporate Laws Committee, Benefit Corporation White Paper, *Bus. Law.* 68 (2013): 1085: "When the corporation faces more general, day-to-day decisions, the conflict between shareholders and other constituencies is less pronounced and directors might more easily be able to arrive at the conclusion that a decision that directly benefits a non-shareholder constituency also increases the long-term value of the corporation's stock, even if, in the view of the short-term market, it appears to come at a cost to shareholders."

11. Committee on Corporate Laws, Other Constituencies Statutes: Potential for Confusion, *Bus. Law* 45 (1990): 2257–58: "It has long been clear that a corporation may properly expend corporate funds, for instance, for employee outings or other employee benefits; for charitable and community purposes in areas where it had operations; and to assist suppliers in staying in business, all at the expense of shareholders (in the sense that they had an equity in the funds used) on the theory that such expenditures advanced the long-term interests of the corporation." See also Einer Elhauge, Sacrificing Corporate Profits in the Public Interest, *NYU L. Rev.* 80 (2005): 770–772.

12. See, e.g., Blair and Stout, "A Team Production Theory," 299–300.

13. Yosifon, "Law of Corporate Purpose," 222–223: "Some scholars claim that corporate board can easily attend to non-shareholders at the expense of shareholders without getting caught or punished."

14. *Weinberger v. UOP, Inc.*, 457 A.2d 701, 710 (Del. 1983): "When directors of a Delaware corporation are on both sides of a transaction, they are required to demonstrate their utmost good faith and the most scrupulous inherent fairness of the bargain. The requirement of fairness is unflinching in its demand that where one stands on both sides of a transaction, he has the burden of establishing its entire fairness, sufficient to pass the test of careful scrutiny by the courts"; *Kahn v. Tremont Corp.*, 694 A.2d 422, 428 (Del. 1997), holding that "when a controlling shareholder stands on both sides of the transaction the conduct of the parties will be viewed under the more exacting standard of entire fairness as opposed to the more deferential business judgment standard"; *Frank v. Elgamal*, No. 6120-VCN, 2014 WL 957550, at *28 (Del. Ch. Mar. 10, 2014): "The Court should subject a transaction to entire fairness review, even if the controlling stockholder does not stand on both sides, where the controlling stockholder and the minority stockholders are 'competing' for the consideration of the acquirer."

15. The Delaware Supreme Court in *Weinberger v. UOP, Inc.*, 457 A.2d at 711, explained the dual analysis of the entire fairness standard as follows: "The concept of fairness has two basic aspects: fair dealing and fair price. The former embraces questions of when the transaction was timed, how it was initiated, structured, negotiated, disclosed to the directors, and how the approvals of the directors and the stockholders were obtained. The latter aspect of fairness relates to the economic and financial considerations of the proposed merger, including all relevant factors: assets, market value, earnings, future prospects, and any other elements that affect the intrinsic or inherent value of a company's stock. However, the test for fairness is not a bifurcated one as between fair dealing and price. All aspects of the issue must be examined as a whole since the question is one of entire fairness."

16. *Kahn v. Lynch Commc'n Sys.*, Inc., 638 A.2d 1110, 1117 (Del. 1994): "It is a now well-established principle of Delaware corporate law that in an interested merger, the controlling or dominating shareholder proponent of the transaction bears the burden of proving its entire fairness."

17. *Gesoff v. IIC Indus., Inc.*, 902 A.2d 1130, 1145 (Del. Ch. 2006).

18. *Reis v. Hazelett Strip-Casting Corp.*, 28 A.3d 442, 457 (Del. Ch. 2011): "[The intermediate standard of review] applies when the realities of the decision making context can subtly undermine the decisions of even independent and disinterested directors."

19. *Reis*, 28 A.3d 442, quoting *Mercier v. Inter-Tel (Del.), Inc.*, 929 A.2d 786, 810 (Del. Ch. 2007).

20. *Revlon*, 506 A.2d 173 at 185 (Del. 1986), holding that, in a change of control situation, a "board's action is not entitled to the deference accorded it by the business judgment rule"; *In re Smurfit-Stone Container Corp. S'holder Litig.*, No. 6164-VCP, 2011 WL 2028076 at *13 (Del. Ch. May 20, 2011): "Heightened scrutiny is appropriate because of an 'omnipresent specter' that a board, which may have secured a continuing interest of some kind in the surviving entity, may favor its interests over those of the corporation's stockholders."

21. *Corwin v. KKR Fin. Hldgs. LLC*, 125 A/3d 304 (Del. 2015).

22. *Arnold v. Soc'y for Sav. Bancorp, Inc.*, 650 A.2d 1270, 1290 (Del. 1994) (internal quotation marks omitted); *Smurfit-Stone Container Corp.*, at *12: ("If, for example, the resulting entity has a controlling stockholder or stockholder group such that the target's stockholders are relegated to minority status in the combined entity, Delaware Courts have found a change of control would occur for *Revlon* purposes. But, if ownership shifts from one large unaffiliated group of public stockholders to another, that alone does not amount to a change of control.").

23. *Trados*, 73 A.3d 17 at 44.

24. Corporate Laws Committee, "White Paper," 1084: "When it becomes inevitable that a target corporation will be sold for cash, the target's shareholders' sole economic interest is limited to maximizing the cash to be received."

25. *Unocal*, 493 A.2d 946 (Del. 1985) at 954: "Because of the omnipresent specter that a board may be acting primarily in its own interests, rather than those of the corporation and its shareholders, there is an enhanced duty which calls for judicial examination at the threshold before the protections of the business judgment rule may be conferred"; *Unitrin, Inc. v. Am. Gen. Corp.*, 651 A.2d 1361 (Del. 1995).

26. *Reis*, 28 A.3d 442 at 457.

27. *Omnicare, Inc. v. NCS Healthcare, Inc.*, 818 A.2d 914, 934 (Del. 2003), holding that "'safety devices' adopted to protect a transaction that did not result in a change of control are subject to enhanced judicial scrutiny under a *Unocal* analysis"; *Reis*, 28 A.3d at 459: "Enhanced scrutiny likewise extends to defensive measures

that have the potential to insulate last period decision-making from market forces or undermine the ability of stockholders to reject the transaction."

28. *Unocal*, 493 A.2d 946 (Del. 1985) at 955: "In the face of this inherent conflict directors must show that they had reasonable grounds for believing that a danger to corporate policy and effectiveness existed because of another person's stock ownership." *Unocal* also states: "If a defensive measure is to come within the ambit of the business judgment rule, it must be reasonable in relation to the threat posed." See also *Moran v. Household Int'l, Inc.*, 500 A.2d 1346, 1356 (Del. 1985).

29. *Unitrin, Inc. v. Am. Gen. Corp.*, 651 A.2d 1361 (Del. 1995) at 1367, stating that the Court of Chancery should have focused its *Unocal* review "first, upon whether the [defensive measure] was draconian, by being either preclusive or coercive and; second, if it was not draconian, upon whether it was within a range of reasonable responses to the threat . . . posed"; see, generally, Allen, Jacobs, and Strine, "Function Over Form."

30. *Unitrin*, 651 A.2d 1361, at 1387 (Del. 1995).

31. *Revlon*, 506 A.2d at 176.

32. *Blasius Indus., Inc. v. Atlas Corp.*, 564 A.2d 651, at 660 (Del. Ch. 1988), reasoning that enhanced scrutiny is necessary because "action designed principally to interfere with the effectiveness of a vote inevitably involves a conflict between the board and a shareholder majority."

33. *Schnell v. Chris Craft Industries, Inc.*, 285 A.2d 437, at 439 (Del. 1971). See also Allen, Jacobs, and Strine, "Function Over Form," 885, note 99: "*Blasius* drew inspiration from the *Schnell* doctrine that action by fiduciaries, even if lawful, could be improper if it was inequitable"; and 885: "*Blasius* reaffirmed the traditional view that director actions primarily motivated to effect a disenfranchisement have a dim chance of being sustained."

34. *Blasius*, 564 A.2d at 659.

35. See *Yucaipa Am. All. Fund II, L.P. v. Riggio*, 1 A.3d 310 (Del. Ch. 2010), aff'd, 15 A.3d 218 (Del. 2011). A rights plan consists of a dividend to each shareholder to purchase more shares at a deep discount if any one shareholder accumulates a set percentage of the outstanding shares (often 15 percent). The rights owned by the shareholder crossing the threshold immediately

become void, however, so that anyone who crosses the line is diluted and suffers severe economic loss. The effect of a poison pill is to prevent anyone from obtaining control of the corporation by purchasing shares on the open market.

36. *Yucaipa*, 1 A.3d 310, at 335–336. See also *Third Point LLC v. Ruprecht*, No. 9469-VCP, No. 9467-VCP, No. 9508-VCP, 2014 WL 1922029, at *15 (Del. Ch. May 2, 2014), quoting *MM Cos. v. Liquid Audio, Inc.*, 813 A.2d 1118, 1130 (Del. 2003): "The *Blasius* and *Unocal* standards of enhanced judicial review . . . are *not* mutually exclusive."

Chapter 4. The Responsible Investing Movement and Shareholder Primacy

1. See Meg Vorhees, "Responsible Investment in the United States," in *The Routledge Handbook of Responsible Investment*, ed. Tessa Hebb et al. (New York: Routledge, 2016), 58, 61: The 2012 U.S. market for "sustainable and responsible investing strategies" was valued at $3.7 trillion, including $2.5 trillion in institutional investment.

2. Principles for Responsible Investment, home page, https://www.unpri.org; Vorhees, "Responsible Investment," 60–61. One hundred sixty-five U.S. owners and asset managers had signed principles.

3. See Eric D. Beinhocker, *The Origin of Wealth* (Boston, MA: Harvard Business Review Press, 2006), 413: "Few employees jump out of bed in the morning fired up to maximize shareholder value. . . . But employees can attach to the concepts of building a great, lasting institution that creates opportunities for people through growth."

4. Researchers have attempted to value reputation. One 2014 study suggested that 17 percent of the S&P 500's market capitalization reflected corporate reputation. Martin P. Thomas and Mark W. McElroy, *The Multicapital Scorecard: Rethinking Organizational Performance* (White River Junction, VT: Chelsea Green, 2016), 25, citing a study by Reputation Dividend, a management consultancy.

5. See Lynn Stout, *The Shareholder Value Myth: How Putting Shareholders First Harms Investors, Corporations, and the Public* (San Francisco, CA: Berrett-Koehler, 2012), 59, describing academic literature and theories that "do suggest, strongly, that the supposed divides between the interests of shareholders and the interests of stakeholders, society, and the environment may be much narrower than conventional shareholder value thinking admits. Public corporations are more likely to do well for their shareholders when they do good"; Gordon L. Clark, Andress Feiner, and Michael Viehs, *From the Stockholder to the Stakeholder: How Sustainability Can Drive Financial Outperformance* (2015), https://arabesque.com/docs/From_the_stockholder_to_the_stakeholder.pdf, a meta-analysis of more than two hundred studies and sources on sustainability, concluding, among other matters, that "companies with strong sustainability scores show better operational performance and are less risky."

6. See Stephen Davis, Jan Lukomnik, and David Pitt-Watson, *What They Do with Your Money: How the Financial System Fails Us and How to Fix It* (New Haven, CT: Yale University Press, 2016), 66, discussing a speech by the chief economist of the Bank of England that cited a study of 624 large-cap U.S. and U.K. companies, showing deep discounting of future earnings.

7. See Sustainability Accounting Standards Board, home page, https://www.sasb.org.

8. See International Integrated Reporting Council, *The International <IR> Framework*, http://integratedreporting.org/wp-content/uploads/2013/12/13-12-08-THE-INTERNATIONAL-IR-FRAMEWORK-2-1.pdf.

9. Kyle Westaway and Dirk Sampselle, The Benefit Corporation: An Economic Analysis with Recommendations in Courts, Boards, and Legislatures, *Emory L. J.* 62 (2013): 1013, note 66 (emphasis in original). Business writers have also called out the paradoxical nature of mission-produced profit. See Jim Collins and Jerry I. Porras, *Built to Last* (New York: HarperBusiness, 1994): "Visionary companies pursue a cluster of objectives, of which making money is only one—and not necessarily the primary one. . . . Yet paradoxically, the visionary companies make more money than the purely profit driven companies," quoted in John Kay, *Obliquity* (New York: Penguin, 2010), 5. This paradox may also be thought of as an instance of what Kay, an esteemed economist, calls "obliquity," the idea that our goals are best achieved indirectly. He discusses this idea in the context of corporations

and profit maximizing: "Today, people who deplore the activities of modern business and those who applaud those activities both agree that business is distinguished from other forms of organization by having profit as its defining purpose. Yet this agreement encompasses evident nonsense. . . . Yet for years I struggled with the idea that if profit could not be the defining purpose of a corporation, there must be something else that was its defining purpose. If business did not maximize profit, what did it maximize? I was making the same mistake as those victims of the teleological fallacy who struggled for centuries with questions like 'What is a tiger for'?" (169).

10. Robert G. Eccles, Jock Herron, and George Serafeim, "Promoting Corporate Sustainability Through Integrated Reporting: The Role of Investment Fiduciaries and the Responsibilities of the Corporation Board," in *Cambridge Handbook of Institutional Investment and Fiduciary Duty*, ed. James P. Hawley et al. (Cambridge: Cambridge University Press, 2014), 412: "Commitment by the board of directors to effectively mediated stakeholder primacy is likely to create the type of well-informed, longer-term horizon, collaborative behavior within the corporate firm that ultimately leads to durable corporate sustainability—a goal that rewards investors as well."

11. See Beinhocker, *Origin of Wealth*, 121: "Humans have strongly ingrained rules about fairness and reciprocity that override calculated 'rationality.'"

12. Bridges Ventures, *To B or Not To B: An Investor's Guide to B Corps* (London: Bridges Ventures, 2015).

13. Laureate Education, S-4/A, filed January 31, 2017, at iv.

14. Colin Mayer, *Firm Commitment: Why the Corporation Is Failing Us and How to Restore Trust In It* (Oxford: Oxford University Press, 2013), 150–151. A reviewer of Mayer's book captured the concept as follows: "If people are to make long-term commitments, trust is the only alternative. But a company whose goal in whatever seems profitable today can be trusted only to renege on implicit contracts. It is sure to act opportunistically. If its managers did not want to do so, they would be replaced." Martin Wolf, "Opportunistic Shareholders Must Embrace Commitment," *Financial Times* (August 26, 2014), cited in Will Hutton, Colin Mayer, and

Philippe Schneider, The Rights and Wrongs of Shareholder Rights, *Seattle Univ. L. Rev.* 40 (2017): 381.

15. Stout, *Shareholder Value Myth*, 85. Observers have also cogently noted that the financial value thinking that predominates in a shareholder primacy model has infected the traditional employment bargain, financializing what was once a relationship of trust. See Davis, Lukomnik, and Pitt-Watson, *What They Do with Your Money*, 176: "Our top executives . . . are 'incented' through huge issues of shares, options, and bonuses, as if we otherwise didn't trust them to do the job well. The predictable outcome is a legitimization of what to outsiders looks like outrageous greed."

16. For a definition of "externalities," see Roger Urwin, Pension Funds as Universal Owners: Opportunity Beckons and Leadership Calls, *Rotman Int'l J. of Pension Management* 4 (2011): 32, note 3: "The definition of *externalities* is of spill-over effects of production or consumption that produce unpriced costs or benefits on other unrelated parties—that could be other companies or society more generally" (emphasis in original). Jane Gleeson-White explains externalities by referring to a World Bank economist's estimation that the real cost of a fast-food hamburger is $200, once the cost of carbon footprint, water use, soil degradation, and the health care costs of diet-related illness are factored in—but all those costs are mostly borne by society and future generations, not by the seller or buyer. Jane Gleeson-White, *Six Capitals, or Can Accountants Save the Planet? Rethinking Capitalism for the Twenty-First Century* (New York: W. W. Norton, 2014). For a view that the failure of markets extends beyond externalities, and imposes costs on imperfectly rational and underinformed market participants, see George A. Akerlof and Robert J. Shiller, *Phishing For Phools: The Economics of Manipulation and Deception* (Princeton, NJ: Princeton University Press, 2015), 166: "It may be standard economics to pretend that economic pathologies are only 'externalities.' But the ability of free markets to engender phishing for phools [the authors' term for transactions in which one party earns a profit by taking advantage of a counterparty's irrational or uninformed behavior] of many different varieties is not an externality. Rather, it is inherent in the workings of competitive markets."

17. Leo E. Strine Jr., Who Bleeds When the Wolves Bite? A Flesh-and-Blood Perspective on Hedge Fund Activism and Our Strange Corporate Governance System, *Yale L. J.* 126 (2017): 1872, arguing for modifications to corporate governance system, and noting that, in the current system, "top corporate managers . . . must focus intently on stock price growth and be willing to treat other corporate constituencies callously if that is necessary to please the stock market's short-term wishes."

18. See New York State Common Retirement Fund, *Environmental, Social, and Governance Report* (2017), 10: https://www.osc.state.ny.us/reports/esg-report-mar2017.pdf.: "As a 'universal owner,' the Fund is focused on ESG issues that affect the market as a whole because it cannot avoid exposure to them."

19. See "The Structure of the Investment Chain" (chapter 1, present volume).

20. Raj Thamotheram and Aidan Ward, "Whose Risk Counts?," in *Cambridge Handbook of Institutional Investment and Fiduciary Duty*, ed. James P. Hawley et al. (Cambridge: Cambridge University Press, 2014), 212: "About 80 percent of the ability of a fund to meet its liabilities comes from beta, the market return"; Davis, Lukomnik, and Pitt-Watson, *What They Do with Your Money*, 50: "Beta drives some 91 percent of the average portfolio's return."

21. See Beinhocker, *Origin of Wealth*, 407, citing a McKinsey & Co. study showing that "from 1991 to 2000, about 70 percent of the returns of individual companies was due to market factors and only 30 percent was due to company-specific factors."

22. James Gifford, "The Changing Role of Asset Owners in Responsible Investment: Reflections on the Principles for Responsible Investment— The Last Decade and the Next," in *The Routledge Handbook of Responsible Investment*, ed. Tessa Hebb et al. (New York: Routledge, 2016), 438. See also David Wood, "What Do We Mean By the S in ESG?," in *The Routledge Handbook*, 553: "There also resides in the theory of responsible investing the belief that the field is itself is a step towards a better world, in which the integration of ESG information into investment decision making is tied to greater social utility from financial activity"; Stout, *Shareholder Value Myth*, 87: "[Shareholders] want to protect the

value of their other investments, keep their jobs, lower their tax bills, and preserve their health. They are, to a greater or lesser extent, 'universal' owners with stakes in the economy, the community, and the planet."

23. Wood, "What Do We Mean," 561. See also Gordon L. Clark et al., "Addressing the Challenges of Transformation through Sustainable Investment," in *The Routledge Handbook of Responsible Investment*, ed. Tessa Hebb et al. (New York: Routledge, 2016), 594; Anne Tucker, The Citizen Shareholder: Modernizing the Agency Paradigm to Reflect How and Why a Majority of Americans Invest in the Market, *Seattle Univ. L. Rev.* 35 (2012): 1319: "The phrase universal investor describes what an investor owns and her interest in the performance of the market as a whole, as compared to an interest in a specific company. The theory of universal investors also describes the reduction in firm-specific risks achieved through portfolio diversification, as well as an increased vulnerability to systemic risks or failures within the market"; Ivan Diaz-Rainey et al., "Institutional Investment in the European Union Emissions Trading Scheme," in *Cambridge Handbook of Institutional Investment and Fiduciary Duty*, ed. James P. Hawley et al. (Cambridge: Cambridge University Press, 2014), 127: "The impact of environmental externalities such as pollution, waste or changes in the use of resources can cause institutional investors to suffer reduced cash flows from investments, increase environmental coasts and augment uncertainty in capital markets"; Strine, "Who Bleeds," 1884: "Offshoring jobs to nations with pitiful wages and little protection for labor as shortcuts to more immediate profits, rather than making profits in an ethical manner that does not involve externalizing the real costs of business, hurts human investors."

24. Strine, "Who Bleeds," 1871: "In the back and forth about the Tobin's Q, survivorship bias, and the like, the flesh-and-blood human beings our corporate governance system is supposed to serve get lost."

25. Thomas and McElroy, *The Multicapital Scorecard*, 10, advocating a "MultiCapital Scorecard" as a means of assessing performance.

26. Tessa Hebb et al., eds., introduction to *The Routledge Handbook of Responsible Investment* (New York: Routledge, 2016), 3. See also Gifford, "The Changing Role of Asset Managers," 442,

note 5: "Most large corporations explicitly recognize the importance of stakeholders, corporate responsibility and the need to retain their
'license to operate' within the communities
in which they operate. *Even the most progres-
sive investors rarely acknowledge this*, and rather
describe their responsible investment in terms
of risk mitigation or being a better investor"
(emphasis added); Wood, "What Do We Mean,"
559: "Advocates [of responsible investing] claim
that the duties of loyalty and impartiality to beneficiaries supports ESG integration as a means
to improve long-term performance and also
the environment in which beneficiaries will
enjoy their retirement benefits"; Thamotheram
and Ward, "Whose Risk Counts?," 207, 213:
"By chasing headline alpha to succeed vis-à-
vis clients, we contend that the industry creates
several risks to beta. . . . Real risk management—
from the perspective of long-horizon, well-diver-
sified investors—drives beta, the underlying real
return on productive investment, by limiting the
negative impact of real economy events."

27. Steve Lydenberg, Integrating Systemic Risk into
Modern Portfolio Theory and Practice, *Jour.
Applied Corp. Fin.* 28 (2016): 56.

28. See Frederick Alexander, Whose Portfolio Is It,
Anyway?, *Stetson Law Review* (forthcoming).

29. Angus Deaton, "It's Not Just Unfair: Inequality
Is a Threat to Our Governance," *New York Times*
(March 20, 2017): "The artificially inflated costs
of health care are powering up inequality by pro-
ducing large fortunes for a few while holding
down wages; the pharmaceutical industry alone
had 1,400 lobbyists in Washington in 2014.
American health care does a poor job of delivering health, but is exquisitely designed as an
inequality machine, commanding an even larger
share of GDP and funneling resources to the top
of the income distribution."

30. David Min, Corporate Political Activity and
Non-Shareholder Costs, *Yale J. on Reg.* 33 (2016):
473.

31. See Steven L. Schwarcz, *Controlling Systemic Risk
Through Corporate Governance*, Policy brief no. 94
(Ontario: Centre for International Governance
Innovation, 2017), 3–4: "Financial regulation
of substance usually lags behind financial innovation, causing unanticipated consequences
and allowing innovations to escape regulatory
scrutiny."

32. Hugues Letourneau, "The Responsible
Investment Practices of the World's Largest
Government-Sponsored Investment Funds," in
The Routledge Handbook of Responsible Investment,
ed. Tessa Hebb et al. (New York: Routledge,
2016), 447: "Responsible investment emerged at
the beginning of the twenty-first century in an
attempt to reconcile sustainability considerations
with profit maximization."

33. See Cary Krosinsky, "Overcoming Distractions
on the Road to Increased Levels of ESG
Integration," in *The Routledge Handbook of
Responsible Investment*, ed. Tessa Hebb et al. (New
York: Routledge, 2016).

34. Fran Seegull, Response to "How Investors Can
(and Can't) Create Social Value," *Stanford Social
Investor Review* (December 8, 2016): "The global
financial markets are more than $212 trillion,
whereas private investment for impact is only
about $77 billion worldwide. If we seek a more
equitable allocation of value, the capital markets
are a place to focus on."

35. Because this argument has been rehearsed ad
nauseam in academic literature, there is little
to be gained by another treatment here. For the
best articulation of this argument, see Stout,
Shareholder Value Myth. Despite the excellent
policy arguments made by the proponents of the
theory that primacy is not the law in the United
States (arguments with which I fully agree), the
relevant authority continues to support primacy
outside of constituency states. Westaway and
Sampselle, "The Benefit Corporation," 1005:
"The prevailing view, even today, is that despite
any decision-making leeway provided by the
constituency statutes, nonshareholder interests
may be considered only insofar as they relate
rationally to the interests of the corporation
and therefore its shareholders: nonshareholder
stakeholder interests may be considered only as
a means to the shareholder wealth maximization
end, not as an end in and of themselves." See,
generally, chapter 2, present volume.

36. David J. Berger, "In Search of Lost Time: What
if Delaware Had Not Adopted Shareholder
Primacy?," https://ssrn.com/abstract=2916960,
page 3. See also Westaway and Sampselle, "The
Benefit Corporation, "1005: "Why would over
half of the states in the United States need to pass
constituency statutes if the shared wealth maximization norm—nay, duty—did not exist?" The

following states have *not* adopted constituency
statutes: Alaska, Arizona, Arkansas, California,
Colorado, Delaware, Kansas, Montana,
Nebraska, New Hampshire, North Carolina,
Oklahoma, South Carolina, Utah, Virginia, and
West Virginia.

37. William Clark and Elizabeth Babson, How
Benefit Corporations Are Redefining the
Purpose of Business Corporations, *Wm. Mitchell
L. Rev.* 38 (2012): 834: "Without a constituency
statute, the interests of other constituencies may
be considered at the directors' own risk."

38. Berger, "In Search of Lost Time," 3.

39. See Robert Daines, Does Delaware Law Improve
Firm Value?, *J. Fin. Econ.* 62 (2001): 525, pre-
senting evidence that Delaware law improves
firm value; Omari Simmons, Branding the Small
Wonder: Delaware's Dominance and the Market
for Corporate Law, *U. Rich. L. Rev.* 42 (2008), discussing the strength and resilience of Delaware
"brand."

40. See David A. Drexler, Lewis S. Black, and A.
Gilchrist Sparks, *Delaware Corporation Law and
Practice* (Newark, NJ: Matthew Bender, 2016),
§ 35.07(2), discussing the effect of mergers on
contracts under "successors and assigns" or "no
assignment" clauses, and otherwise.

41. See, e.g., Regina Robson, A New Look at Benefit
Corporations: Game Theory and Game Changer,
Am. Bus. L. J. 52 (2015): 513: "Even when not
strictly compelled by the case law, a wealth maximization and 'shareholder first' mentality continued to dominate discussions of corporate
purpose."

42. See Antony Page and Robert Katz, Freezing Out
Ben & Jerry: Corporate Law and the Sale of a
Social Enterprise Icon, *Vermont L. Rev* 35 (2010):
232, analyzing whether, at the time Ben & Jerry's
was a publicly traded corporation, it was constrained from pursuing social goals by shareholder primacy norms, and noting that "Ben &
Jerry's could thus always claim that its social activities helped it achieve its financial goals."

43. See Clark and Babson, "How Benefit
Corporations Are Redefining," 835: "While it is
not true that all considerations that reflect consideration of non-shareholder interests lead to
a reduction in shareholder value, and some in
fact may lead to its increase, it is equally true
that some might lead to reduced shareholder
value, *even over the long term*" (emphasis added);

and 832: Under uncertainty surrounding wealth
maximization construct, "management is
encouraged to lie, or at least couch their actions
in terms of long term shareholder maximization.
For companies that may wish to advertise and
openly rely upon their non-shareholder driven
policies, there is clearly a risk associated with
this position." See also David Yosifon, The Law of
Corporate Purpose, *Berkeley Bus. L. J.* 10 (2013):
222: "A first interpretive move that has bred confusion on the law of corporate purpose is con-
flating of what the law requires with speculation
about what directors can get away with."

44. See *"Revlon* Standard: Changes in Control"
(chapter 3, present volume). See also Clark
and Babson, "How Benefit Corporations Are
Redefining," 837: "To ignore the impact of
director duties in a sale situation is a glaring
oversight."

45. See, e.g., Schwarcz, *Controlling Systemic Risk*,
3: "Opponents of a public duty also argue that
managers could not feasibly govern if they had to
take into account the myriad small externalities
that result from corporate risk taking."

46. See Clark and Babson, "How Benefit
Corporations Are Redefining," 850: "Care should
be taken to make sure the election process in a
benefit corporation remains robust so that the
directors cannot abuse the flexibility inherent in
the benefit corporation form."

47. See Stout, *Shareholder Value Myth*, 108: "This perspective ignores the obvious human capacity to
balance, albeit imperfectly, competing interests
and responsibilities. . . . Balancing interests—
decently satisfying several sometimes-competing
objectives, rather than trying to "maximize"
only one—is the rule and not the exception in
human affairs"; see also John Kay, *Obliquity* (New
York: Penguin, 2010), 170: "Businesses do not
maximize anything. . . . A great business is very
good at doing the things we expect a business to
do—rewarding its investors, providing satisfying
employment, offering goods and services of good
quality at reasonable prices, fulfilling a role in
the community—and to fail in any of these is, in
the long run, to fail at all of them."

48. Beinhocker, *Origin of Wealth*, 410: "Profitability is
in fact a multidimensional problem in pleasing
lots of people"; see also 411.

49. Stout, *Shareholder Value Myth*, 60: "Real human
beings have different investing time frames;

different liquidity demands; different interests in other assets (including their own human capital); and different attitudes toward whether they should live their lives without regard for others or behave prosocially."

50. See Akerlof and Shiller, *Phishing For Phools*, 150: "Free markets produce good-for-me/good-for-you's, but they also produce good-for-me/bad-for-you's. They do both, as long as a profit can be made."

51. James P. Hawley, "Setting the Scene: The Basics of Responsible Investment," in *The Routledge Handbook of Responsible Investment*, ed. Tessa Hebb et al. (New York: Routledge, 2016), 30, suggesting that benefit corporations may serve as "an alternative paradigm" that may "set a standard for what is possible, and indeed necessary."

52. J. Haskell Murray, Defending Patagonia: Mergers & Acquisitions with Benefit Corporations, *Hastings Bus. L. J.* 9 (2013): 506.

53. Thomas and McElroy, *The Multicapital Scorecard*, 162.

Chapter 5. The Model Benefit Corporation Legislation

1. See chapter 4, present volume; J. Haskell Murray, An Early Report on Benefit Corporations, *W. Va. L. Rev.* 118 (2015): 29: "Benefit corporation proponents claim that the market is demanding social enterprise laws and that the traditional legal frameworks are insufficient for social entrepreneurs."

2. See "Universal Owners: Making Concessions to Preserve the Commons" (chapter 4, present volume); Sean W. Brownridge, Canning Plum Organics: The Avant-Garde Campbell Soup Company Acquisition and Delaware Public Benefit Corporations Wandering Revlon-Land, *Del. J. Corp. L.* 39 (2015): 724: "Alternative shareholder preferences and interests are still shareholder preferences and interests, and financial investment in public benefit corporations is an affirmation of investor fidelity to those concerns."

3. See Murray, "An Early Report," 41–42: "Both Delaware and the [MBCL] draw on portions of concession theory. Both frameworks require directors to balance or consider the interests of a broad group of stakeholders, benefiting society, likely in part because of the various concessions of the state." Compare Kyle Westaway and Dirk Sampselle, The Benefit Corporation:

An Economic Analysis with Recommendations in Courts, Boards, and Legislatures, *Emory L. J.* 62 (2013): 1006: "[The benefit corporation] marks the return to a corporate form in which the investor limitation on liability is given in exchange for enterprises that are dedicated to benefitting the society and the environment in which the enterprise operates." To be clear, while benefit corporation law echoes concession theory, the statutes do not represent an implementation of it; in order to do so, states would have to make the law mandatory, rather than optional, so that corporate charters would only be granted to entities that considered the interests of all stakeholders.

4. B Lab, "About B Lab," https://www.bcorporation.net/what-are-b-corps/about-b-lab.

5. This view originated with the experience of the three founders, two of whom founded an athletic wear business and the third of whom was an early investor in the enterprise. All three founders believed that the company, AND 1, was managed under strict ethical principles, including searching supply chain audits and positive treatment of employees. Eventually, the company was sold, and the founders were constrained from allowing any element of consideration for stakeholders to enter into the sales process, due to the *Revlon* doctrine (see chapter 3, present volume). It was this experience that led the founders to create B Lab and to seek out a mechanism to allow ethical for-profit businesses to thrive, without sacrificing commitment to all stakeholders. See Ryan Honeyman, *The B Corp Handbook: How to Use Business As A Force For Good* (San Francisco, CA: Berrett-Koehler, 2014), 12–13.

6. See B Lab, "Corporation Legal Roadmap," https://www.bcorporation.net/become-a-b-corp/how-to-become-a-b-corp/legal-roadmap/corporation-legal-roadmap.

7. See Westaway and Sampselle, "The Benefit Corporation," 1010–11.

8. See William Clark and Elizabeth Babson, How Benefit Corporations Are Redefining the Purpose of Business Corporations, *Wm. Mitchell L. Rev.* 38 (2012): 817, note 3.

9. William H. Clark and Larry Vranka, *The Need and Rationale for the Benefit Corporation* (January 18, 2013), http://benefitcorp.net/sites/default/files/Benefit_Corporation_White_Paper.pdf, 1.

10. Joan MacLeod Heminway, Corporate Purpose and Litigation Risk in Publicly Held U.S. Benefit Corporations, *Seattle Univ. L. Rev.* 40 (2017): 612: "The proliferation of benefit corporation statutes . . . can largely be attributed to the active promotion work of B Lab."

11. Colorado: Colo. Rev. Stat. § 7-101-501 et seq. (2017); Delaware: 8 Del C. §§ 361 et seq. (2016); Kansas: H.B. 2125, 2016–2017 Leg. Sess. (Kan. 2017); Kentucky: Ken. Rev. Stat. Chap. 271B, Subtitle 11; Tennessee: Tenn. C. Ann. § 48-28-101 et seq.

12. See Corporate Laws Committee, Benefit Corporation White Paper, *Bus. Law.* 68 (2013). For ease of reference, I have used the term "benefit corporation" to refer to both models, and only use "public benefit corporation" (or PBC) when addressing a specific aspect of the Delaware model.

13. Heminway, "Corporate Purpose," 614.

14. E-mail to author from April M. Wright, corporations administrator, Office of the Delaware Secretary of State (June 27, 2017).

15. J. Haskell Murray, Social Enterprise and Investment Professionals, *Seattle Univ. L. Rev.* 40 (2017): 776.

16. See Natalie Sherman, "Apollo Global, Abraaj Group Invest in Laureat before Possible IPO," *Baltimore Sun* (December 21, 2016); Sherman, "Laureate Becomes Public Again, Raising $440 Million," *Baltimore Sun* (February 1, 2017).

17. Murray, "Social Enterprise," 783: "This profit-focused expectation makes benefit corporations risky bets for ERISA [Employee Retirement Income Security Act] fiduciaries."

18. Christopher Geczy et al., Institutional Investing When Shareholders Are Not Supreme, *Harv. Bus. L. Rev.* 5 (2015): 73.

19. B Lab, *Model Benefit Corporation Legislation* (April 4, 2016), accessed June 12, 2017, http://benefitcorp.net/sites/default/files/Model %20Benefit%20Corp%20Legislation_4_16 ¡.pdf, § 102.

20. B Lab, *Model Benefit Corporation Legislation* § 301 (comment): "This section is at the heart of what it means to be a benefit corporation. By requiring the consideration of interests of constituencies other than the shareholders, the section rejects the holdings in *Dodge v. Ford*, 170 N.W. 668 (Mich. 1919), and *eBay Domestic Holdings, Inc. v. Newmark*, 16 A.3d 1 (Del. Ch.

2010), that directors must maximize the financial value of a corporation." See also § 303.

21. Clark and Vranka, "White Paper," 24.

22. Clark and Vranka, "White Paper," 22–23. But see B Lab, *Model Benefit Corporation Legislation* § 301(a)(3): "[Directors] need not give priority to a particular interest or factor referred to in paragraph (1) or (2) over any other interest or factor *unless the benefit corporation has stated in its articles of incorporation its intention to give priority to certain interests or factors related to the accomplishment of its general public benefit purpose or of a specific public benefit purpose identified in its articles*" (emphasis added). This apparent possibility of opting into a prioritization scheme is not discussed in the literature. In light of the clear intent of the MBCL to eliminate shareholder or other constituency primacy, it is unclear how far such a prioritization provision could go in subverting duties toward any particular class or classes of stakeholders.

23. See Clark and Vranka, "White Paper," 24: "It is important to note that the consideration standard does not require a particular outcome of the directors' decision-making, but rather that there is a decision-making process that considers all of the enumerated stakeholders."

24. See "The Business Judgment Rule" (chapter 3, present volume). To be sure, in a case where the directors are found to be conflicted or to have acted in an uninformed or bad faith manner, courts may intervene and review the substance of a board decision. But the judicial authority to do so is based on concerns over loyalty, and if a court finds no reason to doubt the fidelity of directors, it will not examine the substance of a decision.

25. See, e.g., B Lab, *Model Benefit Corporation Legislation* § 301: "Every corporation incorporated under this Act has the purpose of engaging in any lawful business unless a more limited purpose is set forth in the articles of incorporation"; 8 Del. Code § 102(a)(3): "It shall be sufficient to state [in the certificate of incorporation], either alone or with other business or purposes, that the purpose of the corporation is to engage in any lawful act or activity for which corporations may be organized under the General Corporation Law of the State of Delaware."

26. See, generally, B Lab, *Model Benefit Corporation Legislation* § 304 (comment).

27. B Lab, Model Benefit Corporation Legislation § 201.

28. B Lab, Model Benefit Corporation Legislation § 201(a), § 102.

29. B Lab, *Model Benefit Corporation Legislation* § 201 defines "third-party standard" as follows:

A recognized standard for defining, reporting, and assessing corporate social and environmental performance that is:

(1) Comprehensive because it assesses the effects of the business and its operations upon the interests listed in section 301(a)(i) (ii), (iii), (iv), and (v).

(2) Developed by an entity that is not controlled by the benefit corporation.

(3) Credible because it is developed by an entity that both:

(i) has access to necessary expertise to assess overall corporate social and environmental performance; and

(ii) uses a balanced multistakeholder approach to develop the standard, including a reasonable public comment period.

(4) Transparent because the following information is publicly available:

(i) About the standard:

(A) The criteria considered when measuring the overall social and environmental performance of a business.

(B) The relative weightings, if any, of those criteria.

(ii) About the development and revision of the standard:

(A) The identity of the directors, officers, material owners, and the governing body of the entity that developed and controls revisions to the standard.

(B) The process by which revisions to the standard and changes to the membership of the governing body are made.

(C) An accounting of the revenue and sources of financial support for the entity, with sufficient detail to disclose any relationships that could reasonably be considered to present a potential conflict of interest.

30. See B Lab, *Model Benefit Corporation Legislation* § 201 (comment): "The requirement in section 401 that a benefit corporation prepare an annual benefit report that assesses its performance in creating general public benefit against a third-party standard provides an important protection against the abuse of benefit corporation status." Also: "By requiring that the impact of a business on society and the environment be looked at 'as a whole,' the concept of general public benefit requires consideration of all of the effects of the business on society and the environment. What is involved in creating general public benefit is informed by section 301(a), which lists the specific interests and factors that the directors of a benefit corporation are required to consider."

31. See Clark and Vranka, "White Paper," 22–23.

32. Clark and Vranka, "White Paper," 23.

33. Compare 8 Del. C. Section 362(b), defining "public benefit" to include "reduction of negative effects."

34. B Lab, *Model Benefit Corporation Legislation* § 102. The definition has seven clauses:

(1) providing low-income or underserved individuals or communities with beneficial products or services;

(2) promoting economic opportunity for individuals or communities beyond the creation of jobs in the normal course of business;

(3) protecting or restoring the environment;

(4) improving human health;

(5) promoting the arts, sciences, or advancement of knowledge;

(6) increasing the flow of capital to entities with a purpose to benefit society or the environment; and

(7) conferring any other particular benefit on society or the environment.

35. B Lab, *Model Benefit Corporation Legislation* § 102: "The identification of a specific public benefit under this subsection does not limit the purpose of a benefit corporation to create general public benefit under subsection (a)."

36. See B Lab, Model Benefit Corporation Legislation § 201(c).

37. Elizabeth Babson, a lawyer at Drinker Biddle who was involved in the drafting of both the MBCL and the white paper, explained the provision as follows, in correspondence with the

author: "It makes it clear that a company has the
ability to highlight a particular purpose, with
the higher vote (so hard to change later), provides clarity for directors on that point, gives
the ability to elevate it (if desired) by stating
its priority in the charter, and makes it subject
to specific reporting on performance re: that
purpose." See also Westaway and Sampselle, "The
Benefit Corporation," 1073: "Articulating specific
public benefit. . . . ensures that the corporation is
allowed to pursue activities in furtherance of that
specific public benefit . . . but it also makes the
corporation susceptible to derivative actions for
failure to consider the creation of that specific
public benefit, or perhaps even for the failure to
affirmatively create that specific public benefit."

38. B Lab, *Model Benefit Corporation Legislation* § 305.
In contrast, as we will discuss (chapter 6, present
volume), the drafters of the Delaware model
chose not to include this concept of substantive
judicial review. It should also be noted that
Hawaii, Maryland, Minnesota, New York,
and Oregon do not have benefit enforcement
proceedings, so that shareholders do not have
the express ability to bring suits beyond the
type of procedural fiduciary claim that exist
for conventional corporations. It remains to be
seen whether a shareholder could bring a claim
under Section 201 in those states and assert
that a corporation had failed to meet its benefit
purpose. Such a claim would not be subject to
the Section 305 exclusivity provision discussed
in the next section.

39. Elizabeth Babson, in correspondence with the
author, described this move as providing the
"teeth" "needed to address . . . the nature of the
shift from a 'lawful' purpose to a general public
benefit (and perhaps specific benefit) purpose."

40. B Lab, *Model Benefit Corporation Legislation* § 305.
See also § 201 (comment): "This definition not
only describes the action that may be brought
under section 305, but it also has the effect
of excluding other actions against a benefit
corporation and its directors and officers
because section 305(a) provides that 'no person
may bring an action or assert a claim against
a benefit corporation or its directors or officers' with respect to violation of the provisions
of this chapter except in a benefit enforcement
proceeding."

41. B Lab, *Model Benefit Corporation Legislation*
§§ 305(b); 305(b)(2)(i) and (ii); and 301(d): "A

director does not have a duty to a person that is a
beneficiary of the general public benefit purpose
or a specific public benefit purpose of a benefit
corporation arising from the status of the person
as a beneficiary."

42. B Lab, *Model Benefit Corporation Legislation*
§ 301(e); see also § 301 (comment): "Subsection
301(c) confirms that the business judgment
rule applies to actions by directors under this
section."

43. See *In re Caremark Int'l Inc. Derivative Litig.*, 698
A.2d 959, 967 (Del Ch.): Compliance with the
duty of care "can never appropriately be judicially determined by reference to the content of
the board decision that leads to a corporate loss,
apart from the consideration of the good faith
or rationality of the process employed"; *In re RJR
Nabisco, Inc., S'holders Litig.*, C.A. No. 10389 1989
WL 1 (Del. Ch. Jan. 31, 1989), at *23, note 13:
Substantive review under the business judgment
rule is "really way of inferring bad faith." See,
generally, Frederick Alexander, The Delaware
Corporation: Legal Aspects of Organization and
Operation, 5th ed. (Arlington, VA: Bloomberg
BNA, 2014), 37, note 35, and accompanying text.

44. B Lab, *Model Benefit Corporation Legislation*
§ 305(b): "A benefit corporation shall not be
liable for monetary damages under this [chapter]
for any failure of the benefit corporation to
pursue or create general public benefit or a
specific public benefit."

45. Clark and Vranka, "White Paper," 22: "By including both the failure to 'create' and 'pursue,' the
drafters intended to clarify that the benefit
enforcement proceeding is intended to be the
sole cause of action available to shareholders with respect to general and specific public
benefit purpose and that monetary damages are
not available as a remedy." But see Westaway and
Sampselle, "The Benefit Corporation," 1051–53,
arguing that the only duty under statute should
be to attempt to create general public benefit "in
light of 100 years of judicial wisdom" requiring
directors to carefully and loyally pursue shareholder value, rather than create it; "duty is to aim
the gun, not hit the target."

46. Westaway and Sampselle, "The Benefit
Corporation," 1034–35; also 1077: "Impact measurement has not yet reached the accuracy or
precision of simple mathematics, and benefit
corporation boards should be free to pursue
solutions to social and environmental problems

as they see fit, rather than being forced to adopt a draconian, procrustean mandate to pursue "general public benefit" as a standards organization sees it. Accordingly, courts should be free to find that boards have failed in their benefit related duties despite performing well according to third party standards, and, on the contrary, that they have performed their duties despite performing poorly according to a third party standard" (emphasis added).

47. See B Lab, "B Impact Assessment," http://bimpactassessment.net; GRI, "G4 Sustainability Reporting Guidelines," accessed July 11, 2017, https://www.globalreporting.org/information/g4/Pages/default.aspx, setting out economic, environment, and disclosure requirements without a scoring system; International Organization for Standardization, "Social Responsibility: Discovering ISO 26000," https://www.iso.org/publication/PUB100258.html: "ISO 26000 is not a management system standard. It does not contain requirements and, as such, cannot be used for certification."

48. See B Lab, Model Benefit Corporation Legislation, subchapter 4.

49. See Clark and Babson, "How Benefit Corporations Are Redefining," 842: "To permit monitoring of the performance of the directors of a benefit corporation, the statues also require reporting on performance."

50. See J. Haskell Murray, An Early Report on Benefit Corporations, *W. Va. L. Rev.* 118 (2015): 31: "The resistance to the state-filing requirement may be due to the already strained state resources. . . . A majority of states do not [require a filing]."

51. B Lab, Model Benefit Corporation Legislation § 401.

52. B Lab, *Model Benefit Corporation Legislation* § (a) (1)(i)–(iv); (a)(2).

53. See B Lab, *Model Benefit Corporation Legislation* § 302(c), requiring a report including:

(1) Whether the benefit corporation acted in accordance with its general public benefit purpose and any specific public benefit purpose in all material respects during the period covered by the report.

(2) Whether the directors and officers complied with sections 301(a) and 303(a), respectively.

(3) If the benefit director believes that the benefit corporation or its directors or

officers failed to act or comply in the manner described in paragraphs (1) and (2), a description of the ways in which the benefit corporation or its directors or officers failed to act or comply.

54. See B Lab, *Model Benefit Corporation Legislation* § 102, defining "independent."

55. B Lab, *Model Benefit Corporation Legislation* § 102, defining "minimum status" vote; § 104, requiring minimum status vote for certain amendments and mergers; and § 105.

56. See J. Haskell Murray, "Corporate Forms of Social Enterprise: Comparing the State Statutes" (updated January 15, 2015), accessed June 12, 2017, https://www.law.umich.edu/clinical/internationaltransactionclinic/Documents/May%2011%20Conference%20Docs/Corporate%20Forms%20of%20Social%20Enterprise.pdf (table).

Chapter 6. The Delaware Public Benefit Corporation Statute

1. See "Delaware Division of Corporations 2015 Annual Report," accessed June 12, 2017, https://corp.delaware.gov/Corporations_2015%20Annual%20Report.pdf.: 86 percent of U.S. based initial public offerings in 2015 chose Delaware as corporate home; Startup Documents, "Why Do Startups Incorporate in Delaware?," https://www.startupdocuments.com/incorporation/why-do-startups-incorporate-in-delaware.

2. See, e.g., Omari Simmons, Branding the Small Wonder: Delaware's Dominance and the Market for Corporate Law, *U. Rich. L. Rev.* 42 (2008).

3. See "Delaware Division of Corporations 2015 Annual Report." The state collected nearly $1 billion in filing fees and franchise taxes in 2015.

4. Brett H. McDonnell, Benefit Corporations and Public Markets: First Experiments and Next Steps, *Seattle Univ. L. Rev.* 40 (2017): 724.

5. See J. Haskell Murray, An Early Report on Benefit Corporations, *W. Va. L. Rev.* 118 (2015): 41: "The Delaware public benefit corporation law largely favors private ordering and appears to favor a nexus-of-contracts theory of the firm with fewer mandatory and more enabling provisions than the Model Benefit Corporation Legislation Framework."

6. Colorado: Colo. Rev. Stat. § 7-101-501, et seq. (2017); Kansas: H.B. 2125, 2016–2017 Leg. Sess. (Kan. 2017); Kentucky: Ken. Rev. Stat. Chap. 271B, Subtitle 11; Tennessee: Tenn. C. Ann. § 48-28-101 et seq.; Texas: H.B. 3488 Leg. Sess. (Tex 85[R]). The operational provisions of the Colorado and Kansas statutes largely follow the Delaware public benefit corporation model, while its transparency provisions are closer to the MBCL. As in the case with the MBCL, the PBC statutes are entirely optional. They only apply to corporations that opt to become PBCs.

7. 8 Del. C. § 362(a).

8. See Jane Gleeson-White, *Six Capitals, or Can Accountants Save the Planet? Rethinking Capitalism for the Twenty-First Century* (New York: W. W. Norton, 2014), xix–xx: Sustainability denotes "long-term thinking with a view to the future viability of business in the context of the planet's various and increasingly obvious environmental and social crises."

9. 8 Del. C. § 362(a).

10. 8 Del. C. § 365(a).

11. While the public benefit corporation statute allows entities to form as or become public benefit corporations by following the statutory provisions, the statute expressly states that it has no effect on other corporations. See 8 Del. C. § 368: "This subchapter shall not affect a statute or rule of law that is applicable to a corporation that is not a public benefit corporation, except [for the voting and appraisal requirements of a non-public benefit entity becoming a public benefit corporation]." Accordingly, although the public benefit corporation subchapter provides beneficially oriented entities a legal regime from which to achieve their beneficial business goals, the statute does not disturb Delaware's well-established governing law for traditional corporations.

12. Martin P. Thomas and Mark W. McElroy, *The Multicapital Scorecard: Rethinking Organizational Performance* (White River Junction, VT: Chelsea Green, 2016), 8: "In order for an organization's use of, or impacts on, natural resources, for example, to be sustainable, it must put neither the sufficiency of such resources nor the well-being of those who depend upon them at risk. Rather, it should live within its fair, just, and proportionate share of ecological means." The need

for a concept of "fair share" at the corporate level mirrors the collective action problem raised at the investor level (see chapter 2).

13. United Nations Environmental Programme, *Raising the Bar—Advancing Environmental Disclosure in Sustainability Reporting* (Nairobi: United Nations Environmental Programme, 2015), 52: "All companies should apply a context-based approach to sustainability reporting, allocating their fair share impacts on common capital resources within thresholds of their carrying capacities," cited in Thomas and McElroy, *The Multicapital Scorecard*, 156.

14. See 8 Del. C. § 362(a)(1): The PBC must "identify within its statement of business or purpose [in its certificate of incorporation] one or more specific public benefits to be promoted by the corporation"; John Montgomery, "Delaware Proposes Historic Benefit Corporation Legislation," *Great From the Start* website (March 27, 2013), http://www.greatfromthestart.com/delaware-proposes-historic-benefit-corporation-legislation, quoting B Lab as explaining that, "in other words, Delaware goes a step further than the Model Benefit Corporation Legislation by requiring a declaration of a specific public benefit or benefits in addition to the general public benefit corporation of all stakeholders."

15. 8 Del. C. § 362(b): "'Public benefit' means a positive effect (or reduction of negative effects) on one or more categories of persons, entities, communities or interests (other than stockholders in their capacities as stockholders) including, but not limited to, effects of an artistic, cultural, economic, educational, environmental, literary, medical, religious, scientific or technological nature."

16. See Frederick H. Alexander et al., M&A Under Delaware's Public Benefit Corporation Statute: A Hypothetical Tour, *Harv. Bus. L. Rev.* 4 (2014): 278, recognizing that question could be raised whether "caring for homeless animals" is a public benefit, but concluding that "interests is a flexible term that could be infused with a broad range of content, and could readily be seen as reflecting a legislative intent to be as liberal as possible with regard to permissible public benefits. Consequently, an effort to avoid PBC obligations by this type of technical statutory construction is not likely to succeed."

17. See Alicia Plerhoples, *Nonprofit Displacement and the Pursuit of Charity Through Public Benefit Corporations* (Washington, DC: Georgetown University Law Center, 2016), 11: "[The specific benefit] requirement is not only an attempt to put the stockholders on notice, but also to give shareholders control over the mission of the public benefit corporation and focus directors on a contractually agreed upon public benefit"; J. Haskell Murray, Defending Patagonia: Mergers & Acquisitions with Benefit Corporations, *Hastings Bus. L. J.* 9 (2013): 494, suggesting, before the Delaware statute is adopted, "that the [benefit corporation] statutes should at least require benefit corporations to choose their top priority to guide courts, directors and investors."

18. See 8 Del. C. § 365(a) (PBCs); *accord* 8 Del. C. § 141(a), conventional Delaware corporations.

19. Commercial promotion of such interests has been referred to as managing toward the "triple bottom line" of people, profit, and planet. See, generally, Shruti Rana, Philanthropic Innovation and Creative Capitalism: A Historical and Comparative Perspective on Social Entrepreneurship and Corporate Social Responsibility, *Ala. L. Rev.* 64 (2013): 1121.

20. See 8 Del. C. § 365(a).

21. See Frederick H. Alexander, "Amendments to the DGCL Remove Obstacles to Adoption of Public Benefit Status," Bloomberg BNA (May 1, 2015), https://www.bna.com/amendments-dgcl-remove-n17179926022. The legislative synopsis to the 2013 DGCL amendments, in which the PBCS was added, notes that "directors receive significant protections against claims by stockholders challenging disinterested decisions" and points to § 365(b) and § 365(c) as providing these protections. See Sen. 47, 147th Gen. Assembly, 79 Del. Laws, c. 122 § 8 (2013).

22. See "Clause 1: The Substantive Remedy—Power to the Courts?" (chapter 5, present volume). As discussed, however, the level of substantive scrutiny that will actually be applied under the MBCL remains to be seen.

23. See Alicia E. Plerhoples, Delaware Public Benefit Corporations 90 Days Out: Who's Opting In, *U. C. Davis Bus. L. J.* 1 (2014): 11: "Both statutes [the MBCL and the PBCS] confirm that the business judgment rule will apply."

24. See 8 Del. C. § 365(b). In addition, directors of all Delaware corporations (including PBCs) are "fully protected" if they rely upon employees and officers or upon statements by persons the director has selected for guidance on the subject in question and which the director "reasonably believes are within such person's professional or expert competence" (8 Del. C. § 141[e]). Section 141(e) thus ensures that the directors of PBCs will be able to rely on experts with respect to sustainability questions. This may encourage PBCs to make use of third-party standards even though there is no mandate to do so.

25. See 8 Del. C. § 365(b).

26. See Leo E. Strine Jr., Making It Easier for Directors To 'Do the Right Thing,' *Harv. Bus. L. Rev.* 4 (2014): 248, emphasizing importance of rule that "the board's good faith balancing of the interests of all constituencies would be entitled to the protection of the business judgment rule"; Sean W. Brownridge, Canning Plum Organics: The Avant-Garde Campbell Soup Company Acquisition and Delaware Public Benefit Corporations Wandering Revlon-Land, *Del. J. Corp. L.* 39 (2015): 717–18: "Indeed, Section 365(b) explicitly states that the business judgment rule will apply to the decision making processes of Delaware public benefit corporation directors." Compare B Lab, *Model Benefit Corporation Legislation* § 301(e), applying business judgment rule to benefit corporations.

27. See *Brehm v. Eisner*, 746 A.2d 244, 264 (Del. 2000): If a decision is irrational, it "may tend to show that the decision is not made in good faith, which is a key ingredient of the business judgment rule." Under the business judgment rule, a Delaware court will not second-guess a director's decision, but only "if [it] can be attributed to any rational business purpose." See also *Sinclair Oil Corp. v. Levien*, 280 A.2d 717, 720 (Del. 1971). However, the business judgment rule does not protect irrational decisions entered into "for a reason unrelated to a pursuit of the corporation's best interests," even if that decision does not provide a direct financial benefit to the director. See *In re RJR Nabisco, Inc. S'holders Litig.*, 14 Del. J. Corp. L. 1132, 1159 (Del. Ch. 1989): "Greed is not the only human emotion that can pull one from the path of propriety; so might hatred, lust, envy, revenge, . . . shame or pride. Indeed any human emotion may cause a director to place his own interests, preferences or appetites before the welfare of the corporation." PBC law, of course, broadly expands the conception of

"the corporation's best interests." Compare B Lab, *Model Benefit Corporation Legislation* § 102(c): "The creation of general public benefit and specific public benefit . . . is in the best interests of the benefit corporation."

28. See *Brehm*, 746 A.2d at 261 and 264, describing waste as "an exchange that is so one-sided that no business person of ordinary, sound judgment could conclude that the corporation has received adequate consideration," discussing irrational business behavior as it relates to "waste," and stating that "irrationality may be the functional equivalent of the waste test."

29. More precisely, there is no substantive test when the business judgment rule allies to a transaction. See *Brehm* at 264: "Courts do not measure, weigh or quantify directors' judgments. . . . Due care in the decision-making context is process due care only." When a transaction is subject to a stricter standard of review, there will be substantive review of the decision, as discussed in chapter 8 of the present volume.

30. See 8 Del. C. § 365(b): "A director of a public benefit corporation shall not, by virtue of the public benefit provisions or § 362(a) of this title, have any duty to any person on account of any interest of such person in the [corporation's specific] public benefit . . . or on account of any interest materially affected by the corporation's conduct." Compare B Lab, *Model Benefit Corporation Legislation* § 301(d).

31. James Gifford, "The Changing Role of Asset Owners in Responsible Investment: Reflections on the Principles for Responsible Investment— The Last Decade and the Next," in *The Routledge Handbook of Responsible Investment*, ed. Tessa Hebb et al. (New York: Routledge, 2016), 439. In fact, this idea of stakeholder interests protected by shareholder power was present in the original work that promoted shareholder primacy as a solution to management self-interest. See Will Hutton, Colin Mayer, and Philippe Schneider, The Rights and Wrongs of Shareholder Rights, *Seattle Univ. L. Rev.* 40 (2017): 376, discussing Adolf Berle and Gardner Means, *The Modern Corporation and Private Property* (1932), and stating, "The truth, now largely forgotten, is that this argument [for shareholder primacy] was embedded in a larger vision that wanted economic and political power, in all its guises, to be exercised to benefit the community at large."

32. Robert G. Eccles, Jock Herron, and George Serafeim, "Promoting Corporate Sustainability Through Integrated Reporting: The Role of Investment Fiduciaries and the Responsibilities of the Corporation Board," in *Cambridge Handbook of Institutional Investment and Fiduciary Duty*, ed. James P. Hawley et al. (Cambridge: Cambridge University Press, 2014), 412.

33. See 8 Del. C. § 361, stating that public benefit corporations are subject to the remaining provisions of the DGCL other than those explicitly outlined in the subchapter; 8 Del. C. § 367, permitting derivative suits to enforce the public benefit purpose of the corporation.

34. Specifically, Section 362 mandates the PBC be managed in a balanced fashion, and Section 365 imposes the obligation to so manage the corporation on the board; see 8 Del. C. §§ 362(a) and 365(a). Section 365 then provides that such obligation runs only to shareholders; see 8 Del. C. § 365(b). Similarly, because the statutory statement that PBCs are "intended . . . to operate in a responsible and sustainable manner" is only precatory, and supportive of the balancing requirement, such a derivative suit is also the only mechanism to address that concept in a lawsuit as well. See Brownridge, "Canning Plum Organics," 716: "Section 367 limits actions against public benefit corporation directors for a violation of their duties under Section 365(a) to derivative suits"; Plerhoples, *Nonprofit Displacement*, 11, noting absence of benefit enforcement proceeding implies that derivative suit is "appropriate action . . . for failure to pursue a public benefit," but also noting elimination of duty to benefit beneficiaries might be read to eliminate any duty with respect to stakeholders, although labeling the latter interpretation "unlikely." One exception to this exclusivity might be a situation where board balancing is alleged to have directly harmed shareholders; see *Tooley v. Donaldson Lufkin & Jenrette, Inc.*, 845 A.2d 1031 (2004) at 1033. *Tooley* held that a fiduciary claim against directors may be brought directly if the harm was suffered by shareholders, rather than the corporation, such that shareholders would receive the benefit from a recovery or remedy. Thus, a challenge to the fairness of a merger, where shares are allegedly undervalued, can be brought as a direct claim; see *Parnes v. Bally Entertainment Corp.*, 722 A.2d 1243, 1245 (Del. 1999). Accordingly,

shareholders challenging the balancing decision of a board in connection with a merger might contend that they are entitled to bring a direct claim if the balance harmed them (i.e., if they received a low price because the board went too far in protecting the interests of workers). However, such a claim would appear to constitute an "end run" around the intent of Section 367 that shareholders own a minimum percentage of shares before challenging a balancing decision.

35. See 8 Del. C. § 367.

36. See *In re: Walt Disney Co. Deriv. Litig.*, 825 A.2d 275, 284 (Del. 2003): One test for bad faith is whether the director "consciously and intentionally disregarded responsibilities."

37. See 8 Del. C. § 365(c).

38. 8 Del. C. § 102(b)(7). See David A. Drexler, Lewis S. Black, and A. Gilchrist Sparks, *Delaware Corporation Law and Practice* (Newark, NJ: Matthew Bender, 2016), § 6.02(7). Specifically, Section 102(b)(7) allows "a provision eliminating or limiting the personal liability of a director to the corporation or its stockholders for monetary damages for breach of fiduciary duty as a director." However, the express language of the statute does not allow exculpation of a director's actions or omissions that "breach the director's duty of loyalty to the corporation or its stockholders," are "not in good faith or which involve intentional misconduct or a knowing violation of the law," include the declaration of an unlawful dividend or stock repurchase or redemption, or result in a transaction from which the director receives an improper personal benefit.

39. See Drexler, Black, and Sparks, *Delaware Corporation Law*, § 15.05(1); *Cinerama, Inc. v. Technicolor, Inc.*, 663 A.2d 1134, 1151–54 (Del. Ch. 1994), analyzing the meaning of "interested" director.

40. See Alexander, "Amendments to the DGCL."

41. See *Quadrant Structured Prods. Co., Ltd. v. Vertin*, 115 A.3d 535, 547 (Del. Ch. 2015): "Directors do not face a conflict of interest simply because they own common stock or owe duties to large common stockholders"; *Unocal Corp. v. Mesa Petroleum Co.*, 493 A.2d 946, 958 (Del. 1985): "Nor does this become an 'interested' director transaction merely because certain board members are large stockholders"; *Cheff v. Mathes*, 199 A.2d 548, 554 (1964): "The mere fact that

some of the other directors were substantial shareholders does not create a personal pecuniary interest in the decisions made by the board of directors."

42. See 8 Del. C. § 361.

43. *Lambrecht v. O'Neal*, 3 A.3d 277, 281 (Del. 2010). See, generally, Drexler, Black, and Sparks, *Delaware Corporation Law*, chapter 42.

44. See *Lambrecht* at 281–282, defining double derivative suit; and 285–286: "[The court in *Rales v. Blasband*] held that the traditional *Aronson v. Lewis* demand excusal test would not be employed in considering whether a demand on the parent board was required in a double derivative action. Rather, a different test (the '*Rales* test') would apply, which is whether the particularized factual allegations of the complaint create a reasonable doubt that the parent's board of directors could properly have exercised its independent and disinterested business judgment in responding to a demand. This Court further held that in a double derivative action the *Rales* test would apply as of the time the complaint was filed, as distinguished from the time of the alleged wrongdoing."

45. 8 Del. C. § 365(a).

46. That is to say, derivative plaintiffs in such a case would face the business judgment rule "squared." They would need to show that the parent directors violated the lenient business judgment rule in deciding whether to pursue a claim that the subsidiary directors had violated the lenient business judgment rule. Furthermore, the first business judgment rule inquiry at the parent level is made even more difficult for plaintiffs due to the "Rales test."

47. Compare 8 Del. C. § 366 with B Lab, *Model Benefit Corporation Legislation* § 401.

48. See 8 Del. C. § 366(b).

49. Again, compare 8 Del. C. § 366 with B Lab, *Model Benefit Corporation Legislation* § 401.

50. See 8 Del. C. § 366(c).

51. 8 Del. C. § 220(b), entitling a shareholder to books and records for "a purpose reasonably related to such person's interest as a stockholder." See, generally, Drexler, Black, and Sparks, *Delaware Corporation Law*, chapter 27.

52. Robert G. Eccles and Michael P. Krzus, with Sydney Ribot, *The Integrated Reporting Movement* (Hoboken, NJ: Wiley, 2015), 62: From 1999 to

2012, number of companies issuing sustainability reports using Global Reporting Initiative standards grew from 11 to 3,704.

53. See James P. Hawley, "Setting the Scene: The Basics of Responsible Investment," in *The Routledge Handbook of Responsible Investment*, ed. Tessa Hebb et al. (New York: Routledge, 2016), 30: "Most large firms include a CSR [corporate social responsibility] section in their annual reports, while some issue separate (typically very glossy) CSR reports. But far too much of this is 'green wash,' rather than clearly reflecting actual changed behaviour"; Eccles and Krzus, *Integrated Reporting Movement*, 39: "Very few [companies] are publishing an integrated report. For us, this raises the question of how to separate sincerity from greenwashing."

54. Corporate Laws Committee, Benefit Corporation White Paper, *Bus. Law.* 68 (2013): 1092.

55. European Commission, "Non-Financial Reporting" (updated December 13, 2016), accessed June 13, 2017, ec.europa.eu/finance/company-reporting/non-financial_reporting/index_en.htm.

56. *Small Business Investment Company Program—Impact SBICs*, 81 Fed. Reg. 5666, 5669 (proposed February 3, 2016, to be codified at 13 C.F.R. pt. 107).

57. Jean Rogers, "Investors Ask SEC for Better Sustainability Disclosure," Sustainability Accounting Standards Board blog (August 16, 2016), https://www.sasb.org/investors-sec-sustainability-disclosure, noting that out of 227 non–form letters the SEC received in response to the entire concept release, 66 percent discussed sustainability disclosures, even though "only 3.2 percent of the concept release (11 of 341 pages) discussed sustainability disclosure."

58. McDonnell, "Benefit Corporations and Public Markets," 725–726, citing Sarah Dadush, Regulating Social Finance: Can Social Stock Exchanges Meet the Challenge?, *U. Pa. J. Int'l. L.* 37 (2015): 139.

59. McDonnell, "Benefit Corporations and Public Markets," 732.

60. Such an incorporation could encompass a certificate of incorporation filed in connection with a conversion of another term of entity into a Delaware corporation or the domestication of a non-U.S. entity into a Delaware corporation. See 8 Del. C. §§ 265 and 388, authorizing conversion

and domestication by filing a certificate of conversion or of domestication, respectively, in each case, along with a certificate of incorporation.

61. See 8 Del. C. §§ 363(a) and (b). Compare 8 Del. C. § 363(a) (requiring a supermajority vote to convert from a traditional entity to a public benefit corporation) with 8 Del. C. § 251(c) (requiring "a majority of the outstanding stock of the corporation entitled to vote thereon" to effectuate a merger of a traditional Delaware corporation), and 8 Del. C. § 242 (requiring majority shareholder approval to amend the certificate of incorporation of a conventional Delaware corporation). This high vote only applies if the target corporation is incorporated in the state that has adopted the PBCS.

62. See 8 Del. C. § 363(a) (2013), amended by S. B. No. 75, Section 12, 148th Gen. Assemb. (Del. 2015).

63. See Alexander, "Amendments to the DGCL."

64. 8 Del. C. § 363(c). There is not a supermajority vote required to initially adopt extra-statutory reporting requirements in a benefit corporation certificate of incorporation. Although 365(c)(3), which only uses the terms "amend," would not impose the supermajority vote in a merger effect solely for the purpose of amending the public benefit provisions, see, e.g., *Elliott Assocs., L.P. v. Avatex Corp.*, 715 A.2d 843, 855 (Del. 1998), holding that where a certificate of incorporation grants a class vote on an amendment, alteration, or repeal of the certificate, there is no implicit right to a class vote on a merger that results in such an amendment, alteration, or repeal unless the certificate specifically provides for rights in such context by adding terms such as "whether by merger, consolidation or otherwise." Section 365(c)(2) would, in fact, impose a supermajority vote on such a transaction, because the outstanding shares would "become" shares of non-benefit corporations. Compare 8 Del. C. § 363(c) with 8 Del. C. § 363(a).

65. 8 Del. C. § 363(a)(2).

66. A social purpose corporation is a form of corporation that has been adopted in California, Florida, Minnesota, Texas, and Washington, although these states do not use consistent terminology. These statutes allow companies to create one or more specific purposes but do not require that companies pursue broad, general benefit. social purpose corporations are discussed in chapter 11 of the present volume.

67. 8 Del. C. § 363(c)(2).

68. See, e.g., *Elliot Associates, L.P. v. Avatex Corp.*, 715 A.2d 843 (Del. 1998); *Benchmark Capital Ptnrs. IV, L.P. v. Vague*, 2002 Del. Ch. Lexis 90 (July 15, 2002); *Starkman v. United Parcel Service of Am., Inc.*, C.A. No. 17747 (Del. Ch. October 18, 1999) (transcript).

69. 8 Del. C. § 363(b): To avoid appraisal rights, the shareholder must receive shares of stock (or depository receipts in respect thereof) in a corporation that is traded on a national securities exchange or publicly held by more than two thousand holders of record, cash in lieu of fractional shares (or fractional depository receipts in respect thereof) in a corporation that is traded on a national securities exchange or publicly held by more than two thousand holders of record, or any combination of these types of consideration.

70. Compare 8 Del. C. § 363(b) (public benefit corporations) with 8 Del. C. § 262 (traditional corporations).

71. 8 Del. C. § 262(h): "Through such proceeding the Court shall determine the fair value of the shares exclusive of any element of value arising from the accomplishment or expectation of the merger or consolidation, together with interest, if any, to be paid upon the amount determined to be the fair value. In determining such fair value, the Court shall take into account all relevant factors." See also Alexander et al., "M&A Under Delaware's Public Benefit Corporation Statute," 257–266, stating that "it follows that Delaware's general appraisal statute applies to PBCs," and providing further analysis of how the Court of Chancery might value a public benefit corporation's stock for appraisal purposes.

72. See Drexler, Black, and Sparks, *Delaware Corporation Law*, § 36.02.

73. See 8 Del. C. § 262(d); *Enstar Corp. v. Senouf*, 535 A.2d 1351 (Del. 1987); *Gilliland v. Motorola, Inc.*, 859 A.2d 80 (Del. Ch. 2004), holding that material information necessary for shareholders to decide whether to seek appraisal must be included in the short-form merger context.

74. *Shell Petroleum, Inc. v. Smith*, 606 A.2d 112, 114 (Del. 1992).

75. *Shell Petroleum*, 606 A.2d 112, 114, quoting *Rosenblatt v. Getty Oil Co.*, 493 A.2d 929, 944 (Del. 1985).

76. See Drexler, Black, and Sparks, *Delaware Corporation Law*, 36.06–36.07.

77. Drexler, Black, and Sparks, *Delaware Corporation Law*, 36.06–36.07.

78. See *Weinberger v. UOP, Inc.*, 457 A.2d 701, 714 (Del. 1983).

79. See *Cede & Co. v. Technicolor, Inc.*, 542 A.2d 1182 (Del. 1988).

80. See *Tri-Continental Corp v. Battye*, 74 A.2d 71, 72 (Del. 1950); *accord Rosenblatt v. Getty Oil Co.*, 493 A.2d 929, 942 (Del. 1985); *Weinberger*, 457 A.2d 701, 713 (Del. 1983); *Robbins & Co. v. A.C. Israel Enters., Inc.*, 11 Del. J. Corp. L. 968, 980 (Del. Ch. 1985).

81. See 8 Del. C. § 262(h): "In determining such fair value, the Court shall take into account all relevant factors."

82. See Drexler, Black, and Sparks, *Delaware Corporation Law*, § 36.07(3).

83. Alexander et al., "M&A Under Delaware's Public Benefit Corporation Statute," 260–266.

84. Alexander et al., "M&A Under Delaware's Public Benefit Corporation Statute," 262–263, citing *Tri-Continental Corp.*, 74 A.2d at 72.

85. See 8 Del. C. § 362(a).

86. See 8 Del. C. § 362(c). Compare 8 Del. C. § 362(c) (2015) with 8 Del. C. § 362(c) (2013), amended by S. B. No. 75, § 11, 148th Gen. Assemb. (Del. 2015).

87. See 8 Del. C. § 364.

Chapter 7. Operating Benefit Corporations in the Normal Course

1. B Lab, Model Benefit Corporation Legislation § 201(a).

2. 8 Del. C. § 362: "A 'public benefit corporation' is a for-profit corporation organized under and subject to the requirements of this chapter that is intended to produce a public benefit or public benefits and to operate in a responsible and sustainable manner." See Leo E. Strine Jr., *Making It Easier for Directors To 'Do the Right Thing,'* Harv. Bus. L. Rev. 4 (2014): 244: "A Delaware benefit corporation must be an overall good corporate citizen, and not just be indulgent toward one narrow cause or interest."

3. See 8 Del. C. § 365(b), specifying that the balancing of interests completed by a board of directors will "satisfy such director's fiduciary duties to stockholders and the corporation if such director's decision is both informed and disinterested

and not such that no person of ordinary, sound judgment would approve"; B Lab, *Model Benefit Corporation Legislation* § 301(e), applying business judgment rule to benefit corporations.

4. Furthermore, as we have noted, the statute contains explicit terms in order to ensure that benefit corporation status does not result in increased nuisance litigation. See "Clause 1: The Substantive Remedy—Power to the Courts?" (chapter 5, present volume) and "Duties of Directors" (chapter 6, present volume).

5. As discussed in Argument 3 in "Shareholder Primacy and Responsible Investing" (chapter 4, present volume), some commentators believe that directors of conventional Delaware corporations already have this protection, because they can always *claim* that such decisions ultimately favored shareholders as well. Under the PBCS, however, there is no need to apply such misdirection; directors can explicitly consider the interests of non-shareholders as a primary concern and still receive business judgment protection.

6. This is a fertile area for thought experiments. Posit a billion-dollar-revenue company deciding whether to spend an additional million dollars to expunge child labor in toxic mines from its supply chain. Would a decision to save the million dollars in order to make sure that profits matched or beat expectations test that line? Would directors want to test that proposition?

7. The actual source of this statement, sometimes attributed to business writer Peter Drucker, seems to have been lost.

8. In "Clause 1: The Substantive Remedy—Power to the Courts?" (chapter 5, present volume), we looked at the question of whether it was enough to pursue general public benefit without achieving it. For purposes of this discussion, we note that this issue is likely to be litigated and decided at some point and that, even if the bar is set at mere pursuit, the question whether benefit is being pursued will involve substantive questions that would not be addressed in a pure business judgment proceeding.

9. But see Kyle Westaway and Dirk Sampselle, The Benefit Corporation: An Economic Analysis with Recommendations in Courts, Boards, and Legislatures, *Emory L. J.* 62 (2013): 1051–53, 1057, arguing that courts construing MBCL, as well as PBCS, should "limit their interpretations

of public benefit purpose and consideration to this process-oriented analysis."

10. To be clear, some critics may believe that even the inducement under the MBCL is insufficient to create a real pull toward stakeholder values, particularly in light of the dynamics of corporate governance, where shareholders hold the ultimate power. Compare Leo E. Strine Jr., The Dangers of Denial: The Need for a Clear-Eyed Understanding of the Power and Accountability Structure Established by the Delaware General Corporation Law, *Wake Forest L. Rev.* 50 (2015): 9: "If we believe that other constituencies should be given more protection within corporation law itself, then statutes should be adopted giving those constituencies enforceable rights that they can wield."

11. Joan Heminway of the University of Tennessee College of Law has suggested that the legal accountability under benefit corporation statutes is low. Joan MacLeod Heminway, Corporate Purpose and Litigation Risk in Publicly Held U.S. Benefit Corporations, *Seattle Univ. L. Rev.* 40 (2017): 640: "When layered onto the liability protections that benefit corporation management may have available, the regulation of causes of action in the benefit corporation context complete an overall picture of limited accountability."

12. Bridges Ventures, *To B or Not To B: An Investor's Guide to B Corps* (London: Bridges Ventures, 2015), 10. See also Leo E. Strine Jr., Who Bleeds When the Wolves Bite? A Flesh-and-Blood Perspective on Hedge Fund Activism and Our Strange Corporate Governance System, *Yale L. J.* 126 (2017): 1922, suggesting that pension funds should be managed with regard to the fact that their beneficiaries "need continuing access to quality jobs and wage growth to live a dignified and secure life."

13. Indeed, activist shareholders often pressure companies to "rationalize their capital structure," meaning returning cash to shareholders and taking on debt.

14. See United Nations Environment Programme, *The Financial System We Need: Aligning the Financial System with Sustainable Development* (Geneva: International Environment House, 2015): "Sustainable development is not the same as having a long-term time horizon, as there are many immediate social and environmental externalities that need to be addressed.

Short-termism does, however, aggravate the externalities problem, especially where much of the investment needed for sustainable development is characterized by relatively high up-front costs and returns spread over a longer period."

15. BlackRock, "Annual Letter to CEOs," letter from Laurence D. Fink, chairman and CEO of BlackRock, https://www.blackrock.com/corporate/en-no/investor-relations/larry-fink-ceo-letter. Yet more than 90 percent of large U.S. companies base compensation for top officers on performance over three years or less. Stephen Davis, Jan Lukomnik, and David Pitt-Watson, *What They Do with Your Money: How the Financial System Fails Us and How to Fix It* (New Haven, CT: Yale University Press, 2016), 68.

16. See, e.g., John Kay, *Other People's Money: The Real Business of Finance* (New York: PublicAffairs, 2015), 194–195: "The short time horizons characteristic of actors in the investment channel today are not imposed by the needs of savers or investees—just the contrary. They have been created by the bias to action within the process of intermediation. . . . and aggravated by the use of investment consultants and the pursuit of benchmarks."

17. B Lab, *Model Benefit Corporation Legislation* § 401; 8 Del. C. § 366(b): "A public benefit corporation shall no less than biennially provide its stockholders with a statement as to the corporation's promotion of the public benefit or public benefits identified in the certificate of incorporation and of the best interests of those materially affected by the corporation's conduct"; appendix F includes a rubric that can be used as a starting point for decision making by Delaware PBCs.

18. See 8 Del. C. § 366(b), listing what must be included on the PBCs statement; 8 Del. C. § 366(c)(1): "The certificate of incorporation or bylaws of a public benefit corporation may require that the corporation: (1) Provide the statement described in subsection (b) of this section more frequently than biennially."

19. 8 Del. C. § 366(c)(1); see also appendix F. Using a third-party standard to measure the effects a public benefit corporation has on its stakeholders may also give board decisions greater protection under the relevant statute. For example, the directors of Delaware corporations are "fully protected in relying in good faith" on

experts selected with reasonable care (8 Del. C. § 141[e]).

20. Robert G. Eccles, Ioannis Ioannou, and George Serafeim, The Impact of Corporate Sustainability on Organizational Processes and Performance, *Mgmt. Sci.* 60 (2014): 7.

21. Generally, committees may be delegated to full power of the board, with limited exceptions. See, e.g., 8 Del. C. § 141(c)(2): Committees have full power of board other than as to matters requiring a shareholder vote or amending bylaws.

22. See appendix F; Leo E. Strine Jr., Documenting the Deal: How Quality Control and Candor Can Improve Boardroom Decision-Making and Reduce the Litigation Target Zone, *Bus. Law.* 70 (2015): 699–702.

23. See Joseph W. Yockey, Does Social Enterprise Law Matter?, *Ala. L. Rev.* 66 (2014): 818–819, discussing the contention that "board composition takes on more significance for larger benefit corporations. . . . A specialist on the board can help to ensure that specific issues like social mission feature in every high-level discussion about organizational objectives. She will have the ear of key executives and can apprise them of matters that bear on mission in the face of potential pressure to focus exclusively on profit."

24. B Lab, *Model Benefit Corporation Legislation.* A significant number of jurisdictions following the MBCL do not require benefit directors. J. Haskell Murray, "Corporate Forms of Social Enterprise: Comparing the State Statutes" (updated January 15, 2015), accessed June 12, 2017, https://www.law.umich.edu/clinical/international-transactionclinic/Documents/May%2011%20Conference%20Docs/Corporate%20Forms%20of%20Social%20Enterprise.pdf.

Chapter 8. Operating Benefit Corporations in Extraordinary Situations

1. 8 Del. C. § 365(b); B Lab, *Model Benefit Corporation Legislation* (April 4, 2016), accessed June 12, 2017, http://benefitcorp.net/sites/default/files/Model%20Benefit%20Corp%20Legislation_4_16.pdf § 301. See "The Entire Fairness Standard" (chapter 3, present volume) for further discussion of the standard with respect to conventional corporations; Leo E. Strine Jr., Making It Easier for Directors To 'Do the Right Thing,' *Harv. Bus. L. Rev.* 4 (2014): 249:

"No kind of equity investor has any rational incentive to tolerate self-interested action by top dogs like directors and key executives, because such behavior has a negative effect on all corporate constituencies, not just stockholders."

2. *Rales v. Blasband*, 634 A.2d 927, 936 (Del. 1993).

3. *In re Walt Disney Co. Derivative Litig.*, 731 A.2d 342, 354 (Del. Ch. 1998) aff'd in part, rev'd in part and remanded sub nom. *Brehm v. Eisner*, 746 A.2d 244 (Del. 2000).

4. See *Aronson v. Lewis*, 473 A.2d 805, 812 (Del. 1984). Compare 8 Del. C. § 365(b) ("With respect to a decision implicating the balance requirement in subsection [a] of this section, will be deemed to satisfy such director's fiduciary duties to stockholders and the corporation if such director's decision is both informed and *disinterested* and not such that no person of ordinary, sound judgment would approve" [emphasis added]), with 8 Del. C. § 144(a)(1) (referring to vote of *"disinterested directors"* [emphasis added]). See also B Lab, *Model Benefit Corporation Legislation* § 301 (comment), citing American Law Institute, *Principles of Corporate Governance: Analysis and Recommendations* § 401(c) as the source of the MBCL business judgment rule. Section 4.01(c) notes that the "basic principle to be discussed is that the director should not use his corporate position to make a personal profit or gain or other personal advantage."

5. *Chen v. Howard-Anderson*, 87 A.3d 648, 671 (Del. Ch. 2014), quoting *Orman v. Cullman*, 794 A.2d 5, 27 n. 56 (Del. Ch. 2002), citing *In re Mobile Commc'ns Corp. of Am., Inc. Consol. Litig.*, No. 10627, No. 10638, No. 10644, No. 10656, No. 10697, 1991 WL 1392, at *9 (Del. Ch. Jan. 7, 1991).

6. American Law Institute, *Principles of Corporate Governance* § 401.

7. However, the MBCL, in its criteria for "independence" (which applies to benefit directors), does provide that shareholding of more than 5 percent is disqualifying (B Lab, *Model Benefit Corporation Legislation* § 102). On the other hand, the MBCL does not use that definition for determining whether a director has a conflict for the purpose of determining whether a director receives the benefit of the business judgment rule or exculpation. In those cases, the question is whether the director was "interested," either "in the subject matter of the decision," or "with

respect to the action or inaction," respectively (§§ 301[c][1] and [b][1]).

8. See 8 Del. C. § 367; B Lab, *Model Benefit Corporation Legislation* § 305. Not all states that have adopted the MBCL follow this requirement for standing. See J. Haskell Murray, "Corporate Forms of Social Enterprise: Comparing the State Statutes" (updated January 15, 2015), accessed June 12, 2017, https://www.law.umich. edu/clinical/internationaltransactionclinic/ Documents/May%2011%20Conference%20 Docs/Corporate%20Forms%20of%20Social%20 Enterprise.pdf.

9. See Sean W. Brownridge, Canning Plum Organics: The Avant-Garde Campbell Soup Company Acquisition and Delaware Public Benefit Corporations Wandering Revlon-Land, *Del. J. Corp. L.* 39 (2015): 724, suggesting that one interpretation of the Delaware statute is as providing directors authority "to consider shareholder interests extrinsic to the company's financial performance."

10. See *"Revlon* Standard: Changes in Control" and "The *Unocal* Standard: Defensive Actions" (chapter 3, present volume).

11. See Michal Barzuza, The State of State Antitakeover Law, *Va. L. Rev.* 95 (2009): 1997–2014.

12. See Strine, Making It Easier for Directors To 'Do the Right Thing,' 245; Frederick H. Alexander et al., M&A Under Delaware's Public Benefit Corporation Statute: A Hypothetical Tour, *Harv. Bus. L. Rev.* 4 (2014): 270, addressing the expectation that traditional corporate law precepts requiring the pursuit of maximization of shareholder gain "would operate differently in the case of a PBC."

13. See Strine, "Making It Easier," 245–246, contending that "one of the most important consequences of the Delaware statute is that it makes clear that the *Revlon* doctrine does not apply to benefit corporations" and that "the board must use its own judgment to choose the best sale partner based on a consideration of all corporate constituencies"; Alexander et al., "M&A Under Delaware's Public Benefit Corporation Statute," 270: "It seems clear that stockholder pecuniary gain is no longer the only permissible objective."

14. J. Haskell Murray, Defending Patagonia: Mergers & Acquisitions with Benefit Corporations, *Hastings Bus. L. J.* 9 (2013): 512: "If, however,

the directors decide to sell or break up the benefit corporation, then the directors should be required to sell to the highest bidder, if the state follows *Revlon*"; also 513.

15. See Alexander et al., "M&A Under Delaware's Public Benefit Corporation Statute," 270, expressing doubt that "courts [will] really abandon the level of scrutiny they have come to apply to a sale of the company" and predicting various applications of the *Revlon* doctrine to PBCs.

16. Brownridge, "Canning Plum Organics," 722: "*Revlon* is incongruous with these [Section 365(a)] duties to the extent that it requires, in the first instance, the maximization of shareholder value."

17. See Alexander et al., "M&A Under Delaware's Public Benefit Corporation Statute," 270, explaining the requirement of traditional directors to function to maximize shareholder gain "even in managing the corporation's ordinary business affairs," that all of the interests directors can permissibly take into account must provide "rationally related benefits accruing to the stockholders," and that "one of the motivating factors behind the enactment of the PBC statute was the desire of entrepreneurs for assurance that in their vitally important, last period decision to sell the company, they could still bring to bear the considerations of public purpose that led them to create and operate the PBC." See also Strine, "Making It Easier," 246, stating that the PBC statute gives "directors a clear legal duty to . . . consider how all corporate constituencies and society generally will be regarded by various bidders."

18. 8 Del. C. § 365(b). See Alexander et al., "M&A Under Delaware's Public Benefit Corporation Statute," 271, discussing various ways a court could look at the board's balancing of obligations in the context of a sale of the company. But compare Strine, "Making It Easier," 246, concluding that to act in accordance with the PBC statute, directors, "in a situation involving the sale of a public benefit corporation[,] where two bidders are both offering a substantial premium to the company's shareholders that is within a fair range, the board could—and in fact, *would have to*—prefer a reasonable bidder at $44 per share who has a track record of and is willing to make a binding commitment to managing in manner that is fair to the corporation's other constituencies and society generally, over

a bidder at $46 per share with a track record of poor treatment of workers, consumers, and the environment" (emphasis added).

19. See *Shepard v. Hanke*, No. IP 01–1103-C H/K, 2002 WL 1800311 (S.D. Ind. Jul. 9, 2002): Allegations of misrepresentations and involving a breakup fee could constitute a claim that directors failed to act in the best interests of all constituencies.

20. Alexander et al., "M&A Under Delaware's Public Benefit Corporation Statute," 271.

21. Brownridge, "Canning Plum Organics," 730: "Even with enhanced scrutiny applied [to a Delaware public benefit corporation subject to *Revlon*], good process and a reasonable connection to impact investor interests should shield a director's decision in the wake of a change of control transaction."

22. It should be noted that not all mergers are subject to *Revlon* scrutiny. When a conventional corporation is sold for stock in the acquirer (in a noncontrolled entity), immediate value maximization is not required, and shareholders may continue to benefit from long-term value that may be created through relationships with stakeholders. Nevertheless, such transactions generally are still subject to heightened scrutiny under the *Unocal* test, because of the protective contractual provisions that often make it difficult for third parties to propose competing transactions. See "Intermediate Standards of Review: Enhanced Business Judgment Rule" (chapter 3, present volume).

23. See Antony Page and Robert Katz, Freezing Out Ben & Jerry: Corporate Law and the Sale of a Social Enterprise Icon, *Vermont L. Rev* 35 (2010): 226–228, describing terms of sale, including the right of the independent board of Ben & Jerry's to enforce terms of merger agreement after the sale closed.

24. See Alexander et al., "M&A Under Delaware's Public Benefit Corporation Statute," 272, suggesting that *Unocal* will continue to apply to deal protections, as "it might be argued that the statute was only meant to address matters within board authority, and not to allow the board more authority or influence over matters that come within stockholder authority, such as votes on mergers so that *Unocal* will still apply"; Murray, "Defending Patagonia," 494, recognizing that the *Unocal* test is "used in evaluating a benefit

corporation's takeover defense, but the threats
and the reasonableness of the response would be
evaluated in light of the purpose of the benefit
corporation." But compare Barzuza, "State of
State Antitakeover Law," 1998–2008, finding that
most courts interpreted expanded director discretion under constituency statutes as eliminating the *Unocal* test.

25. See *eBay Domestic Holdings, Inc. v. Newmark*,
16 A.3d 1, 28 (Del. Ch. 2010): "The decision to deploy a rights plan will fall within the
range of reasonableness if the directors use the
plan in a good faith effort to promote stockholder value. . . . Using a rights plan to promote
stockholder value is a legitimate exercise of
board authority that accords with the directors'
fiduciary duties"; *Air Prods. & Chems., Inc. v.
Airgas, Inc.*, 16 A.3d 48, 112–13 (Del. Ch. 2011),
illustrating the concept in Delaware law that a
board can appropriately deploy defensive devices
to protect shareholders from threat of mistakenly
tendering into an inadequate offer; *Unitrin, Inc. v.
Am. Gen. Corp.*, 651 A.2d 1361, 1376 (Del. 1995),
noting that a board can "properly employ a
poison pill as a proportionate defensive response
to protect its stockholders from a 'low-ball' bid"
if the board has a good faith belief that an offer is
inadequate.

26. See Alexander et al., "M&A Under Delaware's
Public Benefit Corporation Statute," 272: "The
range of permissibly identifiable threats to a
PBC would extend to threats of the accomplishment of the PBC's stated public purpose, as well
as threats of a more traditional, financial type";
Murray, "Defending Patagonia," 511, giving an
example of a threat to Patagonia's mission of
protecting the environment and arguing that it
"could be considered, even to the extreme detriment of shareholder wealth"; Kyle Westaway
and Dirk Sampselle, The Benefit Corporation:
An Economic Analysis with Recommendations
in Courts, Boards, and Legislatures, *Emory L. J.*
62 (2013): 1062–1063: "The traditional [*Unocal*]
substantive test should be applied to scenarios
involving defensive measures. Of course, the test
must be reconstructed to account for the additional purposes of the corporation, but the principles upon which the test is founded—concern
over directors' self-interested attempts to regain
control of the expense of shareholders or, in
the case of benefit corporations, stakeholders—
remain valid."

27. See Alexander et al., "M&A Under Delaware's
Public Benefit Corporation Statute," 273,
explaining that the "range of reasonableness
standard" that courts employ to evaluate defensive devices "would be even looser in the case of
a PBC."

28. See Alexander et al., "M&A Under Delaware's
Public Benefit Corporation Statute," 272;
Westaway and Sampselle, "The Benefit
Corporation," 1063: "Courts should be skeptical
of benefit corporation board claims of pursuing
public benefit in a given defensive measure when
the board's record does not reflect actual consideration of public benefit and stakeholder interest in the reasoning and discussion of the board
meeting."

29. *Third Point, LLC v. Ruprecht*, WL19220 (Del. Ch.
2014) at 21–22.

30. *Versata Enters, Inc. v. Selectica, Inc.*, 5 A.2d 586
(Del. 2010), permitting a rights plan with a 5
percent trigger to protect a company from losing
valuable tax assets upon certain ownership
changes.

31. Murray, "Defending Patagonia," 506; see also
504: "The benefit corporation [signals] that it
is interested in a different type of investor—an
investor focused on multiple bottom lines."

32. See "Standards for the Exercise of Shareholder
Voting Rights" (chapter 3, present volume); 8
Del. C. § 367; B Lab, *Model Benefit Corporation
Legislation* § 305. But compare Murray,
"Corporate Forms of Social Enterprise,"
showing some states that have unclear standing
requirements.

33. See Barzuza, "State of State Antitakeover Law,"
2014–18, concluding that, with one exception,
courts in states that had adopted other consti-
uency statutes continued to follow *Blasius*. For
more discussion of this issue, see "Application to
Voting Rights" (chapter 9, present volume).

34. See *Blasius Indus., Inc. v. Atlas Corp.*, 564 A.2d
651, 660 (Del. Ch. 1988).

35. See Strine, "Making It Easier," 249, noting that
PBC directors cannot take "actions that might be
motivated by a desire to remain in office."

36. Alexander et al., "M&A Under Delaware's Public
Benefit Corporation Statute," 273.

37. Robert P. Bartlett III, Shareholder Wealth
Maximization as Means to an End, *Seattle Univ.
L. Rev.* 38 (2015): 255–256.

Chapter 9. Constituency Statutes: A Viable Alternative for Stakeholder Governance?

1. See, generally, Christopher Geczy et al., Institutional Investing When Shareholders Are Not Supreme, *Harv. Bus. L. Rev.* 5 (2015), providing an overview of constituency statutes; William T. Allen, Our Schizophrenic Conception of the Business Corporation, *Cardozo L. Rev.* 14 (1992): 276: "The entity conception was even more clearly endorsed by the law in a remarkable series of legislative acts adopted . . . over the course of the last few years of the 1980s."

2. See Geczy et al., "Institutional Investing," 94; 114: "Constituency statutes did not open litigation floodgates as some critics cautioned"; 127: "We cannot rule out that constituency statutes had some effect on [high fiduciary duty institution] investment, but we can rule out that these investors significantly altered investment behavior after the passage of the statutes"; Roberta Romano, What Is the Value of Other Constituency Statutes to Shareholders?, *U. Toronto L. J.* 43 (1993): 537.

3. See, e.g., Committee on Corporate Laws, Other Constituencies Statutes: Potential for Confusion, *Bus. Law* 45 (1990): 2253: "These statutes variously authorize . . . directors to take into account the interests of other 'constituencies'—persons or groups other than shareholders—in performing their duties, including the making of change-of-control decisions."

4. See Geczy et al., "Institutional Investing," 95: "Constituency statutes expand the protection of the business judgment rule," citing Stephen M. Bainbridge, *Corporate Law*, 2nd ed. (New York: Thomson Reuters/Foundation Press, 2009), 96–102.

5. See, e.g., Jonathan D. Springer, Corporate Constituency Statutes: Hollow Hopes and False Fears, *Ann. Surv. Am. L.* (1999): 99, noting that official comment on the Indiana statute "implies that, like Pennsylvania, Indiana rejects the *Revlon* duty to auction"; 92–94, explaining statutes' origins in anti-takeover movement of 1980s; John H. Matheson and Brent A. Olson, Shareholder Rights and Legislative Wrongs: Toward Balanced Takeover Legislation, *Geo. Wash. L. Rev.* 59 (1991): 1448–50, discussing how increased discretion from statutes "bolster[s] the board's anti-takeover decisions."

6. Brett McDonnell, Corporate Constituency Statutes and Employee Governance, *Wm. Mitchell L. Rev.* 30 (2004): 1228: "Many commentators have charged that [the statutes'] main intent and effect is to help entrench incumbent managers"; and 1235, observing how management initiation of statutes "helps explain why the statutes are permissive rather than mandatory."

7. See Committee on Corporate Laws, "Other Constituencies Statutes," 2261, listing factors permitted for consideration in constituency statutes.

8. Springer, "Corporate Constituency Statutes," 98: "Most statutes do not address [whether constituency interests may trump those of shareholders] directly," discussing statutes rejecting dominance of any single interest over others.

9. See Geczy et al., "Institutional Investing," 96–97.

10. See Edward S. Adams and John H. Matheson, A Statutory Model for Corporate Constituency Concerns, *Emory L. J.* 49 (2000): 1089: "Permissive statutes authorize directors to consider a wider group of interests when making corporate decisions if they so choose. Accordingly, permissive statutes allow consideration of stakeholder interests without demanding it."

11. Ind. Code Ann. § 23-1-35-1(d) (2015).

12. See Eric W. Orts, Beyond Shareholders: Interpreting Corporate Constituency Statutes, *Geo. Wash. L. Rev.* 61 (1992): 29, providing original language of Connecticut statute, which mandated that directors "shall consider" non-shareholder interests.

13. See Adams and Matheson, "A Statutory Model," 1089: "Mandating statutes strictly require directors to take into account a wider group of interests when making corporate decisions. Instead of granting authority, these statutes impose a strict obligation on directors to consider stakeholder interest when making corporate decisions."

14. Conn. Gen. Stat. § 33-756(d) (2015). The new provision reads: "(d) [A] director of a corporation [with registered securities] *may* consider, in determining what he reasonably believes to be in the best interests of the corporation, (1) the long-term as well as the short-term interests of the corporation, (2) the interests of the shareholders, long-term as well as short-term, including the possibility that those interests may be best served by the continued independence

of the corporation, (3) the interests of the corporation's employees, customers, creditors and suppliers, and (4) community and societal considerations including those of any community in which any office or other facility of the corporation is located. A director may also in his discretion consider any other factors he reasonably considers appropriate in determining what he reasonably believes to be in the best interests of the corporation" (emphasis added).

15. See Geczy et al., "Institutional Investing," 96: "Idaho provides a slight deviation from the permissive grant."

16. Idaho Code Ann. §§ 30-1602, 30-1702 (2015) Comparison of the hybrid language in the Idaho statute with the more conventional language in the Indiana and Connecticut statutes suggests that a literal reading of a typical constituency statute frees directors from the obligation to give *any* consideration to shareholder interests.

17. See Leo E. Strine Jr., The Dangers of Denial: The Need for a Clear-Eyed Understanding of the Power and Accountability Structure Established by the Delaware General Corporation Law, *Wake Forest L. Rev.* 50 (2015): 25–26: "Furthermore, when other states moved to adopt express constituency statutes that allowed their boards of directors to consider the interests of other constituencies on equal footing with stockholders, Delaware did not join them."

18. See Geczy et al., "Institutional Investing," 102, explaining that constituency statutes apply to all corporations in a state; Springer, "Corporate Constituency Statutes," 101–102, describing the optional nature of some constituency statutes: in opt-in states, "constituency statutes are not default measures, but rather are language that a corporation may choose to include in its charter"; Geczy et al., "Institutional Investing" 97, identifying two jurisdictions, Georgia and Maryland, as having these "opt-in" statutes; Tenn. Code Ann. § 48-103-204, allowing consideration of other interests "if such factors . . . *are permitted to be considered by the board of directors under the charter* for such resident domestic corporation in connection with a merger, exchange, tender offer or significant disposition of assets" (emphasis added).

19. Ga. Code Ann. § 14-2-202(b)(5) (2015).

20. See Committee on Corporate Laws, "Other Constituencies Statutes," 2253: "The Committee has reviewed the so-called 'other constituencies' statutes enacted during the last several years by at least twenty-five states to determine whether or not the Model Act should include such a provision."

21. Committee on Corporate Laws, "Other Constituencies Statutes," 2270–71.

22. Committee on Corporate Laws, "Other Constituencies Statutes," 2261: "We believe the Delaware courts have stated the prevailing corporate common law in this country."

23. Committee on Corporate Laws, "Other Constituencies Statutes," 2269. Such ramifications included confusion of directors caused by balancing interests, deterrence from serving on boards due to a new class of plaintiffs, reduction of shareholders' ability to monitor director conduct, and a lack of director accountability. See also 2269–70, identifying potential unintended consequences of constituency statutes.

24. See Allen, "Our Schizophrenic Conception."

25. See McDonnell, "Corporate Constituency Statutes," 1232–33, noting opposition to constituency statutes was not surprising because they challenge the dominant view of shareholder primacy: "The traditional argument for [shareholder primacy] is that shareholders are the owners of the corporation. Hence they have the right to expect that their property is managed in their interest." Adams and Matheson, "A Statutory Model," 1090, provide an overview of the historical debate. On the other hand, proponents of stakeholder governance welcomed constituency statutes as a vehicle for promoting corporate social responsibility. See Springer, "Corporate Constituency Statutes," 102–104, explaining proponents' hopes for constituency statutes to protect stakeholder interests.

26. Springer, "Corporate Constituency Statutes," 106. See also Adams and Matheson, "A Statutory Model," 1095: "Not only do opponents believe constituency statutes are contradictory to shareholder supremacy, some argue that existing law already adequately protects the interests of stakeholders"; Jonathan R. Macey, An Economic Analysis of the Various Rationales for Making Shareholders the Exclusive Beneficiaries of Corporate Fiduciary Duties, *Stetson L. Rev.* 21 (1991): 23; Mark E. Van Der Wide, Against Fiduciary Duties to Corporate Stakeholders, *Del. J. Corp. L.* 21 (1996): 27.

27. Committee on Corporate Laws, "Other Constituencies Statutes," 2255; 2268; 2269: "When directors must not only decide what their duty of loyalty mandates, but also to whom their duty of loyalty runs (and in what proportions), poorer decisions can be expected."

28. See, e.g., Committee on Corporate Laws, "Other Constituencies Statutes," 2262: "[Constituency statutes] seem designed to protect directors against claims of breach of fiduciary duty if they choose to take into account interests other than those of shareholders."

29. Brian J. M. Quinn, Constituency Provisions and Intermediate Scrutiny Outside of Delaware, *M&A Law Prof Blog* (November 23, 2009), http://lawprofessors.typepad.com/mergers/2009/11/unocal-duties-outside-of-delaware.html.

30. See Roberta Romano, A Guide to Takeovers: Theory, Evidence, and Regulation, *Yale J. on Reg.* 9 (1992): 171: "The statutes, ironically, protect managers more effectively than workers. Workers have no right to challenge board decisions for failing to consider their interest, while shareholders' ability to sue managers successfully for opposing a bid is diminished"; Stephen M. Bainbridge, In Defense of the Shareholder Wealth Maximization Norm: A Reply to Professor Green, *Wash. & Lee L. Rev.* 50 (1993): 1438–39, noting that, under a "multi-fiduciary duty" standard, "management could freely pursue its own self-interest by playing shareholders off against nonshareholders. When management's interests coincide with those of shareholders, management could justify its decision by saying that shareholder interests prevailed in this instance, and vice-versa"; McDonnell, "Corporate Constituency Statutes," 1231, "The statutes reduce the disciplinary pressure of shareholder suits on directors without a concomitant increase in pressure from other groups. The statutes are a shield for managers, not a sword for employees or other non-shareholder groups."

31. J. Haskell Murray, Defending Patagonia: Mergers & Acquisitions with Benefit Corporations, *Hastings Bus. L. J.* 9 (2013): 505. One correspondent has noted that shareholder value dominates board decision making at public companies, even at corporations in constituency statute states. John Montgomery, in an e-mail to the author (April 2, 2017), pointed out that when Medtronic, a public company incorporated in Minnesota, merged with Covidien and redomiciled in Ireland, a so-called inversion that reduced its taxes significantly, its proxy statement had "pages of the required disclosure about board process and . . . next to nothing about considerations to other stakeholders or Medtronics' elaborate mission and values, one of which was to be a good corporate citizen." See also David Min, Corporate Political Activity and Non-Shareholder Costs, *Yale J. on Reg.* 33 (2016): 443: "While these theories [stakeholder and team production models that reject shareholder primacy] may be theoretically compelling, they have not been widely adopted by practitioners, policy makers, or judges, who have tended to view corporate law as prioritizing the interests of shareholders over those of other corporate stakeholders or team members."

32. See Steven L. Schwarcz, *Controlling Systemic Risk Through Corporate Governance*, Policy brief no. 94 (Ontario: Centre for International Governance Innovation, 2017), 5: "Any given legislature would be unlikely to want to pioneer [a public governance] duty because it could discourage firms from incorporating in its state."

33. See Geczy et al., "Institutional Investing," 111: "The number of enforcement cases reviewed in this study, forty-seven in total, is not large, but not unexpectedly small given the limited enforcement mechanisms in all statutes, and further restrictions in state variations limiting the scope to takeovers, public companies, or both"; Springer, "Corporate Constituency Statutes," 109–110, noting the infrequency of constituency statute litigation, and "the fact that cases generally do not turn on constituency statutes alone is a function of . . . the availability of other anti-takeover mechanisms that do not seem to call into question directors' fiduciary duties."

34. See Geczy et al., "Institutional Investing," 112, observing the cases concerned statutes from thirteen jurisdictions, with Ohio, Pennsylvania, and Nevada analyzed most frequently, and that thirty-two cases were resolved after 2000; 113 (table 3): seventeen cases claimed breach of fiduciary duty in a takeover setting, twelve in bankruptcy or insolvency, and eleven in other situations.

35. Geczy et al., "Institutional Investing," 111, provides an overview of results of study and enforcement coding.

36. See Geczy et al., "Institutional Investing," 106–112. The Positive category was subdivided into two categories, Subcategory A, which addressed directors' expanded rights, and Subcategory B, which addressed lack of standing for non-shareholder constituents. Similarly to the Positive category, Neutral/Positive cases were divided into subcategory A, where the court discussed expanded director rights, and B, where the court discussed the absence of a right of action for nonshareholders. Subcategory A Neutral cases simply had citations to constituency statutes, and Subcategory B cases had references by name or "other nonsubstantive discussions." "Only four court opinions were classified as Neutral/Negative because they did not recognize expanded director duties nor depart from Revlon duties in takeover settings." Finally, "We did not find cases that fell under the Negative category."

37. See Geczy et al., "Institutional Investing," 106–107.

38. *Kloha v. Duda*, 246 F. Supp. 2d 1237 (M.D. Fla. 2003) at 1244: "Plaintiff claims that Defendant Directors caused the Company to remain in the losing operations of vegetables and citrus because they were beholden to F. S. Duda, who wanted to ensure continued family employment"; see also 1246.

39. See *Safety-Kleen Corp. v. Laidlaw Envtl. Servs. Inc.*, No. 97 C 8003, 1999 WL 601039 (N.D. Ill. Feb. 4, 1998) at *18; also *12: "Directors have fiduciary duties to the shareholders which cannot be ignored."

40. *Shepard v. Humke*, No. IP 01–1103-C H/K, 2002 WL 1800311 (S.D. Ind. Jul. 9, 2002) at *8–*9.

41. *Warehime v. Warehime*, 777 A.2d 469 (Pa. Super. Ct. 2001), *rev'd on other grounds*, 860 A.2d 41 (2004) at 480–481. The court ultimately determined the "directors impermissibly exercised their power to retain their own positions by purposely depriving the majority shareholders of any real opportunity to affect the outcome of any vote. Such abuse of position, even if exercised in the belief that the company was thereby well served, violates the principles of corporate democracy that enable shareholders to control their own company." See Michal Barzuza, The State of State Antitakeover Law, *Va. L. Rev.* 95 (2009): 2014–17, finding three cases in which courts applied the *Blasius* standard where a constituency statute was in effect.

42. *Invacare Corp. v. Healthdyne Techs., Inc.*, 968 F. Supp. 1578 (N.D. Ga. 1997).

43. See Barzuza, "State of State Antitakeover Law," 1996–2014.

44. See Geczy et al., "Institutional Investing," 115: "[Constituency statutes] did not create an enforceable right in any of the nonshareholder constituents"; Steven M. H. Wallman, The Proper Interpretation of Corporate Constituency Statutes and Formulation of Director Duties, *Stetson L. Rev.* 21 (1991): 188–189: "[Constituency] statutes are not intended to create in these other constituencies any legally enforceable rights, or to provide nonshareholder constituents with a direct voice in corporate governance."

45. See, e.g., *Washington Penn Plastic Co., Inc. v. Creative Engineered Polymer Prods., LLC*, No. 5:06CV1224, 2007 WL 2509873, at *2 (N.D. Ohio Aug. 30, 2007): "The permissive language of the statute forecloses the contention that the directors' duty to the corporation's creditor is fiduciary in nature."

46. *Official Comm. of Unsecured Creditors of PHD, Inc. v. Bank One*, No. 1:03CV2466, 2004 WL 3721325 (N.D. Ohio Apr. 23, 2004) at *5.

47. *In re I.E. Liquidation, Inc.*, No. 08–6007, 2009 WL 2707233 (Bankr. N.D. Ohio Aug. 25, 2009) at *5: "The Court cannot conclude that the law imposes a mandatory obligation on a director to consider creditor interests, even when the entity is insolvent or operating in the zone of insolvency. The Court will therefore dismiss count five to the extent that it attempts to hold Counter-defendants liable for a breach of fiduciary duty for failing to consider creditor interests, as well as any other counts that similarly attempt to improperly impose upon a director the duty to act on behalf of creditors."

48. See 8 Del. C. § 365(b), providing directors have "no duty to any person" under balancing obligation; 8 Del. C. § 367, providing shareholders with minimum holdings a right to bring derivative such as challenging the balancing; Geczy et al., "Institutional Investing," 102, noting that under both statutory regimes non-shareholders lack enforcement rights.

49. See William Clark and Elizabeth Babson, How Benefit Corporations Are Redefining the Purpose of Business Corporations, *Wm. Mitchell L. Rev.* 38 (2012): 849: "The [MBCL] explicitly

does not create a fiduciary duty to anyone who cannot bring a 'benefit enforcement proceeding.'" This is limited to directors, shareholders with a threshold percentage interests, and other persons identified in the articles of incorporation.

50. But see Geczy et al., "Institutional Investing," 117: "If under constituency statutes creditors were denied standing because directors had permission, but no obligation, to consider creditors, the mandatory 'shall' language in benefit corporation statutes may prove a viable argument." Benefit corporation legislation seems to do away with that concern by explicitly denying any duty to third parties.

51. See Geczy et al., "Institutional Investing," 114: "It is clear that constituency statutes were seen, for the most part, as a true expansion of directors' authority and not merely a codification of earlier common law. The low number of Negative and Neutral/Negative cases supports this assertion."

52. Geczy et al., "Institutional Investing," 115; Barzuza, "State of State Antitakeover Law," 229.

53. See Geczy et al., "Institutional Investing," 115: "Constituency statutes expanded directors' authority to consider nonshareholder constituents, but that expansion only protected directors and did not create an enforceable right in any of the nonshareholder constituents."

54. Romano, "What Is the Value," 283. Romano examined twenty-five states with constituency statutes and the change in stock prices on the day the bill was introduced, the first day the bill got a favorable vote, and the day the bill was signed into law (536–37, detailing the methodology of event study). Romano identifies a number of factors that could have impacted the results of the study, such as combined impact with other anti-takeover legislation, problems with use of dates that may have been prior to public announcements, and variations in firm characteristics (537–41). Alternatively, and "most compelling," Romano speculates that "other constituency statutes are not perceived to have a negative wealth effect because they do not create dramatic changes in the common law of takeovers or in management's behaviour in responding to hostile bids" (541).

55. See Geczy et al., "Institutional Investing," 75, 80.

56. Geczy et al., "Institutional Investing," 127. However, the difference between constituency statutes and the benefit corporation legislation

may pose certain challenges for benefit corporations not indicated by the study.

57. Caroline Flammer and Aleksandra Kacperczyk, The Impact of Stakeholder Orientation on Innovation: Evidence From a Natural Experiment, *Management Reference* (November 12, 2015); Julian Atanassov, "Corporate Governance, Non-Financial Stakeholders, and Innovation: Evidence From a Natural Experiment" (June 2013), https://ssrn.com/abstract=2181766.

Chapter 10. Could a Conventional Delaware Corporation Adopt Stakeholder Values Without Becoming a Public Benefit Corporation?

1. See, e.g., Frank H. Easterbrook and Daniel R. Fischel, Contract and Fiduciary Duty, *J. L. & Econ.* 36 (1993): 427: "Fiduciary duties are not special duties; they have no moral footing; they are the same sort of obligations, derived and enforced in the same way, as other contractual undertakings"; David Rosenberg, Making Sense of Good Faith in Delaware Corporate Fiduciary Law: A Contractarian Approach, *Del. J. Corp. L.* 29 (2004): 493: "The relationship between corporate directors and stockholders can be viewed, then, essentially as a contract, the terms of which may be crafted according to the parties' own understanding of what the market will bear." But also: "Opponents of this point of view believe that fiduciary duties originate from the unique ethical and moral implications of relationships in which one party entrusts his wealth or property to another. Further, they believe that the law must make these obligations unwaivable to protect potential victims from the misuse of the extraordinary degree of power entrusted to corporate directors."

2. See *Jones Apparel Grp., Inc. v. Maxwell Shoe Co.*, 883 A.2d 837, 845 (2004): "Delaware's corporate statute is widely regarded as the most flexible in the nation because it leaves the parties to the corporate contract (managers and stockholders) with great leeway to structure their relations, subject to relatively loose statutory constraints and to the policing of director misconduct through equitable review"; Lynn A. Stout, Bad and Not-So-Bad Arguments for Shareholder Primacy, *S. Cal. L. Rev.* 75 (2002): 1206: "Delaware corporate law, like most corporate

law, is an enabling system. This means that most
of the rules provided by Delaware are default
rules that corporate promoters are free to modify
through charter and bylaw provisions."

3. 8 Del. C. § 102(b)(7), permitting inclusion
of a provision in the certificate of incorporation of a traditional Delaware corporation that
would eliminate or limit the personal liability of
a director to the corporation or its shareholders for monetary damages for certain fiduciary
duty breaches; but not permitting exculpation
for (i) breach of the duty of loyalty, (ii) acts or
omissions not in good faith, (iii) liability under
the distribution provisions of the statute, or (iv)
transactions from which the director derived an
improper personal benefit.

4. 8 Del. C. § 122(17), empowering a traditional
Delaware corporation to "renounce, in its certificate of incorporation or by action of its board of
directors, any interest or expectancy of the corporation in, or in being offered an opportunity
to participate in, specified business opportunities or specified classes or categories of business
opportunities that are presented to the corporation or one or more of its officers, directors or
stockholders."

5. 6 Del. C. § 17-1101, permitting limitations or
elimination of any and all liabilities for "breach
of duties" in limited partnership agreement; 6
Del. C. § 18-1101, permitting the same with
respect to limited liability agreements. These
provisions have been interpreted to authorize the
complete elimination of the duties of care and
loyalty in limited partnerships and limited liability companies. See *Lonergan v. EPE Holdings, LLC*,
5 A.3d 1008, 1017 (Del. Ch. 2010): "The complaint frames each of these theories using the
implied covenant of good faith and fair dealing
because the Holdings LP Agreement eliminates default fiduciary duties in accordance with
the authority granted by the Delaware Limited
Partnership Act"; *Fisk Ventures, LLC v. Segal*, No.
3017-CC, 2008 WL 1961156, at *11 (Del. Ch.
May 7, 2008), dismissing breach of fiduciary
duty claims because "the LLC Agreement, in
accordance with Delaware law, greatly restricts
or even eliminates fiduciary duties" (*aff'd*, 984
A.2d 124 [Del. 2009]).

6. 8 Del. C. § 102(b)(1).

7. See *Sterling v. Mayflower Hotel Corp.*, 93 A.2d
107, 118 (Del. Ch. 1952): "The stockholders of a
Delaware corporation may by contract embody
in the charter a provision departing from the
rules of the common law, provided that it does
not transgress a statutory enactment or a public
policy settled by the common law or implicit
in the General Corporation Law itself"; *Jones
Apparel Grp.*, 883 A.2d 837 at 846, noting that
when evaluating a certificate provision, the
court must "only invalidate a certificate provision if it 'transgress[es]'—i.e., vitiates or contravenes—a mandatory rule of our corporate code
or common law."

8. *Jones Apparel Grp.*, 883 A.2d 837 at 848. For
example, in *Rohe v. Reliance Training Network,
Inc.* No. 17992, 2000 WL 1038190, at *10-*11
(Del. Ch. July 21, 2000), the Delaware Court of
Chancery held that a certificate of incorporation could not contain a provision eliminating
the annual meeting requirement and purporting
to give directors on a nonstaggered board three-
year terms. The court determined that those
particular certificate provisions were contrary to
Delaware's public policy and therefore violate the
limitation in § 102(b)(1).

9. *Siegman v. Tri-Star Pictures, Inc.*, 15 Del. J. Corp.
L. 218, 236 (Del. Ch. 1989): "At least one sce-
nario (and perhaps others) could plausibly be
constructed where Article Sixth [the charter
provision purporting to limit the liability of the
corporation's directors in certain circumstances]
would eliminate or limit the liability of Tri-Star
directors for breach of their fiduciary duty of
loyalty-a result proscribed by § 102(b)(7)."

10. Victor Brudney, Contract and Fiduciary Duty
in Corporate Law, *B.C. L. Rev.* 38 (1997): 627,
and 627, note 82: "Not only do traditional
fiduciary loyalty restrictions thus differ from
classic contract rules in content, but fiduciary
strictures are not designed like contract background rules to fill gaps in, or enforce, explicitly
specified preferences or protective provisions
that the parties selected. . . . The functional role
of management, as actor for the stockholders,
and the structural bargaining incapacity and
passive posture of the public stockholder which
result in the state thus imposing broad fiduciary
restrictions, preclude a court from 'interpreting'
the meaning or scope of these so-called
background rules as if they were deliberately
and freely adopted by contracting parties."

11. Frederick H. Alexander, An Optimal Mix of Clarity and Flexibility, *Delaware Lawyer* 26 (2008): 31: "Given the capitalistic milieu of the business corporation, it may seem counterintuitive to preclude participants from opting out of any rule. The theoretical answer is that too much freedom may sow confusion. By assuring a minimum level of governance, mandatory rules provide important clarity—an investor in a Delaware corporation need not read the charter of bylaws to know that there are certain bottom-line protections."

Chapter 11. Limited Liability Companies and Social Purpose Corporations

1. See *Auriga Capital Corp. v. Gatz Props., LLC*, 40 A.3d 839, 852 (Del. Ch. 2012), expressing a view that default fiduciary duties exist in the LLC context, but that they can be supplanted or modified by clear contractual provisions; *Auriga Capital Corp. v. Gatz Props., LLC*, 59 A.3d 1206, 1218 (Del. 2012), *aff'g* 40 A.3d 839, noting that the Court of Chancery's "statutory pronouncements" regarding existence vel non of default fiduciary duties in the LLC context "must be regarded as dictum without any precedential value."

2. 6 Del. C. § 18-1104: "In any case not provided for in this chapter, the rules of law and equity, including the rules of law and equity relating to fiduciary duties and the law merchant, shall govern."

3. 6 Del. C. § 18-1101(c).

4. See, e.g., *Greenmont Capital Partners I, LP v. Mary's Gone Crackers, Inc.*, No. 7265-VCP, 2012 WL 4479999, at *6, note 24 (Del. Ch. Sept. 28, 2012), quoting *Seidensticker v. Gasparilla Inn, Inc.*, No. 2555-CC, 2007 WL 4054473, at *3 (Del. Ch. Nov. 8, 2007).

5. 6 Del. C. § 18–1101(c).

6. See *Nemec v. Shrader*, 991 A.2d 1120, 1125 (Del. 2010), *aff'g* No. 3878-CC, 3934-CC, 2009 WL 1204346 (Del. Ch. Apr. 30, 2009): "The implied covenant of good faith and fair dealing involves a 'cautious enterprise,' inferring contractual terms to handle developments or contractual gaps that the asserting party pleads neither party anticipated."

7. *Nemec v. Shrader*, 991 A.2d 1120 at 1125–26, quoting *Dunlap v. State Farm Fire & Cas. Co.*, 878 A.2d 434, 441 (Del. 2005).

8. *Dunlap v. State Farm Fire & Cas. Co.*, 878 A.2d 434, 442 (Del. 2005), quoting *Wilgus v. Salt Pond Inv. Co.*, 498 A.2d 151, 159 (Del. Ch. 1985).

9. See B Lab, "Find a B Corp," https://www.bcorporation.net/community/find-a-b-corp.

10. William H. Clark Jr., and Larry Vranka, The Need and Rationale for the Benefit Corporations: Why It Is the Legal Form That Best Addresses the Needs of Social Entrepreneurs, Investors, and, Ultimately, the Public, White paper (January 18, 2013), http://benefitcorp.net/sites/default/files/Benefit_Corporation_White_Paper.pdf., appendix C at 3: "While some LLCs have gone public, LLCs still represent a small minority of initial public offerings over the last decade."

11. See B Lab, "What Is a Benefit Corporation?," http://benefitcorp.net/attorneys.

12. See J. Haskell Murray, Social Enterprise and Investment Professionals, *Seattle Univ. L. Rev.* 40 (2017):767–769.

13. See ORS 65.750 (1), defining Oregon benefit company as either corporation or LLC; Md. C. Ann., §§ 4A-1201 to 4A-1303, establishing Maryland Benefit LLCs; Pennsylvania Uniform Limited Liability Company Act of 2016.

14. See Rev. Wash. 23B25.005 et seq.; Cal. Corp. Code § 2500 et seq.; Tx. Bus. Ore. Code § 23.001 et seq.; Fla. State. Ann. § 607.501 et seq.; Minn. Stat. Ann. § 304A.001 et seq., combining benefit corporation and social purpose corporation authorization into one statute, and using terminology of "general benefit corporation" and "specific benefit corporation."

15. See B Lab, "Social Purpose Corporations and the B Corp Legal Requirement for Certification," accessed July 11, 2017, https://www.bcorporation.net/sites/default/files/documents/legalreq/SPC_Legal-Requirement_9222016.pdf.

Further Reading

Rather than a complete bibliography, the following is a list of resources I have found very enlightening, for those who want to delve deeper into some of the topics covered in the book. The list is by no means exhaustive.

Shareholder Primacy and Stakeholder Governance

Allen, William T. "Our Schizophrenic Conception of the Business Corporation." *Cardozo Law Review* 14 (1992): 261.

Berger, David J. "In Search of Lost Time: What If Delaware Had Not Adopted Shareholder Primacy?" https://ssrn.com/abstract=2916960.

Jensen, Michael C., and William H. Meckling. "Theory of the Firm: Managerial Behavior, Agency Costs, and Ownership Structure." *Journal of Financial Economics* 3, no. 4 (1976): 305–360.

Masouros, Pavlos E. *Corporate Law and Stagnation: How Shareholder Value and Short-Termism Contribute to the Decline of the Western Economies*. The Hague: Eleven International, 2013.

Mayer, Colin. *Firm Commitment: Why the Corporation Is Failing Us and How to Restore Trust in It*. Oxford: Oxford University Press, 2013.

Orrick, UnLtd, and Thomson Reuters. *Balancing Purpose and Profit: Legal Mechanisms to Lock in Social Mission for "Profit with Purpose" Business Across the G8*. Thomson Reuters Foundation, December 2014. http://www.trust.org /contentAsset/raw-data/1d3b4f99-2a65-49f9-9bc0-39585bc52cac/file.

Stout, Lynn. *The Shareholder Value Myth: How Putting Shareholders First Harms Investors, Corporations and the Public*. San Francisco, CA: Berrett-Koehler, 2012.

Strine, Leo E., Jr. "Who Bleeds When the Wolves Bite? A Flesh-and-Blood Perspective on Hedge Fund Activism and Our Strange Corporate Governance System." *Yale Law Journal* 126, no. 6 (2017): 1600–1971.

Tucker, Anne. "The Citizen Shareholder: Modernizing the Agency Paradigm to Reflect How and Why a Majority of Americans Invest the Way They Do." *Seattle University Law Review* 35, no. 4 (2012): 1299–1367.

Williams, Cynthia A., and Peer Zumbansen. *The Embedded Firm: Corporate Governance, Labor, and Finance Capitalism.* Cambridge: Cambridge University Press, 2011.

Yosifon, David G. "The Law of Corporate Purpose." *Berkeley Business Law Journal* 10, no. 2 (2013): 181–230.

The Investment Chain

Davis, Stephen, Jon Lukomnik, and David Pitt-Watson. *What They Do with Your Money: How the Financial System Fails Us and How to Fix It.* New Haven, CT: Yale University Press, 2016.

Kay, John. *Other People's Money: The Real Business of Finance.* New York: PublicAffairs, 2015.

History of Corporations

Berle, Adolf A., and Gardiner C. Means. *The Modern Corporation and Private Property.* 1932. Reprint, New Brunswick: Transaction, 1991.

Mayer, Colin. "Reinventing the Corporation." *Journal of the British Academy* 4 (2016): 53–72.

McBride, David. "General Corporation Laws: History and Economics." *Law and Contemporary Problems* 74, no. 1 (Winter 2011): 1–18.

Universal Ownership and Responsible Institutional Investing

3 Corp. Governance Int'l Rev, 2007, Universal Owner Issue.

Hawley, James P., Andreas G. F. Hoepner, Keith L. Johnson, Joakim Sandberg, and Edward J. Waitzer. *Cambridge Handbook of Institutional Investment and Fiduciary Duty.* Cambridge: Cambridge University Press, 2014.

Hawley, James, Keith Johnson, and Ed Waitzer. "Reclaiming Fiduciary Balance." *Rotman International Journal of Pension Management* 4, no. 2 (Fall 2011): 4–16.

Hebb, Tessa, James P. Hawley, Andreas G. F. Hoepner, Agnes L. Neher, and David Wood, eds. *The Routledge Handbook of Responsible Investment.* New York: Routledge, 2016.

Lydenberg, Steve. "Integrating Systemic Risk into Modern Portfolio Theory and Practice." *Journal of Applied Corporate Finance* 28, no. 2 (Spring 2016): 56–61.

Sullivan, Rory, Will Martindale, Elodie Feller, and Anna Bordon. *Fiduciary Duty in the 21st Century.* 2015. http://www.unepfi.org/fileadmin/documents/fiduciary _duty_21st_century.pdf.

Urwin, Roger. "Pension Funds as Universal Owners: Opportunity Beckons and Leadership Calls." *Rotman International Journal of Pension Management* 4, no. 1 (2011): 26–33.

Youngdahl, Jay. "The Time has Come for a Sustainable Theory of Fiduciary Duty in Investment." *Hofstra Labor and Employment Law Journal* 29, no. 1 (2011): 115–139.

Sustainability Reporting

Eccles, Robert G., and Michael P. Krzus, with Sydney Ribot. *The Integrated Reporting Movement: Meaning, Momentum, Motives, and Materiality.* Hoboken, NJ: Wiley, 2015.

Gleeson-White, Jane. *Six Capitals, or Can Accountants Save the Planet? Rethinking Capitalism for the Twenty-First Century.* New York: W. W. Norton, 2014.

International Integrated Reporting Council. *The International <IR> Framework.* December 2013. http://integratedreporting.org/wp-content/uploads/2013/12 /13-12-08-THE-INTERNATIONAL-IR-FRAMEWORK-2-1.pdf.

Thomas, Martin P., and Mark W. McElroy. *The MultiCapital Scorecard: Rethinking Organizational Performance.* White River Junction, VT: Chelsea Green, 2016.

Benefit Corporations

Alexander, Frederick H., Lawrence A. Hamermesh, Frank R. Martin, and Norman M Monhait. "M&A under Delaware's Public Benefit Corporation Statute: A Hypothetical Tour." *Harvard Business Law Review* 4 (2014): 255–279.

"Berle VIII: Benefit Corporations and the Firm Commitment Universe." *Seattle University Law Review* 40, no. 2 (2017) (Symposium issue): 299–302.

Clark, William H., Jr., and Elizabeth K. Babson. "How Benefit Corporations Are Redefining the Purpose of Business Corporations." *William Mitchell Law Review* 38, no. 2 (2012): 817–851.

Clark, William H., Jr., and Larry Vranka. *The Need and Rationale for the Benefit Corporations: Why It Is the Legal Form That Best Addresses the Needs of Social Entrepreneurs, Investors, and, Ultimately, the Public.* White paper, January 18, 2013. http://benefitcorp.net/sites/default/files/Benefit_Corporation_White_Paper.pdf.

Corporate Laws Committee. "Benefit Corporation White Paper." *Business Lawyer* 68, no. 4 (August 2013): 1083–1110.

Loewenstein, Mark J. "Benefit Corporations: A Challenge in Corporate Governance." *Business Lawyer* 68, no. 4 (August 2013): 1007–1038.

Murray, J. Haskell. "Defending Patagonia: Mergers & Acquisitions with Benefit Corporations." *Hastings Business Law Journal* 9, no. 3 (2013): 485–517.

Murray, J. Haskell. "An Early Report on Benefit Reports." *West Virginia Law Review* 118 (2015): 25–57.

Plerhoples, Alicia. "Delaware Public Benefit Corporations 90 Days Out: Who's Opting In?" *U.C. Davis Business Law Journal* 14 (2014): 247–280.

Plerhoples, Alicia. *Nonprofit Displacement and the Pursuit of Charity Through Public Benefit Corporations.* Washington, DC: Georgetown University Law Center, 2016. https://ssrn.com/abstract=2817881.

Robson, Regina. "A New Look at Benefit Corporations: Game Theory and Game Changer." *American Business Law Journal* 52, no. 3 (2015): 501–555.

Steingard, David S., and William H. Clark Jr. "The Benefit Corporation as an Exemplar of Integrative Corporate Purpose (ICP): Delivering Maximal Social and Environmental Impact with a New Corporate Form." *Business and Professional Ethics Journal* 35 (2016): 73.

Strine, Leo E., Jr. "Making it Easier for Directors to 'Do the Right Thing'?" *Harvard Business Law Review* 4 (2014): 235–253.

Westaway, Kyle, and Dirk Sampselle. "The Benefit Corporation: An Economic Analysis with Recommendations to Courts, Boards, and Legislatures." *Emory Law Journal* 62 (2013): 999–1085.

Index

About the Author

Frederick ("Rick") H. Alexander is a frequent writer and speaker on corporate law, particularly on matters of stakeholder governance.

Following law school at Georgetown University, Rick practiced law for 26 years at Morris, Nichols, Arsht & Tunnell LLP, including four years as managing partner. He remains counsel to the firm. During that time, he was selected as one of the ten most highly regarded corporate governance lawyers worldwide, as Delaware Mergers & Acquisitions Lawyer of the Year, as Delaware Corporate Law Lawyer of the Year, and as one of the 500 leading lawyers in the United States.

In 2015, Rick became the Head of Legal Policy at B Lab, a non-profit organization dedicated to enabling people to use business as a force for good. In that position, Rick works with lawyers, companies, investors, legislators and regulators around the world, seeking to create corporate governance structures that lead corporations to contribute to a healthy and stable society and planet.

Rick prepared the initial drafts of both the Delaware public benefit corporation legislation and the American Bar Association's Benefit Corporation White Paper, and serves as Special Consultant to the ABA's Corporate Laws Committee. He is also a member of the Delaware Access to Justice Commission, co-chairs the Content Committee of the American College of Governance Counsel, and is a member of the Commonwealth Climate and Law Initiative Advisory Board. He also serves as a board member of the Transgender Legal Defense and Education Fund.

Rick lives in Wilmington, Delaware.

Berrett–Koehler
Publishers

Berrett-Koehler is an independent publisher dedicated to an ambitious mission: Connecting people and ideas to create a world that works for all.

We believe that the solutions to the world's problems will come from all of us, working at all levels: in our organizations, in our society, and in our own lives. Our BK Business books help people make their organizations more humane, democratic, diverse, and effective (we don't think there's any contradiction there). Our BK Currents books offer pathways to creating a more just, equitable, and sustainable society. Our BK Life books help people create positive change in their lives and align their personal practices with their aspirations for a better world.

All of our books are designed to bring people seeking positive change together around the ideas that empower them to see and shape the world in a new way.

And we strive to practice what we preach. At the core of our approach is Stewardship, a deep sense of responsibility to administer the company for the benefit of all of our stakeholder groups including authors, customers, employees, investors, service providers, and the communities and environment around us. Everything we do is built around this and our other key values of quality, partnership, inclusion, and sustainability.

This is why we are both a B-Corporation and a California Benefit Corporation—a certification and a for-profit legal status that require us to adhere to the highest standards for corporate, social, and environmental performance.

We are grateful to our readers, authors, and other friends of the company who consider themselves to be part of the BK Community. We hope that you, too, will join us in our mission.

A BK Business Book

We hope you enjoy this BK Business book. BK Business books pioneer new leadership and management practices and socially responsible approaches to business. They are designed to provide you with groundbreaking and practical tools to transform your work and organizations while upholding the triple bottom line of people, planet, and profits. High-five!

To find out more, visit **www.bkconnection.com.**

Berrett–Koehler
Publishers

Connecting people and ideas
to create a world that works for all

Dear Reader,

Thank you for picking up this book and joining our worldwide community of Berrett-Koehler readers. We share ideas that bring positive change into people's lives, organizations, and society.

To welcome you, we'd like to offer you a free e-book. You can pick from among twelve of our bestselling books by entering the promotional code BKP92E here: http://www.bkconnection.com/welcome.

When you claim your free e-book, we'll also send you a copy of our e-newsletter, the *BK Communiqué*. Although you're free to unsubscribe, there are many benefits to sticking around. In every issue of our newsletter you'll find

- A free e-book
- Tips from famous authors
- Discounts on spotlight titles
- Hilarious insider publishing news
- A chance to win a prize for answering a riddle

Best of all, our readers tell us, "Your newsletter is the only one I actually read." So claim your gift today, and please stay in touch!

Sincerely,

Charlotte Ashlock
Steward of the BK Website

Questions? Comments? Contact me at bkcommunity@bkpub.com.